Morrells of Oxford

The Family and their Brewery
1743–1993

B R I G I D   A L L E N

OXFORDSHIRE BOOKS

First published in 1994 by Oxfordshire Books

Copyright © Brigid Allen, 1994

All rights reserved. No part of this publication may be reproduced, stored in a retrieval system, or transmitted, in any form, or by any means, electronic, mechanical, photocopying, recording or otherwise, without the prior permission of the publishers and copyright holder.

British Library Cataloguing-in-Publication Data. A catalogue record for this book is available from the British Library.

ISBN 0–7509–0634–0

Library of Congress Cataloging-in-Publication Data applied for.

OXFORDSHIRE BOOKS
Publishing imprint of
Oxfordshire County Council
Department of Leisure and Arts
in collaboration with
Alan Sutton Publishing Limited
Phoenix Mill · Far Thrupp · Stroud
Gloucestershire

Typeset in 11/13 Sabon.
Typesetting and origination by
Alan Sutton Publishing Limited.
Printed in Great Britain by
Redwood Books, Trowbridge, Wiltshire

CONTENTS

Foreword	iv
Acknowledgements	vi
Introduction	vii
1. The Morrells of Wallingford and Oxford	1
2. Brewers and Bankers, 1797–1815	16
3. Country Gentlemen, 1815–34	29
4. Deaths and Gains, 1835–56	40
5. The Landed Magnate, 1856–63	53
6. Trusteeship, 1863–85	63
7. Expansion, 1885–1906	80
8. Pre-War and Wartime, 1906–18	97
9. Morrell's Trustees, 1918–43	109
10. Morrells Brewery Limited, 1943–65	123
11. Morrells Brewery Limited, 1965–93	133
Appendix 1: '1782'	149
Appendix 2: Pubs Lost or Renamed	150
Appendix 3: Pubs Lost, *c.* 1880–90	156
Notes	158
Index	167

FOREWORD

As a child I knew that the first Thursday of every month was Brewery Meeting Day and my mother would be away. She would return in the evening with a supply of bottled beer for the family and the occasional small wooden cask of something called College Ale. Indeed one of my enduring childhood memories is going down to the dark, damp cellar and drawing off a jug of this wonderful aromatic brew for my parents' lunch. At the time I took all this for granted and never thought to question the family association with a brewery called Morrell's.

At the age of fourteen, on the death of my maternal grandmother, I and each of her other eight grandchildren inherited a small shareholding in the brewery. By this time I was aware that the company was based in Oxford and that my uncle was the managing director, as his father had been before him. My new-found status as a shareholder entitled me to attend the Annual General Meetings of the company, which were held in the splendid Victorian clutter of the chairman's office. Although much of the content of the meetings was lost on me, I enjoyed the family gathering, an excellent lunch and a sense of belonging.

Fourteen years later, after deciding to resign my commission in the Royal Artillery, my uncle invited me to join the brewery and begin training to be his successor. Quite by chance, I started work in Oxford in 1982, which was thought to be the bi-centenary of the company and I witnessed the celebrations of this milestone. However, as I became more involved with trying to understand the complexities of the brewing industry, other questions about the founding of the brewery and the Morrell family history came to mind. For example, when had brewing actually started on the site and how did Mark and James Morrell become brewers? Why was the business run by Trustees for nearly eighty years and what happened to the sizeable land holdings built up by the Morrells in the nineteenth century?

A few years ago, Brigid Allen was commissioned to write another local company's history. Reading the published version, I felt that this had the right combination of accurate historical research and fascinating narrative, and I asked Brigid if she would write a definitive history of the Morrell family and the brewery. This book is the outcome of her original and painstaking research, not only in record offices and on foot in

FOREWORD

Oxford, but while archiving a jumble of old company papers stored in the brewery strong-room and attic.

Now, not only do we have the story of eight generations of a brewing family but also the development of brewing in the Parish of St Thomas's over a period of 500 years. I have found it fascinating to discover so much about the past and I hope that you will enjoy reading our history.

Charles Eld
Managing Director
Morrells Brewery Ltd

ACKNOWLEDGEMENTS

Many people have contributed towards the completion of this history. At Morrells brewery, Charles Eld and his staff have been endlessly patient and accommodating. Louis Gunter, a former head brewer and former director of Morrells Brewery Ltd, has been unstinting in sharing his time and technical knowledge with me. I am also grateful to Charles Smith and Tony Worth, both former directors, and to Mrs Margaret Eld and her sister, the late Mrs Mary Luard, for talking to me about the brewery. I have received help and information of various kinds from Mrs Elizabeth Maxwell, Julian Munby and Dr Mary Prior; members of staff of the Berkshire Record Office, Bodleian Library, Oxford City Council (City Solicitor's Office), Oxfordshire Archives, Oxfordshire Local Studies Centre, Oxford University Archives, Oxford University Officers' Training Corps, Public Record Office (Chancery Lane) and Surrey Record Office (Guildford Muniment Room); Dr John Jones, archivist of Balliol College; John Wing, librarian of Christ Church; Clare Hopkins, former archivist of Lincoln College; Dr Janie Cottis, archivist of Magdalen College; Mr J.M. Kaye and Miss Helen Powell, archivist and librarian of The Queen's College; Dr Malcolm Vale, archivist of St John's College; Mr F.R. Williamson of Morrell, Peel and Gamlen (solicitors); and Fiona Wood of the Brewers' Society. As always in matters connected with local topography and history, I have shared every problem and discovery with my husband David Sturdy, who has helped me in a number of practical ways and whose understanding and enthusiasm for places, buildings, people, maps and archives has been my greatest support.

I would like to acknowledge permission to reproduce illustrations from the following sources: Bodleian Library, Oxford, pp. 30 (MS Top. Oxon. b. 89, fol. 102), 42, 43 (MS Top. Oxon. c. 211, fol. 131); Morrells Brewery Ltd, pp. 19, 24, 50, 84, 91, 99, 107, 114, 118, 120; Col. and Mrs H.W.J. Morrell, p. 113; Oxfordshire Local Studies Centre, pp. xx, 7, 11, 13, 35, 36, 37, 54, 59, 64, 65, 73, 92, 93, 94, 98, 103, 116, 117, 125, 128, 130, 132, 134, 135, 136, 137, 139, 140; David Sturdy, p. xxii.

INTRODUCTION

Morrells Brewery in St Thomas's, Oxford, is the oldest surviving family-run business in the city, and the longest established of Oxford's commercial breweries, either past or present. Since the late eighteenth century it has been owned, directed or managed by six generations of the same family, of whom the first, the brothers Mark and James Morrell, took over an existing brewery business established by Richard Tawney and bequeathed in 1756 to his son, the future alderman Sir Richard, who left it in 1791 to his brother Edward, like him an alderman and three times Mayor of Oxford.

The elder Richard Tawney, formerly a boatmaster, is first named as a brewer in a lease of premises just round the corner from the brewery in Lower Fisher Row in 1743. Two years later he established himself legally as the tenant of a brewhouse and dwelling-house on the present brewery site, which had been occupied since 1718 by the brewers Thomas and William Kenton, and then by William's widow Hannah until her remarriage.[1] Tawney, who was sixty at the time and a near neighbour of the Kentons, may have taken up brewing as a lucrative retirement occupation when William Kenton died, borrowing or renting his brewhouse and brewing-vessels until Hannah remarried and was ready to assign the remainder of her lease. Whether he inherited the goodwill of a surviving concern from the Kentons, or whether he created a substantially new one of his own, it seems safe enough to regard him as the originator of the present brewery business, whose continuing prosperity allowed him to be elected Mayor of Oxford in 1748 and to provide for both the sons of his second marriage – Richard as a brewer and Edward as a miller and maltster with premises almost immediately next door at the Castle Mill.

Brewing in Oxford, as in most other towns and cities, had been widespread on a domestic scale since the Middle Ages. Monasteries such as Oseney Abbey and Rewley Abbey, colleges, inns and large family town houses all had private brewhouses, sometimes little more than a shed off the backyard where brewing might take place every week or as the occasion demanded. Commercial breweries, owned or leased by individual common brewers, also operated on a larger or smaller scale throughout the city. Brewer Street off St Aldate's, less than half a mile from Morrell's premises in St Thomas's, was originally Brewer's Lane, named for the powerful seventeenth-century Smyth family who lived in a large house on the corner of the two streets and farther down St Aldate's at the Old Palace, and whose brewhouse probably had a water-wheel turned by the open Trill Mill Stream, which flowed in a sweeping curve from St Thomas's round the Paradise Garden in St Ebbe's.

The nearest rival to Morrell's Brewery, the Swan or Swan's Nest Brewery almost immediately adjoining it in St Thomas's, on a spit of land lying to the west of Paradise Street, came into being in about 1700. At that time the future Morrell's site did not include a working brewhouse; while a previous brewhouse 'at the west end of the bridge below the Castle Mills', roughly on the site of the builders' merchants Cooper Callas, had ceased to be used for brewing and become a malthouse.[2] The Swan's Nest, later Hall's Brewery, co-existed with the Tawney- and later Morrell-owned brewery from the middle of the eighteenth century until its take-over by Allsopps in 1926. The brewery buildings have now been demolished or converted to other purposes, while the handsome red-brick brewery house built by the late eighteenth-century brewer, Alderman Sir John Treacher, no longer stands. The Swan's Nest itself, a willow-fringed peninsula, now contains a car-park with a fine view of the multi-layered rear wall of Morrell's brewhouse, its waterwheel still in position, and the plate-glass and concrete offices of British Telecom.

In the 1980s Hall's name was revived by Allied Breweries as Hall's Oxford and West Brewery Company Ltd, a subsidiary company selling traditional ales brewed at Burton-on-Trent, with its headquarters at the former Hall's bottling plant in the old Eagle Steam Brewery premises in Park End Street. Those premises, however, have now been demolished, and the company's offices moved to Messrs Ind Coope's premises at Bourne End, Bucks.

While brewhouses existed all over central Oxford, decreasing in number only towards the end of the eighteenth century, they seem to have been most numerous in the parishes of St Ebbe's, St Aldate's and St Thomas's, near the water-power and transport provided by the Castle Mill Stream and its continuation, the Trill Mill Stream. St Thomas's, the home of the two great medieval abbeys of Oseney and Rewley, is a watery, low-lying parish roughly occupying the area between Oxford Castle and the former prison to the east, Worcester College to the north, the Thames at Osney to the west, and Osney Lane, which divides it from St Ebbe's parish, to the south. The Castle Mill Stream, probably a medieval canalization of a natural, southward-running channel of the Thames, leaves the main river south of Medley, runs parallel with the Oxford Canal as far as its termination in Hythe Bridge Street, then continues past Middle and Lower Fisher Row and under Quaking Bridge between St Thomas's Street and the castle, gathering momentum as it passes through the sluice which once belonged to the (now demolished) Castle Mill. Near the north end of Lower Fisher Row the smaller Back Stream runs off this, controlled by a sluice, to pursue its course behind the remaining houses of the row, under Bookbinder's Bridge in St Thomas's Street, and through a culvert between the Marlborough Arms and the brewery just upstream from the waterwheel behind the brewhouse, reconverging with the Castle Mill Stream beyond the farthest point of the Swan's Nest. Yet another sub-branch detached itself from this behind Lower Fisher Row, flowed parallel with it for several hundred yards, then passed under the (now non-existent) Knowles's Bridge in St Thomas's Street, to reconverge with it at the tip of the brewery garden. The brewery premises in the eighteenth century were thus largely defined by watercourses: to the east the Back Stream running under Bookbinder's Bridge, to the south and west the stream running under Knowles's Bridge, and to the north St Thomas's Street.

To the brewers of St Thomas's these various streams provided not only power but also a surprising degree of navigability. The Castle Mill Stream, now culverted as the Trill Mill Stream between the Swan's Nest and Christ Church Memorial Garden in St Aldate's (and providing, before the culvert was sealed off at both ends by gratings, a challenging terror-ride with bicycle lamp and canoe)[3] was once the main navigation stream for goods being delivered to the castle or for grain and flour being taken to and from the Castle Mill. The Back Stream, now virtually unnavigable, was a channel for goods being taken in large punts through Oxford or to local destinations other than the castle and the mill. Supplies of malt for brewing came from one or another of the malthouses in the neighbourhood of the Castle Mill, since malting and milling went together, using the same transport system for grain. Wells sunk in the gravelly alluvium of the Castle Mill Stream area produced good clean brewing water, hard like all Oxford water but free from muddy clay deposits.

One of the major medieval and later brewhouses in the parish was erected at the castle end of the present Tidmarsh Lane, on a site now occupied by the former malthouse (partly rebuilt to house the University surveyor's department) which belonged, between the 1790s and the 1950s, to Morrell's Brewery. Until the Dissolution of the Monasteries much of the land in St Thomas's was the property of Oseney Abbey, from which it passed in 1546 to the new Royal college, Christ Church. From the thirteenth century onwards the monks of Oseney had encouraged the development of St Thomas's as an industrial suburb; and in 1452 they agreed to build a brewhouse on a piece of land that they had leased five years earlier to William Newman and his family, just below the castle on the road leading northwards from Quaking Bridge in the direction of Brokenheyes, the rough, open ground on the west side of the city.

On a plot of land measuring in all 15 perches (80 yd) long and 4 perches (64 ft) wide, from the corner of the castle ditch northwards, the monks agreed to erect a building 66 ft long and 18 ft wide, with a loft at least 30 ft long, roofed *'cum tegulis vel tylys'*. The Newmans were to provide the interior building materials *'pro floryng'* and other purposes, and all the brewing-vessels. These comprised:

> duo magna vasa plumbea & unum growtlede, duos magnos vates, & unum chykefatte, xxxi kevers vel plures ... cum xvi covelys & tubbys, paylys & omnibus aliis vasis & utensilibus necessariis, quot sufficere possint & valeant ad sexdecim quarteria brasianda. (Two great lead vessels and one wort-back, two great vats and one chickfat[?], 31 or more kevers ... with 16 covelys [coolers?] and tubs, pails and all other vessels and utensils necessary for the brewing of sixteen quarters [of malt at a time].)

All these, *'cum uno horsmylle'*, were liable to be handed over to the monks in good condition for the next tenant if the Newmans' lease expired and failed to be renewed.[4]

Although 16 quarters of malt (16 x 336 lb) were only about half the amount brewed on any one day by Morrell's Brewery in the 1850s, the Newmans' brewery was evidently on a large enough scale to be intended for commercial use rather than (say) as a replacement for the monks' own domestic brewhouse. The number of vessels required in the brewing operation suggests a certain complication in the procedure, which contrasts with the relative simplicity of a small common brewer's equipment in the mid-eighteenth century. We have no record of the number or kind of vessels used by Richard Tawney and his sons; but in 1752 Edward Allen, a brewer of St Aldate's, left the following items, which were listed in his inventory:

> A New Ale Tun
> An Old Ditto
> A Small Beer Tun
> An Under Back
> A Mash Tun
> An Old Float
> Two Old Coolers
> A Copper
> The Cask
> A Dray
> A Cart
> Five Troughs

INTRODUCTION

A Hand Mill
A Horse Mill
The Kiln Plate [for malting]
Four Horses[5]

While beer remained unrivalled until the mid- to late seventeenth century as the chief sustaining drink for all classes and age-groups of English people, in Oxford it had an additional importance of its own, as the standard drink of undergraduates (and the less sophisticated dons) from the fourteenth to the eighteenth century or beyond. Before colleges acquired their own brewhouses or systematized their arrangements for communal eating, undergraduates were expected to buy their own bread and ale from local tradesmen. The mutual resentment between town and gown which was expressed in, or caused by, overcharging led to the St Scholastica's Day riots of 1355, after which the Chancellor of the University claimed the right to regulate local prices at the annual assizes of bread and ale. In the early seventeenth century the Laudian statutes forbade undergraduates to enter alehouses, but the assizes continued until their abolition in the tradesmen's interest in 1836.[6] Meanwhile most colleges acquired or rebuilt existing brewhouses, and some employed local brewers to come in and brew in them, or, if they had no brewhouse (like Lincoln College from the 1640s), to come into the beer-cellar to install, tap and season barrels of bought-in beer.[7]

Having breakfasted on ale, or having studied on an empty stomach until midday dinner, restless undergraduates still liked to escape and spend the afternoons walking to a country alehouse such as Joan's or Mother Gurden's at Headington, where they would indulge in mock disputations, exchange Latin epigrams, and drink steadily to fortify themselves for the cold and damp walk home. Others, less energetic, simply sloped off to the nearest town alehouse, hoping that they would not be informed on to the proctors or to the college authorities. To counteract this tendency some colleges made a practice of brewing particularly strong beer so that the young men would not be driven out in search of a more satisfying alternative. As John Aubrey wrote in the mid-seventeenth century of Dr Ralph Kettell, the President of Trinity College:

> He observed that the Howses that had the smallest beer had the most drunkards, for it forced them to goe into the towne to comfort their stomachs, wherefore Dr Kettell always had in his College excellent Beere, not better to be had in Oxon, so that we could not goe to any other place but for the worst, and we had the fewest drunkards of any howse in Oxford.[8]

Between the mid-seventeenth and the mid-eighteenth century, most English adults other than manual workers abandoned the practice of beer-drinking at breakfast in favour of chocolate, coffee, tea or bread and milk. At public treats, where free beer for all had once been the norm, a certain social distinction began to creep in at about the time of the Restoration, with wine being provided for the gentry or civic dignitaries and beer for the ordinary members of the crowd. On similar academic occasions wine appeared for the fellows of colleges, beer for undergraduates. Only at very special festivities, such as the Oxford celebrations for the accession of King James II in 1685, was Carfax Conduit allowed to run with claret. Yet wine had become available in taverns to any casual drinker who cared to pay for it, as we can see from the Oxford chronicler Anthony Wood's account of his early life, in which, describing the winter of 1642–3 when he was eleven, he noted that the taverns of Oxford ran dry of wine for several weeks after Christmas, 'and insted thereof sold ale and beere'.[9]

By the middle of the eighteenth century, therefore, beer was principally the drink of certain classes of people, such as farm workers, labourers, domestic servants and children at boarding school or young men in college, rather than the obvious accompaniment to any meal in any English home. Country houses continued to brew their own beer for the servants' hall, farm workers and children, just as they continued to bake their own bread well into the mid-nineteenth century. When Simon, 1st Earl Harcourt, built Nuneham Park near Oxford in 1756–7 he included a brewhouse in a wing of his new house; and when his son employed Capability Brown to redesign the domestic offices twenty-five years later a new brewhouse was built, detached from the main house but near the recently added kitchen wing. In towns, on the other hand, few large houses were built with facilities for brewing. Farm labourers, forced out of home brewing by a depressed economy, took to drinking at alehouses when they had the time and money to do so, and to beginning the day with a meagre breakfast of bread and tea, or just bread and water. The Oxford colleges continued to provide undergraduates with beer as a wholesome and cheaper alternative to wine, which became increasingly a feature of the ever-later dinner (at midday in the seventeenth century, mid-afternoon by the late eighteenth and early evening by the end of the nineteenth). A college fellow such as the beer-loving Dr Thomas Anyan, President of Corpus Christi College in the early seventeenth century, who ordered the building or rebuilding of the college brewhouse and was reported by Wood to have been drunk on beer at breakfast-time, appeared comically antiquated even to his immediate successors. All colleges continued to have ale brewed on the premises, but by the end of the eighteenth century only three of them were employing their own staff to do so. Sixteen of the colleges, in 1793, employed Bolton, a Witney brewer, since the prices charged by local brewers had become so exorbitant.[10]

Small-time brewing by publicans, too, became an antiquated practice once it was less and less economically viable to maintain and equip a small private brewhouse and to bring in the requisite supplies of malt. Peter Mathias has estimated that in 1700 there were about forty thousand brewing victuallers in England, in 1750 about fifty thousand, and by 1800 a rapidly diminishing twenty-four thousand. This did not indicate that less beer, overall, was being drunk, but rather that more power and money were becoming concentrated in the hands of the common brewers. They had begun the practice of owning or leasing groups of tied public houses, either simply through sale on the open market or as the result of foreclosing on mortgages, and could supply the occupants of non-tied houses more cheaply than these could produce their own beer. When a brewery acquired a public house all brewing on the premises automatically stopped. Thus in 1782, when Sir Richard Tawney bought the Wheatsheaf in St Aldate's, he acquired the farmyard-like back premises but not the brewhouse that occupied the plot next door.[11]

In the centre of Oxford, then, many former brewhouses quietly decayed, or became transformed into stables, workshops or small factories, or were pulled down to make way for gardens or extended living accommodation. In St Thomas's, on the other hand, the serious commercial brewhouses rarely underwent such drastic changes of use. At most, a large brewhouse which had for some reason become disused might be converted into a malthouse or be temporarily used for some other industrial purpose, often one needing a supply of running water, before reverting to its original function.

A fine example of this is the large Elizabethan brewhouse built by a speculator, Robert Linke, on the Morrell's Brewery site. Linke, a Christ Church singing-man who earned his living as a member of the cathedral choir, leased various properties around Oxford, including a brewhouse in St Giles on the site of the present offices of the law firm Morrell, Peel and Gamlen.[12] In 1563 he took out a lease from Christ Church of the nucleus of the present brewery site, a rough triangle of land fronting the south side of St Thomas's Street and tapering to a point, occupied by a garden or orchard, between the two streams. Ralph Agas's bird's-eye-view map of Oxford, surveyed in 1578, tells us that the street frontage consisted of a row of small, gabled houses, probably with a yard and workshops behind them which could be reached for loading and unloading purposes by punt along the Back Stream. Earlier leases tell us that in the thirteenth century, when there must have been some means of access from the street between the houses, the yard had contained a horse-mill, a dye-works and a forge.[13] Linke's brewhouse appears on David Loggan's bird's-eye-view

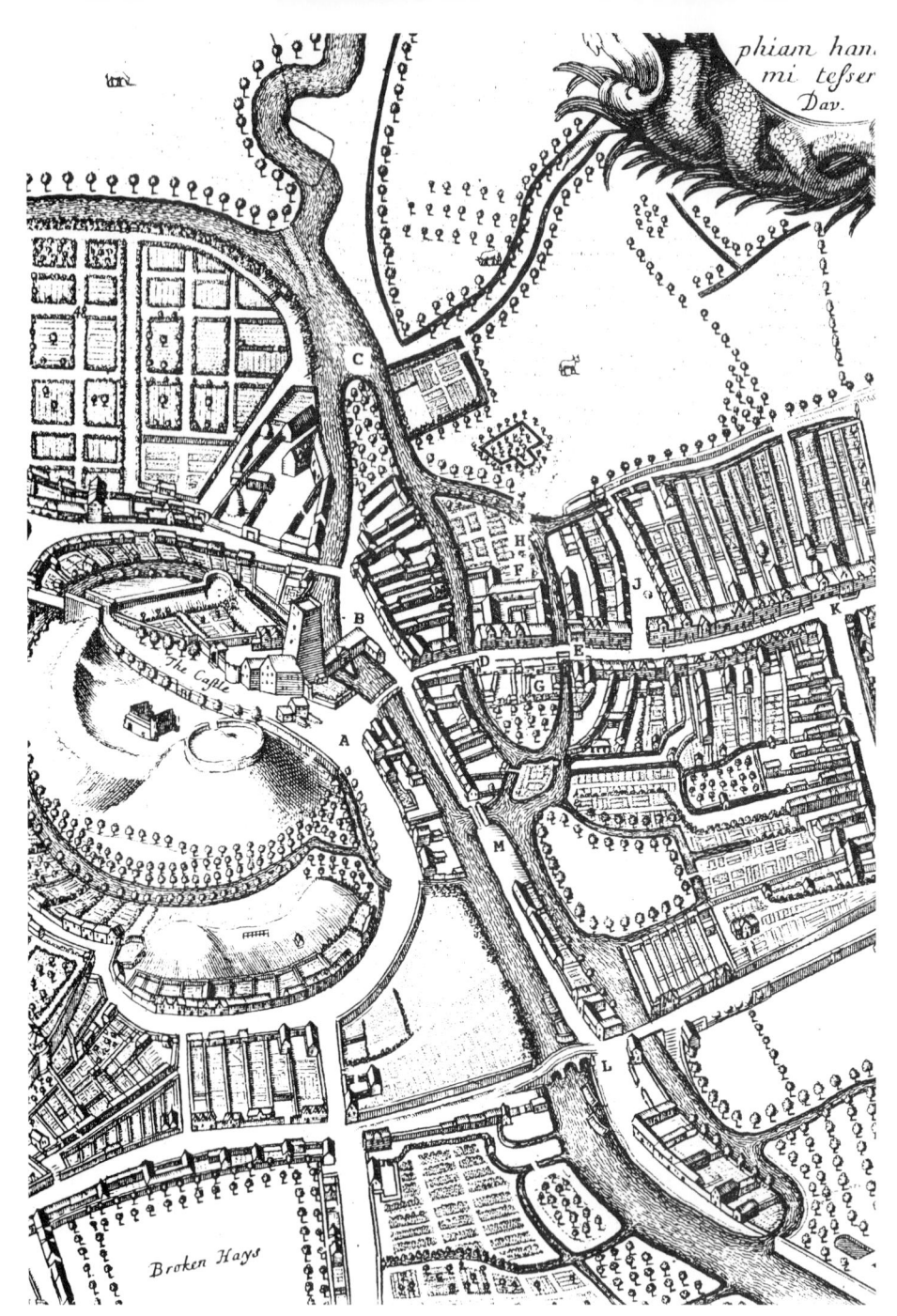

The brewery and its surroundings, 1675: a detail, facing southwards, from David Loggan's plan of Oxford, published in *Oxonia Depicta* (1675). The main watercourse shown here is the Castle Mill Stream, of which an eastward-swinging branch becomes the Trill Mill Stream as it skirts the corner of the Paradise Garden in St Ebbe's. Key: A: Tidmarsh Lane and former fifteenth-century Oseney Abbey brewhouse; B: Castle Mill; C: Swan's Nest peninsula; D: Bookbinder's Bridge over Back Stream; E: Knowles's Bridge; F: Robert Linke's sixteenth-century brewhouse on future Morrell's Brewery site; G: early seventeenth-century brewhouse, later Morrell's Brewery stables; H: Linke's, later Morrell's brewhouse garden; J: The Hamel; K: Junction of St Thomas's Street and Hollybush Row; L: Hythe Bridge; M: Fisher Row plan of 1675 as one of a complex of buildings behind the row of houses, with two long back additions, one directly fronting the stream, joined by a barn-like building lying parallel with the street frontage across a yard, and with a smaller yard at an angle to this adjoining the Back Stream. Behind the buildings a garden still occupies roughly half the area, but can be reached only through the outbuildings or by water. Two of the four houses on the street front have tiny fenced-off yards within the main rear yard. There is no means of access to the outbuildings except by entering one of the two houses that communicate directly with them, or by punt or small barge along one of the side-streams.

Linke probably never operated his own brewhouse, but left the property as an investment to his son Robert, an Oxford graduate and schoolmaster, who sublet it to a variety of under-tenants. By the time that the younger Robert's widow had taken over the lease early in the seventeenth century, brewing had temporarily come to an end on the site. Not all the sub-tenants are identified by their occupations, but of those who are, throughout the seventeenth century, none was in a trade connected with brewing. At least one, however, John Cope in the 1650s, of unnamed occupation, was almost certainly a maltster.[14] A 'Book of Evidences' drawn up for Christ Church towards the end of the century describes the nucleus of the present brewery site:

> The Eighteenth Tene[me]nt alwaies call'd by the name of a Brew-house, is bounded thus, The Back Streame [sic] running from Knowles's bridge West, the streame or river running from Bookbinders bridge East, The street leading from the Castle toward St Tho[mas's] par[ish] Church North And the water-course running by Oxe Close wall South. This, as has been s[ai]d was always call'd a Brewhouse, but is now a Malthouse, besides many Tene[ment]s let to poor people, a garden ground, Orchard, backe side & waters . . .[15]

It was this malthouse and its appurtenances that, in 1718, Thomas Kenton leased as a single property from Christ Church and set about reconverting into a brewhouse, while probably making his home in one or two of the improved, street-fronting houses at the east end of the row, nearest to the Back Stream. Either he or his son or (less probably) Richard Tawney demolished part of the street frontage to give access to the yard for horses and wagons, while keeping the barn-like Elizabethan building that enclosed the yard to the south. Behind and in front of this long building a complex of brewhouses arose on the east side of the yard near the Back Stream, with a row of stores, and a privy at one end, backing on to the smaller stream to the west.

Meanwhile, round about, other breweries consolidated themselves as family businesses or fell into abeyance as family interest in them waned. In Tidmarsh Lane, just across the Castle Mill Stream, the fifteenth-century brewhouse formerly let out to tenants by the monks of Oseney Abbey was still standing, disused, in 1782, when Christ Church commissioned a detailed plan of the area. Since the Reformation Christ Church had let this property to a succession of tenants, some brewers, others obviously investors. In 1679, when John Bishop, brewer, leased the property directly from Christ Church, it was said to include a 'brewhouse, malthouse and all outhouses and offices necessary to them with a large garden ground and orchard'. But thirty years later, when John Bishop, gentleman (and therefore no longer a tradesman), passed on the lease to another John Bishop, gentleman, we may assume either that brewing had come to an end on that site or that the Bishops had begun to sublet to other, financially less secure brewers. The brewhouse remained in the Bishop family's hands until Christ Church found a new lessee in 1758. Two years later the new lessee made way for the twenty-five-year-old Edward Tawney, younger son of the late brewer of St Thomas's Street, Richard Tawney, who, with a brother in brewing, evidently wished to set up in a usefully supplementary business, and leased the property in order to work it as a maltster.[16]

On the small triangular island across St Thomas's Street from the Morrell's Brewery site, now the home of the brewery surveyor's department, Christ Church leased a group of cottages and buildings with an orchard behind them to two successive local brewers, Henry Bosworth and William Chillingworth, in 1628 and 1650. Earlier these premises had been used as a dye-works, and from the 1670s they were used, equally messily, by a fellmonger; but it is perhaps more than coincidental that the brewhouse here (which could be reached from the street by an alleyway between the houses) operated at a time when Robert Linke's former brewhouse was no longer used as such, perhaps proving impractical to work without direct access for wagons and horses from the street.[17]

Meanwhile, round the corner off Paradise Street, on the promontory where swans must have nested at the confluence of two waters, the future Hall's brewery became established when Francis Loader began to brew there in about 1700. Two landlords, Christ Church and the City of Oxford, owned adjacent pieces of land there, the Christ Church land lying near Quaking Bridge and the City-owned land, which was vacant until the mid-seventeenth century, lying nearer the tip of the Swan's Nest where the two waters met. Between these two was a former brewhouse, converted into a malthouse by the late seventeenth century, and paying a quit-rent to Christ Church after its sale to a private occupant. One tenant of the brewhouse, a Mrs Sheppery or Shepreve, had also leased the City-owned waste plot of land, before a miller named John Plaisteed built two houses there in about 1650. The farther of these, near the tip of the Swan's Nest, was described in 1709 as containing two ground-floor rooms with a bedchamber and cockloft above, and had been occupied since about 1695 by a brewer, Francis Loader, whose wife's trustees had originally leased it for her from the City.[18]

In 1700 Loader became a tenant of the adjoining Christ Church piece of land, on which he must have built a brewhouse; and in 1729 Thomas Loader leased both the City-owned pair of houses, probably knocking them into one to make a reasonably spacious family house. Deborah, Thomas's widow, renewed his leases from the City and Christ Church in the early 1740s, and, unlike Hannah Kenton round the corner in St Thomas's Street, kept the business under her control until her daughter married a brewer, Alderman John Treacher, ten years later. Treacher's lease of the City-owned portion of the Swan's Nest, dated 1755, states that a brewing firm, Messrs Collins and Bew, occupied the premises to the north of Deborah's former City leasehold, evidently as her sub-tenants in her late husband's brewhouse. Treacher died, reputedly worth £40,000, in 1780; and his son, Alderman Sir John Treacher, a municipal grandee like his brewing neighbour Sir Richard Tawney, bought the freehold of the Christ Church-owned portion of the Swan's Nest in 1796. With his partner William Hall, who eventually took over the business, he continued at the brewery until his death in 1807, leaving the Hall family his impressive, square, Georgian brewery house with its large rear garden facing westwards across the mill stream and the riverside meadows to the south of Osney Lane.[19]

Among the Loaders' neighbours in Lower Fisher Row, where they had leased a property between 1700 and 1757, had been the Tawneys, boatmen for a century or so before Richard Tawney retired into brewing. Mildly disreputable at first (Nicholas and William Tawney were accused in 1637 of unlawfully digging up clay on Port Meadow to sell it to brewers),[20] the family evidently gained from the widowed Elizabeth Tawney's remarriage in 1691 to a bargemaster, John Clarke. This brought her a substantial leasehold property in Lower Fisher Row, since she outlived John Clarke and, once her younger son Richard had reached his majority, continued to live there with Richard as lessee occupying the adjoining house. Only seven at the time of his mother's remarriage (when she sold her late husband's equipment, including his boats),[21] Richard may have taken over a share in his stepfather's business as well as his leasehold. His brother Robert, five years older than he was, also worked as a bargemaster, but described himself for some purposes as a yeoman of Binsey, a couple of miles up the Thames from Fisher Row. Richard, too, in his later years as a boatmaster, claimed to be of Binsey; and he, his elder son Sir Richard and younger son Edward are all impressively commemorated in monuments in Binsey church.[22]

Richard's first wife Jane died in 1717, leaving him with an only daughter, Jane, who later married the son of his elder brother Robert. By his second wife, Elizabeth Rowles of Yarnton, he had Richard, born in 1721, and Edward, born in 1735. Both were aldermen and each was three times Mayor of Oxford, at a time when corruption and graft were rampant in city politics. Richard, while owner of the brewery in 1768, spent some days in prison at Newgate as a salutary warning for his part in an attempt by the city councillors to bribe the two sitting Members of Parliament. A few years later, as deputy mayor, he was knighted during a visit by King George III to Oxford, voluntarily substituting himself for the mayor who was unwilling to pay the expenses that went with the honour.[23]

Few direct records of the brewery have survived from the period of ownership by the Tawneys, between the 1740s and the late 1790s. We know that in 1759 the younger Richard bought the freehold of the brewery's first tied public house, the King and Queen at Wheatley, which cost him £350. For twenty years he made no apparent effort to acquire others; then, in a spate of activity during the last twelve years of his life, he bought the Anchor in New Road, the Jolly Post Boy in High Street, the Three Cups in Queen Street near St Martin's churchyard, the Wheatsheaf in St Aldate's and (probably) the Boar's Head in Queen's Lane, which the Morrells exchanged for the Red Lion in High Street in 1801. Outside Oxford he bought the Red Lion at Tetsworth, the Red Lion at Eynsham and the White Hart at Benson.[24] For supplies of malt for brewing he leased a malthouse on Christ Church-owned land at Rewley, near the present Oxford railway station, to supplement the output of his brother Edward's small malthouse behind the old brewery in Tidmarsh Lane. (This large malthouse, in the ruins of the former Rewley Abbey, later belonged to the Rowland family, bakers and millers, who were close friends of the Tawneys and a powerful family in St Thomas's.) To graze the horses that pulled his drays, and for meadowland to provide them with hay, Tawney leased several fields belonging to Rewley on either side of the present Park End Street, and further land in Alley Meads, an expanse of pasture stretching westwards from St Thomas's church across what is now the main railway line towards Osney and the river.[25]

Sir Richard's marriage had left him with no surviving direct heir, and when he died in 1791 the brewery passed to his bachelor brother Edward, then in his fifties and already fully occupied with local politics and his own private form of empire-building. In 1763, three years after establishing himself as a maltster behind the disused brewhouse in Tidmarsh Lane, he had become the first independent tenant of the City-owned Castle Mill. Previously rented out, rather than leased, to tenants nominated by the City, this had enjoyed a theoretical monopoly of a high proportion of local milling, the profits from which had gone directly to the City.[26]

INTRODUCTION

Milling and malting were often combined in the late eighteenth and early nineteenth centuries, and Edward Tawney, like his brother, profited from a sound, increasingly prosperous business. Once the Mileways Act had been passed in 1771 (allowing Oxford colleges to sell freehold property, initially for the rebuilding of Magdalen Bridge and other, similar improvements), Christ Church was able to begin selling off properties in St Thomas's, a process that continued over the next two hundred years. In 1773 Tawney bought the freehold of the Tidmarsh Lane brewhouse and malthouse, and in 1796 the freeholds of a row of properties in Lower Fisher Row, including the former leasehold tenement occupied by his father, grandmother and John Clarke before him, and others on which he built (or designated to be built) his almshouse for four poor men and four poor women and a fine, square, Georgian red brick house for himself.[27] Both of these remain standing, close to Morrell's Brewery, as 1 to 3 Lower Fisher Row, Tawney's own house at No. 1 having accommodated two successive generations of Morrells, one brewery manager, his widow and their unmarried daughters in the period between 1800 and the Second World War.

Two months before his brother died, Edward Tawney had renewed his lease of the Castle Mill. He probably assigned this to another lessee almost at once, since he stopped referring to himself as 'mealman' and began to call himself 'brewer'.[28] Yet a different life altogether, one of country or suburban retirement, had begun to suggest itself to him. Having no children as heirs to the brewery, he probably saw no reason to continue nurturing his brother's business until the day he died. His much older half-sister Jane, married to her first cousin Robert Tawney, a carpenter near Magdalen Bridge, had had sons: Bradnam, an Oxford graduate, chaplain of Winchester and New College, and Henry, who inherited his father's carpenter's business. (These apparent social oddities, breaching the supposedly impenetrable divide between town and university, were much more common in the eighteenth and early nineteenth century than late-Victorian, suburban donnish snobbery cared to admit.) Henry's two sons – Richard, who became a canal engineer, and Charles, a future partner with Henry Hall in the Swan Brewery in St Thomas's – had been seventeen and eleven when their great-uncle Sir Richard Tawney died, and too far removed from him to be considered as his or his brother Edward's heirs. Charles's share in the Swan Brewery, then known as Hall and Tawney, may have passed down to him from his mother's first cousin, the childless Sir John Treacher; and, as a cousin of his later married the young James Morrell, a network of family relationships bound the early nineteenth-century owners of the two rival breweries, if not always amicably, together.

Edward's closest personal heir was his half-niece Ann, Bradnam and

Henry Tawney's younger sister, who had married a High Street apothecary named Theophilus Wharton. Perhaps with her eventual comfort in mind, Edward built himself a gentleman's farmhouse at Headington, on the hill to the east of Oxford, and directed in his will that the house and its contents (excluding only his horses and carriage) should go to Ann for her lifetime and to her eldest son Theophilus after her death. The Fisher Row house was to be sold at auction after he died, and the proceeds added to the rest of his estate.[29]

At the brewery, Edward employed a brewer, William Morgan, and a maltman, John Hiscock, each of whom received £50 under the directions of his will. The absence of a bequest to a clerk (an important figure in the early nineteenth-century history of the brewery, before James Morrell's son appointed the first manager) suggests that Edward may have done much of the necessary paperwork for the business himself. Unlike Sir Richard he seems to have taken little interest in expanding the brewery business, and acquired no new freehold tied public houses. On the Tidmarsh Lane site he converted, or had already converted, the former brewhouse into a second malthouse, and amalgamated the malting business with the brewery once he gave up the lease of the Castle Mill.[30]

Nos 1–3 Fisher Row, Oxford, built by Edward Tawney in about 1790. The house on the left (No. 1) was occupied by Tawney, then from 1800 to 1856 by members of the Morrell family. Thomas Sherwood, Brewery Manager, moved into the house in 1857; members of his family continued living there until early in the Second World War. The house on the right (Nos 2–3) contained Tawney's Almshouses

Even so the malting capacity of Tidmarsh Lane was far from satisfactory, and needed supplementing or updating within a very few years of his retirement from the brewery in 1798, followed by his death early in 1800.

In September 1797 Tawney entered on his third and last term as Mayor of Oxford. Two months later he entered into an agreement with Mark and James Morrell, the young nephews of Oxford's most prominent solicitor, James Morrell, to take them into a nominal partnership with him while they began to buy out his interest in the brewery, the whole of which (including the freeholds of the Tidmarsh Lane malthouse and the various tied public houses) he valued at £9,975. Just over a year later, at the end of 1798, he placed an advertisement in the local newspaper stating that the partnership had come to an end and that the Morrells would in future carry on the brewery without him.[31] The freehold properties, and the lease of the brewery premises from Christ Church, remained in Tawney's name until his death in March 1800. By then, the Morrells had paid only part of the lump sum on which they had agreed; but in August 1800 Tawney's executors placed them officially in possession of the freehold property, and in the same month James Morrell (probably the solicitor, acting for his nephews, to whom he had lent large sums of money), bought the freehold of the Brewery House, 1 Fisher Row, for them at auction for £586.[32]

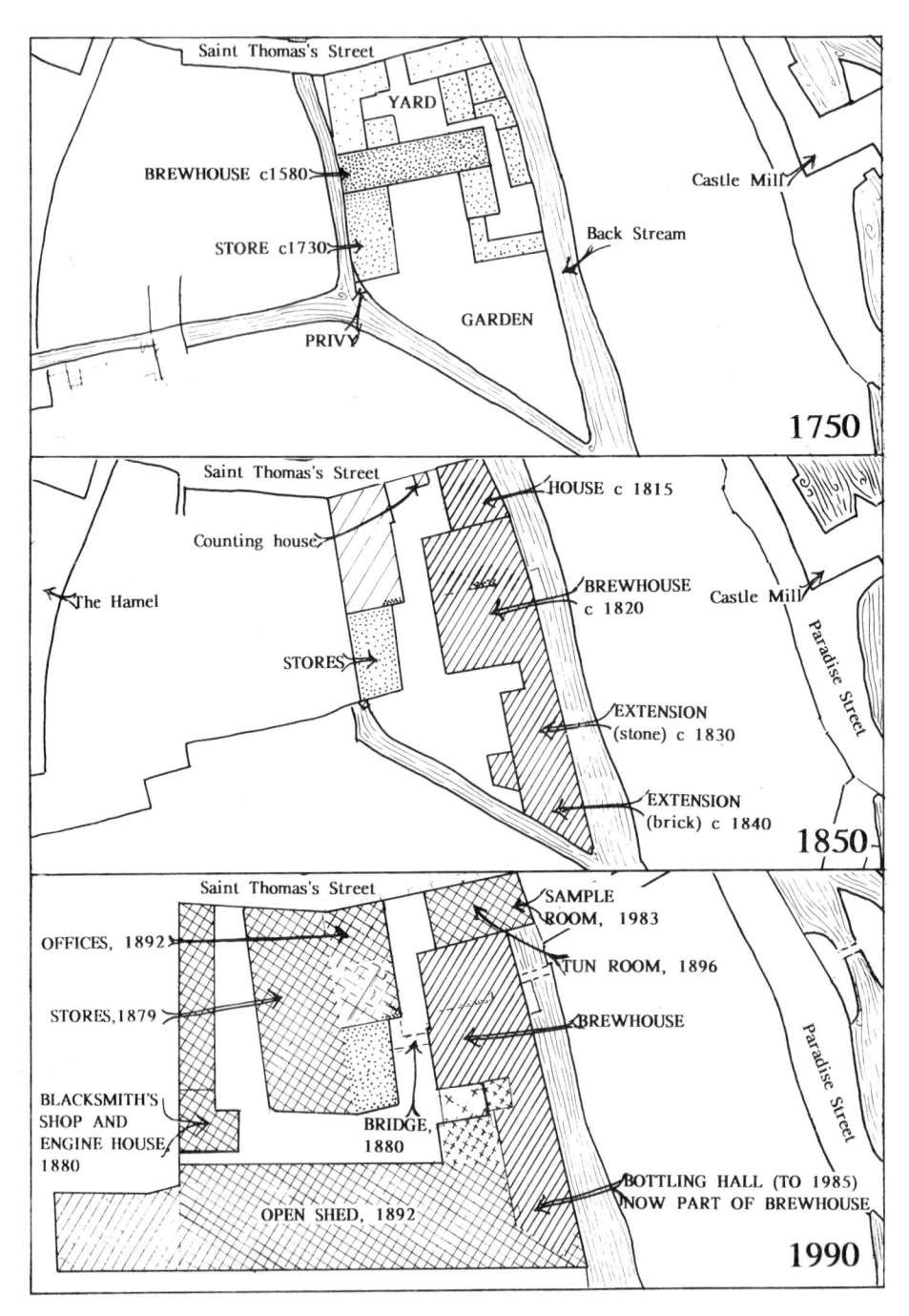

Morrells Brewery site plan, 1750, 1850 and 1990

CHAPTER ONE

THE MORRELLS OF WALLINGFORD AND OXFORD

The surname Morrell, traditionally pronounced 'Murrell' with the accent on the first syllable, is a familiar one in Oxford and its immediate surroundings. Few people who do not work there ever penetrate the brewery buildings, in a secretive, little-visited part of central Oxford dominated by the castle mound as it rises steeply above the Castle Mill Stream. Many, however, must be aware of the nourishing, malty smell of brewing which is sometimes carried towards the city centre on a westerly wind. Anyone living in or passing through Oxford is likely to see Morrell's name on advertisement hoardings, the sides of city buses, and the façades of any of about fifty local public houses. The alternative name, Lion Brewery, used officially from the 1870s when the brewery was in the hands of family trustees, never really caught on, despite the fact that its principal local competitors were the Eagle and the Swan. For two centuries, less a few years, the brewery has been Morrell's; and the family name remains all that is necessary to identify it, as it has been from the late 1790s onwards.

Elsewhere in Oxford the name has other associations. Morrell Avenue, the steep, tree-lined road of superior late-1920s council houses leading down from the Churchill and Warneford hospitals into St Clement's, commemorates the family's long residence on Headington Hill, where James Morrell, the younger of the two brewery brothers, built the house that developed into the present Headington Hill Hall. South Park, bordered on one side by Morrell Avenue, and Headington Hill Park, the lower part of the original shrub-planted grounds of the rebuilt Victorian Headington Hill Hall, now belong to the City of Oxford, but in the late nineteenth century were both part of the family's private pleasure-grounds, sweeping down from the summit of the hill as far as London Place and the edge of the River Cherwell in St Clement's.

In St Giles, again, there were Morrells, commemorated now by the solicitors' firm of Morrell, Peel and Gamlen in Beaumont Street and at 1 St Giles. James Morrell the attorney, the uncle of Mark and James at the brewery, came to Oxford in the 1750s as an adolescent articled clerk, and in time established himself as the most powerful attorney in the city. He and three generations of his descendants lived and practised on the east side of St Giles from 1766, when he acquired the lease of a large family house, now rebuilt as part of Balliol College, until 1908, when his great-grandson Frederick Parker Morrell of Black Hall, otherwise 21 St Giles, died. Frederick's son Philip Morrell, the Liberal Member of Parliament and pacifist opponent of the First World War, was the long-suffering husband of Lady Ottoline, the eccentric, much celebrated literary hostess. The country house where they lived and entertained, Garsington Manor, a few miles east of Oxford, stands next to the church where James Morrell the attorney's first wife was buried in 1765, and in a village where his family owned farmland from the late eighteenth century onwards.

The brothers Mark and James Morrell, aged twenty-six and twenty-four, were comparative strangers to Oxford when they first came there in the autumn of 1797 to take over their new business venture. Their background, however, was one that Edward Tawney would have found familiar, with milling, malting and corn-dealing as a strong element among the last few generations, and the Thames Valley, from Wallingford in Berkshire, thirteen miles south of Oxford, to London as their home.

Like Edward's father, the young men's grandfather Jeremiah Morrell had apparently taken up brewing towards the end of his life, having previously been the Wallingford miller. When he died in 1766 Jeremiah had left their father Mark, his third surviving son, all his brewing and malting utensils, together with all the account books and other items used in his counting-house. The implication seems to be that Jeremiah had handed over the running of the mill to Mark some years previously and had set up a separate malting and brewing business with a sideline in water-transport up and down the Thames. In addition to a sub-lease of Wallingford Mill, Jeremiah had also left Mark all his 'Horses Waggons Carts Harness Barge Sacks and Barge poles and Tackle', and a two-thirds share in the wharf in St Peter's parish near Wallingford Bridge, with a house, malthouse, pigeon house, gardens, outhouses and other buildings.[1] None of this, however, descended to Mark or James, who as younger sons were expected to leave Wallingford and fend for themselves.

The elder Mark had died in 1787 at the age of nearly fifty. When he had made his will four years earlier he had had four sons, Charles, Mark, James and an apparently short-lived Jeremiah, and three daughters to provide for. Charles, who was twenty-three when his father died, inherited the sub-tenancy of the mill and all the freeholds of the malthouses, warehouses, granaries, wharf and other premises in St Peter's parish. Mark, who had attended a boarding academy in Reading, perhaps to wean him from Wallingford in preparation for a more successful life elsewhere, had been apprenticed the previous year, aged fifteen, to a London brewer, William Tunnard of Southwark. James was still a schoolboy awaiting apprenticeship, his future unclear.[2]

THE MORRELLS OF WALLINGFORD AND OXFORD

SPW - St. Peter's Church, Wallingford
SMW - St. Mary's Church, Wallingford
SNG - St. Nicholas Church, Guildford
SMM - St. Mary Magdalen Church, Oxford
STC - St. Thomas's Church, Oxford
SCC - St. Clement's Church, Oxford

JEREMIAH MORRELL (1700?-1766) = Mary Smith (1706/07-1775)
of Wallingford and Guildford, SNG of Guildford, bur. SPW
bur. SPW. Miller and brewer. 1726

Jeremiah	William	Charles	**MARK**	**James**	Robert	Mary
(1729-1795) of London, bap. and bur. SNG, corn-factor and brewer, = Sarah Tew 1754	(1731-) bap. SNG	(1735-)	(1737-1787) of Wallingford, bap. SNG, bur. SPW, miller	(1739-1807) of Oxford, bap.SNG, bur. SMM, attorney	(1741-1816) of London, bap. SPW, hosier	(1745-1765), bap., bur. SPW
Thomas, Jeremiah, James, Robert, Sarah, Henry, all bap. St. Giles, Cripplegate			⊤ Phyllis Greenwood, bur. SPW 1780	= (1) Elizabeth 1764 Sheen of Wheatley (1741-1765), bur. Garsington (2) Ann Baker 1769 of Moulsford (1741-1819), bur. SMM. (See **Morrell/Baker Connection**.)	= Ann Jaques 1771 of Wallingford (1750-1773), bap. and bur. SPW Robert (1773-1849), of Oxford, bur. SPW, solicitor and banker	

Charles (1764-1846?), of Wallingford, bap. SMW, bur. SPW, miller, = Elizabeth Fludger, bap. SMW, bur. SPW (1772-1850)	Sarah (b.1765), bap. SMW, = Robert Dalzell 1790	Mary (b.1767), bap. SMW, = William Stone of Basildon, Berks.	**MARK** (1771-1843), of Oxford, bap. SPW, bur. STC, BREWER	Phyllis (b.1772)	**JAMES** (1773-1855), of Oxford, bap. SPW, bur. SCC, BREWER, BANKER
Charles, Jeremiah, Mark (1), Frances, James, Mark (2), all bap. SPW, 1795-1804		William Henry, Barrister = Emily, 1830 daughter of JAMES MORRELL, brewer			= Jane 1807 Wharton (see Tawney/Wharton/ Morrell Connection and next page)

Morrell family tree

Morrell family tree

- **MARK MORRELL** (1771-1843), of Oxford, BREWER
- **JAMES MORRELL** (1773-1855), of Oxford, BREWER, BANKER = Jane Wharton (1790-1814) of Headington (1807)

Children of James Morrell and Jane Wharton:
- Jane (bap. and bur. 1809, STC)
- **JAMES** (1810-1863), bap. STC, bur. SCC, of Headington Hill Hall, BREWER, JP, MFH = Alicia Everett (1822-1864), 1851
- Emily (1811-1891), bap. STC, of Streatley House, Berks. = William Henry Stone, her first cousin
  - Jane (1832-1848)
- Mark Theophilus (1813-1842), bap. STC, bur. SCC, of Headington

Child of James and Alicia:
- **EMILY ALICIA** (1854-1938) of Headington Hill Hall and Streatley House, bap. St. Giles, Oxford, bur. Streatley = **GEORGE HERBERT MORRELL** (1845-1906), MP, her third cousin, 1874
  (see **Morrell/Baker Connection**)

Children:
- **JAMES HERBERT** (1882-1965), of The Rise, Headington Hill, MANAGING DIRECTOR AND CHAIRMAN, MORRELLS BREWERY LTD. = Julia Denton, 1913
- George Mark (1884-1939)

Sir George Denton, Governor-General, The Gambia, 1902-1910
  - Julia Denton

Children of James Herbert and Julia:
- Mary (Luard) (1914-1993), DIRECTOR, MORRELLS BREWERY LTD.
  - Tom (1942-), DIRECTOR, MORRELLS BREWERY LTD.
- **BILL** (1915-), MANAGING DIRECTOR, CHAIRMAN AND PRESIDENT,
  - David (1959-), DIRECTOR, MORRELLS BREWERY LTD.
- George (1918-1936)
- Margaret (Eld) (1920-)
  - **CHARLES ELD** (1952-) MANAGING DIRECTOR, MORRELLS BREWERY LTD.

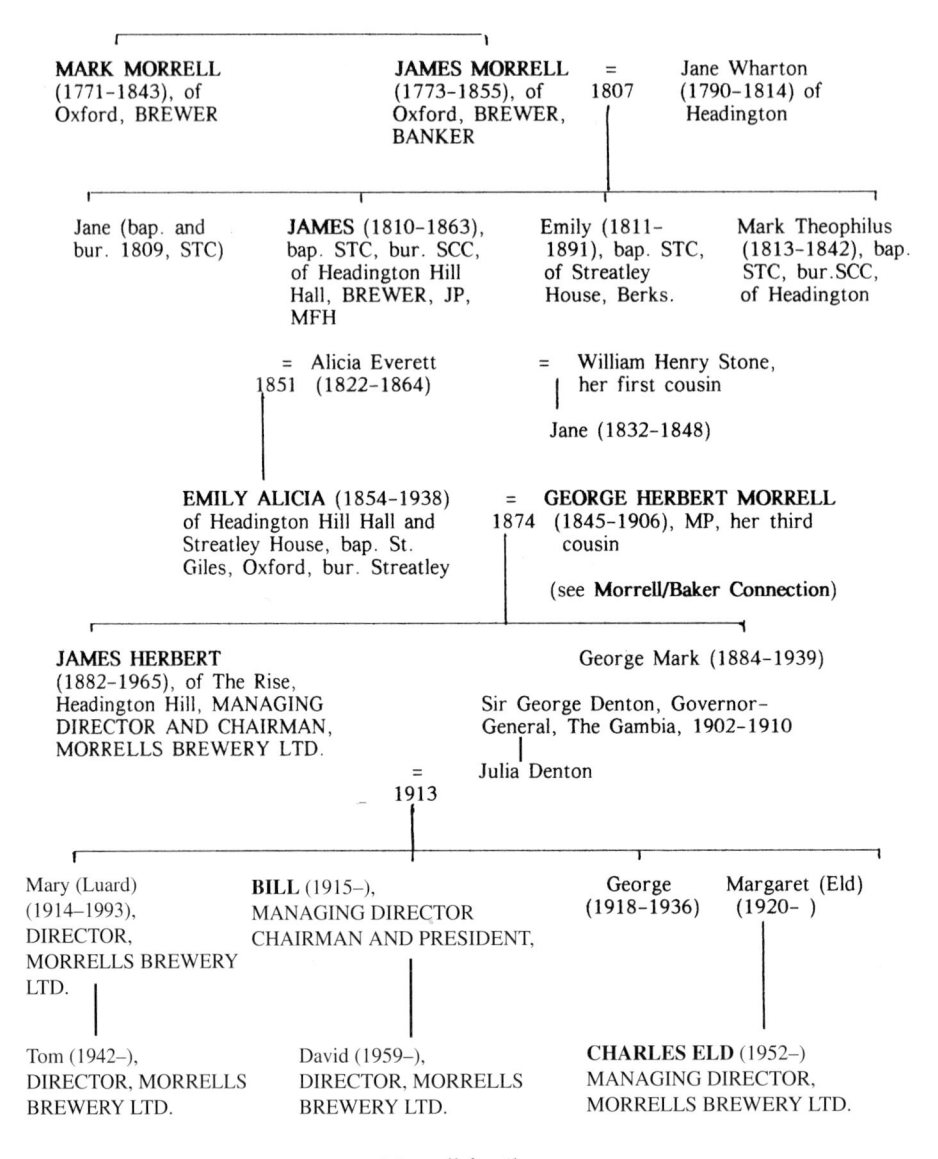

Morrell family tree

The earlier origins of the Morrells, before the eighteenth century, are hard to disentangle from those of the many other farming Morrells (and Murrells) who were to be found all over Berkshire and in other counties in southern England, but especially in the triangle of downland and river valley lying between Wallingford, Newbury and Swallowfield, south of Reading. Much of this is corn country, the downland near Wallingford being especially suitable for barley. As one travels by train from Oxford towards Reading, the rounded curve of Down Hill to the left of the line

THE MORRELLS OF WALLINGFORD AND OXFORD

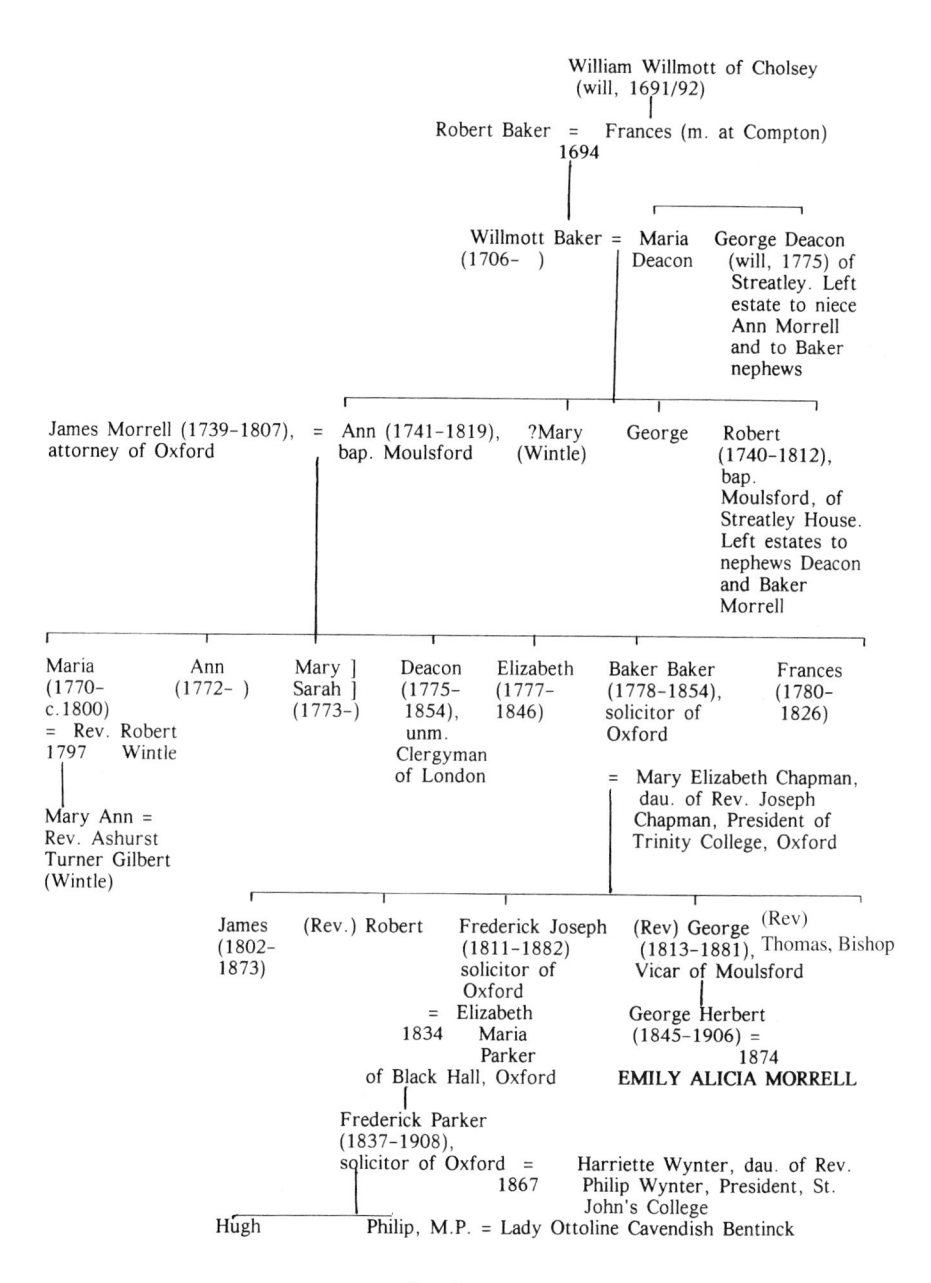

```
                                William Willmott of Cholsey
                                      (will, 1691/92)
                                            |
                        Robert Baker  =  Frances (m. at Compton)
                                    1694
                                       |
                        Willmott Baker = Maria    George Deacon
                           (1706-  )    Deacon    (will, 1775) of
                                                  Streatley. Left
                                                  estate to niece
                                                  Ann Morrell
                                                  and to Baker
                                                  nephews

James Morrell (1739-1807), = Ann (1741-1819),  ?Mary    George   Robert
attorney of Oxford           bap. Moulsford    (Wintle)          (1740-1812),
                                                                 bap.
                                                                 Moulsford, of
                                                                 Streatley House.
                                                                 Left estates to
                                                                 nephews Deacon
                                                                 and Baker
                                                                 Morrell
```

Maria	Ann	Mary]	Deacon	Elizabeth	Baker Baker	Frances
(1770-	(1772-)	Sarah]	(1775-	(1777-	(1778-1854),	(1780-
c.1800)		(1773-)	1854),	1846)	solicitor of	1826)
= Rev. Robert			unm.		Oxford	
1797 Wintle			Clergyman			
			of London		= Mary Elizabeth Chapman,	
Mary Ann =					dau. of Rev. Joseph	
Rev. Ashurst					Chapman, President of	
Turner Gilbert					Trinity College, Oxford	
(Wintle)						

```
         James      (Rev.) Robert   Frederick Joseph   (Rev) George    (Rev)
         (1802-                     (1811-1882)        (1813-1881),   Thomas, Bishop
         1873)                      solicitor of       Vicar of Moulsford
                                    Oxford
                                      = Elizabeth      George Herbert
                                   1834  Maria         (1845-1906) =
                                         Parker                    1874
                                    of Black Hall, Oxford   EMILY ALICIA MORRELL
                                         |
                                    Frederick Parker
                                    (1837-1908),
                                    solicitor of Oxford  =   Harriette Wynter, dau. of Rev.
                                                       1867  Philip Wynter, President, St.
                                         |                   John's College
          Hugh                     Philip, M.P. = Lady Ottoline Cavendish Bentinck
```

Morrell/Baker connection

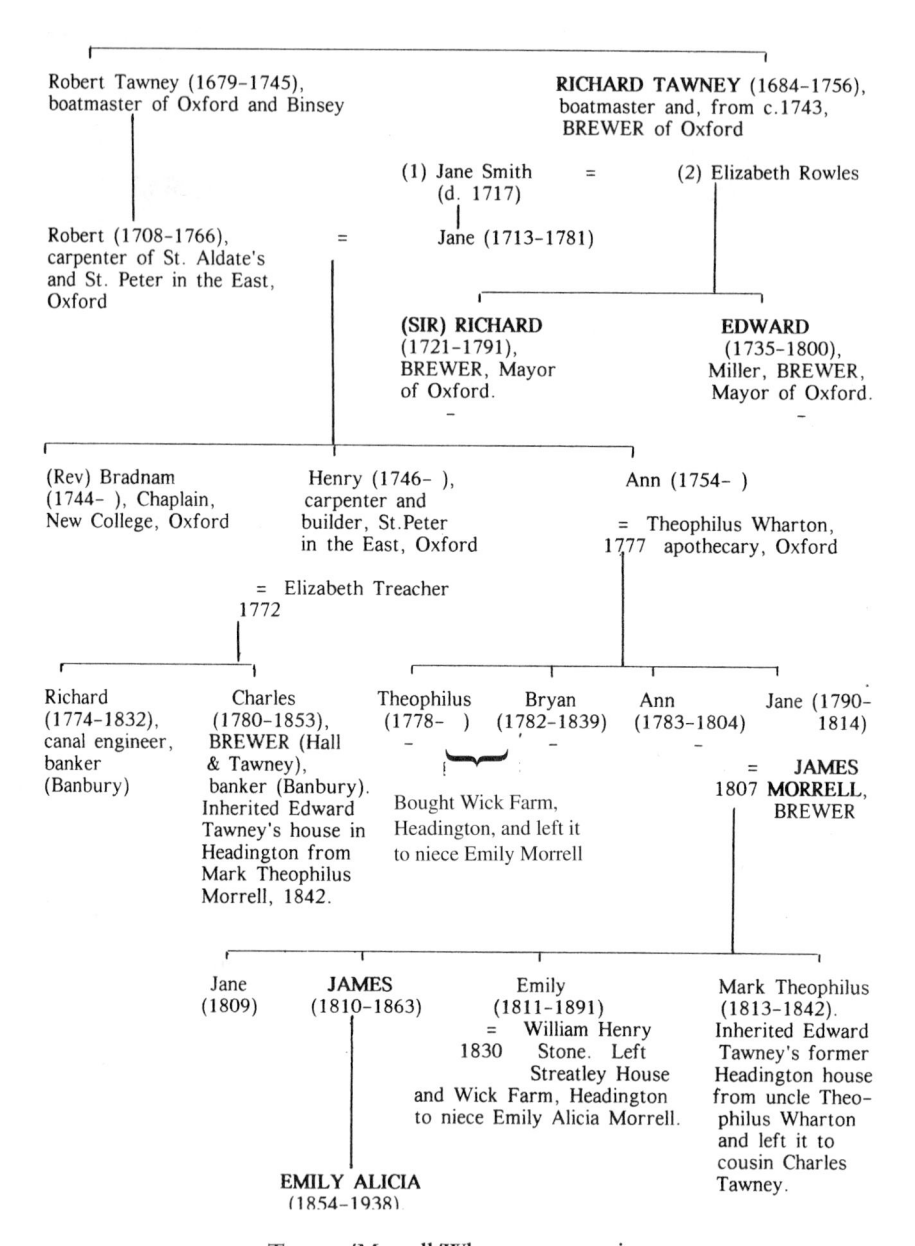

Tawney/Morrell/Wharton connection

- Robert Tawney (1679–1745), boatmaster of Oxford and Binsey
  - Robert (1708–1766), carpenter of St. Aldate's and St. Peter in the East, Oxford = Jane (1713–1781)

- **RICHARD TAWNEY** (1684–1756), boatmaster and, from c.1743, BREWER of Oxford
  - (1) Jane Smith (d. 1717) = (2) Elizabeth Rowles
    - Jane (1713–1781)
    - **(SIR) RICHARD** (1721–1791), BREWER, Mayor of Oxford.
    - **EDWARD** (1735–1800), Miller, BREWER, Mayor of Oxford.

Children of Robert (1708–1766) and Jane (1713–1781):
- (Rev) Bradnam (1744–), Chaplain, New College, Oxford
- Henry (1746–), carpenter and builder, St. Peter in the East, Oxford = Elizabeth Treacher 1772
- Ann (1754–) = Theophilus Wharton, 1777 apothecary, Oxford

Children of Henry and Elizabeth Treacher:
- Richard (1774–1832), canal engineer, banker (Banbury)
- Charles (1780–1853), BREWER (Hall & Tawney), banker (Banbury). Inherited Edward Tawney's house in Headington from Mark Theophilus Morrell, 1842.

Children of Ann and Theophilus Wharton:
- Theophilus (1778–)
- Bryan (1782–1839)
  - Bought Wick Farm, Headington, and left it to niece Emily Morrell
- Ann (1783–1804)
- Jane (1790–1814) = **JAMES MORRELL**, BREWER, 1807

Children of Jane and James Morrell:
- Jane (1809)
- **JAMES** (1810–1863)
  - EMILY ALICIA (1854–1938)
- Emily (1811–1891) = William Henry Stone, 1830. Left Streatley House and Wick Farm, Headington to niece Emily Alicia Morrell.
- Mark Theophilus (1813–1842). Inherited Edward Tawney's former Headington house from uncle Theophilus Wharton and left it to cousin Charles Tawney.

Tawney/Morrell/Wharton connection

Wallingford bridge and St Peter's church in the eighteenth century

just outside Didcot half obscures the large, modern malting installation at Wallingford, a replacement at several removes for the Morrells' small malting business of the late eighteenth and early nineteenth century. A few miles further south, in the hills to the west of Streatley, lie the villages of East Ilsley and Compton, where late eighteenth-century farming Morrells may have kept up some connection with their Wallingford cousins. James Morrell, the Oxford attorney, who had grown up at Wallingford in the 1740s and 1750s, had a summer home at Compton towards the end of his life, when a family of Morrells, perhaps distant, less successful relations, farmed there. By the river in the churchyard at Basildon, below Streatley, near the agriculturalist Jethro Tull, lie the grandparents-in-law of one of James's Wallingford nieces, William and Susannah Stone, whose descendants were closely associated with the brewery family at Streatley and Oxford for several generations.

Despite the lack of known antecedents for Jeremiah Morrell, the former Wallingford miller by the time of his death in 1766, an unnamed Morrell is also known to have been the miller there a century or so earlier. In the 1670s or thereabouts, this Mr Morrell complained that Edward Wells, a member of the powerful Wallingford brewing family, was using a private windmill to grind his own and other people's corn, thus infringing the civic monopoly that the town mills had enjoyed for at least the past forty years, since Charles I was on the throne.[3] Like Edward Tawney at the Castle Mill in Oxford, the Morrells were tenants responsible to the municipal authority, which in this case had derived its powers from the royal Honour of Wallingford early in the sixteenth century. In 1675 the Wallingford Mills and a large part of the town were destroyed by fire. The miller's complaint therefore almost certainly preceded the time of the fire, since private enterprise must have taken over from civic monopoly immediately after this.

If the late seventeenth-century Wallingford miller also had the distinctive family Christian name of Jeremiah, he may have been the Jeremiah, son of Jeremiah and Emma Morrell, who was baptized at St Martin in the Fields church, London, in 1638. Certainly the Wallingford Morrells were a fairly mobile family within the confines of south-eastern England and within an intricate network of family and local relationships. Jeremiah, the eighteenth-century Wallingford miller, who was probably born in the town in about 1700, spent his last twenty-five years there and was buried under a large oblong tomb on the north side of St Peter's church, also lived in Guildford, Surrey, between 1726 and about 1740. His wife Mary, whom he married in Guildford in October 1726, was the daughter of William Smith, a prosperous local coal merchant. Another important family in the town were the Flutters or Fludders, possibly a branch of the equally prosperous Wallingford Fludyers, of whom Elizabeth later married Jeremiah's grandson, the miller Charles. Apart from his marriage, however, no obvious explanation exists for Jeremiah's presence in Guildford, where his first five sons, Jeremiah, Charles, William, Mark and James were born between 1729 and 1739. Alone among the family, Jeremiah the eldest seems to have felt an attachment to the place, and was buried there, at the church where he had been baptized, after a lifetime spent in London, in 1795.[4]

Back in Wallingford, meanwhile, half a century had passed between the fire of 1675 and the reconstruction of the town mills. The first successful bid to reconstruct the mills occurred in 1723, when William Hucks and Thomas Tew promised to rebuild them within two years in exchange for a ninety-nine year lease of the premises.[5] Hucks and Tew were evidently entrepreneurs, and Tew may be identified as a member of a corn-dealing family of the parish of St Giles, Cripplegate, in the City of London, which seems to have moved there from Reading in about the late sixteenth century. Tew died, unfortunately intestate, in 1733, leaving the administration of his estate to his widow Ann.[6] The Sarah Tew who married Jeremiah, eldest son of Jeremiah Morrell of Wallingford and Guildford, at the church of St Benet Fink in 1754, and settled down with him as he pursued his occupation of corn-dealer in St Giles, Cripplegate parish, must have been at the remotest a great-niece of Thomas Tew. Their children, baptized at St Giles, Cripplegate, included a Jeremiah and a Thomas Tew Morrell. More significantly, Sarah had inherited a half-share in the remainder of the ninety-nine year lease of the mill. When her father-in-law Jeremiah in

Wallingford made his will, he remarked in it that he had not yet assigned his sub-lease of the mill to his son Mark, who was already milling there, but that he wished his executors to do so for him, and hoped that his son Jeremiah would eventually grant Mark a new sub-lease when the original one expired.

How the Morrells came back into occupation of Wallingford Mill in about 1740 (Jeremiah and Mary's two youngest children, Robert and Mary, were baptized at St Peter's, Wallingford, in 1741 and 1745) remains a mystery that is open to deduction from later events. Possibly Jeremiah's father, son of the original miller, had sub-leased the mill from William Hucks and Thomas Tew as soon as it had been rebuilt. The connection between Morrells and Tews was evidently strong enough to send the younger Jeremiah to London, where he may have taken over his father-in-law's business after marrying Sarah Tew. (A Richard Tew, baptized at St Giles, Cripplegate in 1696, may have been Sarah's father. Richard Tew, husband of Mary, fathered Rebekah, who was baptized at St Giles, Cripplegate in 1729. Richard Tew, husband of Ann, was the father of Sarah, baptized at St Andrew's, Holborn in 1736.)

Probably the most interesting fact about the London corn dealer Jeremiah is that, like his father, he turned in middle age to brewing. In 1786 his eldest surviving son Thomas Tew Morrell was living in the Minories, where his eldest son Jeremiah was baptized at Holy Trinity church. At just that time, according to a London trade directory, a brewing firm listed as 'Morrall and Collins' existed in the Minories. In his will, made in 1795, Jeremiah referred to himself as a brewer, although in earlier trade directories he had always appeared as a cornbroker. He left his premises in Red Cross Street, next to a bakehouse (perhaps a dependency of the corn trade), to his sons Thomas Tew and Robert Morrell, and his share in the head-lease of Wallingford Mill to his second son Jeremiah. He also had a summer home at Walworth, where his nephew Robert recorded a visit to him the previous year in his diary, and an estate at Guildford inherited from his mother's family, which may explain his wish to be buried there.[7]

Of the six sons of Jeremiah Morrell of Wallingford five were living, in their twenties and thirties, when he made his will in 1766; but only one, Mark, is known to have remained in Wallingford. This small riverside market town, with its tight oligarchy of Wellses and Fludyers, offered little opportunity to young men with their way to make in the world. The brewing firm operated by the Wellses (who later became close friends of Jeremiah's grandson, the miller Charles Morrell and his family) was too successful to allow a serious rival firm to flourish – a fact which may explain why Jeremiah's descendants apparently discontinued the brewing side of his business. Neither Jeremiah nor Mark made much effort to succeed as members of the Wallingford Corporation, whose business was mainly ceremonial and social. Representatives of the Wells family were Mayors of Wallingford twenty-seven times during the hundred years between 1745 and 1845; but no member of the Morrell family was mayor once during this period. Jeremiah, having joined the Corporation soon after his return from Guildford, was eventually fined for non-attendance and did not hold office. Mark, who had been elected a town bailiff in his twenties, was soon overtaken in public life by a keener contemporary, Charles Greenwood (possibly a brother of his wife, Phyllis Greenwood) and similarly dropped out. In his son Mark's apprenticeship indenture he described himself as a 'dealer', which suggests that he may have given up milling in his forties and handed over the business to his son Charles, while setting up some small independent concern of his own.[8]

The most successful Wallingford man, Sir William Blackstone, was a constitutional lawyer of international reputation, whose classic *Commentaries on the Laws of England* appeared in fascicle form between 1765 and 1769. During that period, as Recorder of Wallingford, he lived in a house inside the former castle, and caused St Peter's church to be rebuilt (as yet without its spire) in the classical style. In the 1750s, while a Fellow of All Souls' College, Oxford, and still quite a young man, he may have spared time for Cornelius Norton, an elderly Wallingfordian with an attorney's practice in Oxford. Blackstone's intervention may have persuaded Norton to accept as his articled clerk the adolescent James Morrell, who had been born in Guildford in 1739 as Jeremiah and Mary's fifth son, and was clearly the ablest of the family. James was working for Norton by 1757, and in early 1761 took out his freedom to practise in the Oxford Mayor's Court. At about that time Norton must have retired back to Wallingford, where he died a few years later aged over eighty.[9] The only member of his family to take up a profession rather than going into business, James used all the Morrell acumen to further his career, and profited especially from his skill at cultivating the rich and influential to build up a private attorney's practice which was a model of how to succeed in a provincial but increasingly political, fast-moving world.

In 1763 James joined forces with his chief potential rival, Thomas Walker, town clerk from 1756 until his death in 1795, and a man with many useful connections among the country gentry and heads of colleges. The young partners' account book, which covers the three years of their partnership together, shows them doing business with several colleges and with various important individual clients, such as the Earl of Abingdon at Wytham Abbey, the first Earl Harcourt at Nuneham Park, and Jane Austen's future relations, the Leighs or Leigh Perrots. In 1766 the partnership ended when the fourth Duke of Marlborough, James's exact

East side, St Giles, Oxford, late nineteenth century, showing St John's College (left) and Balliol College (right). The pedimented house (rebuilt in 1907 as part of Balliol College) belonged to James Morrell the attorney from 1766 until his death in 1807, and later to his descendants. To the left is 1 St Giles, offices of Morrell, Peel and Gamlen, solicitors

contemporary, invited Walker to become his man of business. The duke's town house in St Giles, Oxford (a pedimented stone mansion, later the Judge's Lodging and now part of St John's College) made him James's neighbour when in the same year James, having lost his first wife in childbed, took a sub-lease of a house farther down St Giles, now replaced by a neo-Georgian Balliol College building in vivid dark golden ironstone. The Morrells later became frequent visitors to Blenheim Park at Woodstock, where the duke encouraged them to make use of his grounds; and the brewery Morrells continued the friendship with the next two generations, the penurious fifth duke, his illegitimate daughters and his son, the highly respectable sixth duke.[10]

During his partnership with Walker James had often consulted Blackstone, Vinerian Professor of English Law since 1758, who had been happy to charge the young men a token fee of 1 gn. for advice when they first set up in business, but had later raised his charge as high as 7 gns for more complicated cases. In the 1760s Blackstone was Member of Parliament for two successive constituencies in Wiltshire, and by the 1768 election James was helping him with constituency work as well as acting as a kind of electoral agent for one of the candidates for Oxford City. Blackstone also employed him to devil for him as a parliamentary draftsman, drawing up private members' bills, engrossing petitions and riding up from Oxford to bring him documents at Westminster. Later James began to act as solicitor for the University, as well as for several of the individual colleges; and in the 1790s his nephew Robert Morrell, who kept a diary, recorded that his uncle was still busy from time to time at Westminster, and still riding back and forth between there and Oxford rather than travelling by coach.[11]

In 1769 James married Ann Baker of Moulsford, on the Thames near Wallingford, whose landowning family eventually passed on to his descendants a huge complex of property at Cholsey, Moulsford and Streatley. This included Streatley House, the home during the late nineteenth century of the brewery heiress Emily Morrell, whose position as lady of the manor caused her to rebuild much of the village round the church in arts and crafts style, evidently preferring it to her other inherited mansion, the squarely Italianate Headington Hill Hall.

Ann's father, Willmott Baker of Moulsford, was the son of Robert Baker, who had married Frances, daughter of William Willmott of Lollingdon Farm, Cholsey, at Compton, Berkshire, in 1694. From the Willmotts came Lollingdon and Breach Farms at Cholsey; while from the Deacons, the family of Willmott Baker's wife Elizabeth Maria, came property at Streatley and at North Stoke and Ipsden. Almost the entire estate descended to Ann's childless brother Robert Baker of Streatley House, and on his death in 1812 it was divided between Deacon and Baker Morrell, the two sons of James and Ann.[12] Deacon, educated at Westminster and Christ Church in conformity with his father's ambitions and status in life, became a clergyman and remained unmarried. Baker, an attorney, inherited the residue of James's practice when his father died in 1807. The couple also had six daughters, of whom we catch occasional glimpses (together with their Wallingford cousins, the young Mark and James) in the diary of their London-born cousin Robert Morrell, the son of Robert, Jeremiah and Mary's youngest-but-one child.

Robert, an only child, had been born in 1773 and was the same age as James, the youngest of the Wallingford family of brothers. He had grown up in Finsbury, where his father was a hosier and carpet manufacturer of Chiswell Street, and in Islington, to which his father had retired early. His mother Ann Jaques, a Wallingford ironmonger's daughter, had died when he was only a few months old. Robert had attended an academy in Hackney, then had left home at sixteen to be articled to a solicitor in Newbury. An unwilling Londoner, Robert always looked on Wallingford as the warm centre of family life, and his happiest times as a young man seem to have been those spent visiting the Jaqueses or the family at The

Wallingford bridge, *c.* 1890. In the background are (from left) the early nineteenth-century Bridge House, built by the miller and wharf-owner Charles Morrell, St Peter's church and the wharf

Wharf, the home of his cousin Charles, the elder brother of Mark and James.

We first meet Mark and James in 1792, on a painfully hilarious expedition to watch the military manoeuvres on Bagshot Heath. (Early the following year Britain went to war with Revolutionary France, but this is the only allusion to France in the whole of Robert's diary, which begins in 1789 and ends with his arrival in Oxford, a few months before Mark and James, in 1797.) The party consisted of four men and three ladies: Robert, Mark, James, and a cousin of the Oxford Morrells on their mother's side, Robert Wintle (formerly at school with Robert Morrell at Hackney and with Deacon Morrell at Westminster, and a future clergyman, who on leaving Christ Church in 1797 would marry Maria Morrell, the eldest of James Morrell the attorney's daughters), his future bride, and two sisters of Mark and James from Wallingford, Sarah Dalzell and Mary Morrell.

Meeting at Basildon on the Thames, at the home of William Stone, who was shortly to marry Mary Morrell, the four young men ride off together to spend the night in bug-infested lodgings in Reading. Mark Morrell stoically sleeps through the onslaughts of the bed-bugs, but the others lie awake suffering until dawn. They are then joined by the ladies, who have evidently been driven from Wallingford in a hired post-chaise. After breakfast they set off together, the ladies in the post-chaise, the men riding behind them, for Bagshot Heath. Robert, a lonely, awkward and self-conscious figure, soon finds the crowds, the dust and his borrowed horse exhausting. He cannot understand the manoeuvres and becomes separated from his cousins. Finding the post-chaise he consoles himself with grog, and after a long ride back to The Wharf at Wallingford he falls thankfully asleep at the end of a wasted twenty-four hours, sacrificed (as it might have been in one of the novels of his contemporary Jane Austen) to social politeness and cousinly conviviality.

Two years after the Bagshot episode, Robert reached the end of his five-year period as an articled clerk, but on his uncle James's advice decided to continue working for his former master in Newbury. A prudent young man, he was shocked, while on holiday at his father's house in London, by the sudden arrival of his Wallingford cousin James. Apprenticed, probably to a local miller or maltster other than his elder brother Charles (a James Morrell, maltster, was briefly in trade in Wallingford a year or two later),[13] he had quarrelled with his master and left home. In Robert's opinion James should have played safe and contained his irritation; 'but Morrell-like hot and not giving a Thought to the Consequences resulting from such hasty Steps', he had made a possibly disastrous bid for independence.[14] New starts, and even complete changes of trade or profession, were both theoretically and practically possible within the restrictive middle-class framework of late eighteenth-century England, as Robert himself would shortly find out. For a young man without power or influence, however, and without the savings amassed during a first few years' hard work and self-denial, it could be difficult to do more than carry out a routine of drudgery, passing from apprenticeship to a position as an employee in the hope that, at best, he might marry his master's daughter and in that way be promoted to a partnership in the family firm.

The following spring, when Robert was in Newbury, James turned up again, still in quest of work. He and Mark, both unsettled and unhappy, hoped to be able to work together in a place where Mark could continue as a brewer and James find a position in the milling or malting trade. (Mark's London apprenticeship had long since ended, and we know only that, in the spring of 1797, he was in lodgings with one S. Garrard, paying £11 17s. a quarter for room and board.)[15] In Newbury James had arranged to see William Stone of Englefield, probably the father of his sister Mary's husband, William Stone of Basildon, with a view to finding work at a Newbury mill. A bereavement, however, meant that he could not be interviewed, and this attempt apparently came to nothing. Both James and Mark had stood to inherit about £3,000 each from their father: a large enough sum to help them begin to buy their way into a business, but hardly enough to enable them to set up together from scratch on their own.[16]

In the spring of 1797 Robert brought to an end his unhappy and lonely eight years in Newbury. The Townsends, with whom he had lived, had a pretty, nubile but disagreeable daughter, Honoria. After agonizing into his diary about Honoria's feelings, or lack of feelings, for him, Robert clumsily proposed to her at half past seven one morning as she sat practising in the music parlour. He was rebuffed. 'She . . . told me . . . that she was particularly obliged to me for my Civilities to her but that we never could be – for that it was impossible for Us to be happy. . . . She kindly wished me happy with some other Lady this altho intended as kindness was severely cutting. She returned to her Harpsichord and I left the Room. . . .'[17]

With this botched proposal ended Robert's hopes of a steady family business in Newbury and, apparently, his thoughts of ever marrying. Two days later on 1 April, as he left the Townsends' house for ever, he may have reproached himself for this 'Morrell-like' act of rashness. Happily, however, on arriving in London he heard that his uncle James in Oxford had recently inherited some property, and so could afford to take on an employee. Ten days later, when James 'had transacted some weighty business at the Commons', Robert travelled back to Oxford with him, his aunt Ann and his cousin Maria. During the happy summer of that year, with expeditions to Blenheim Palace and Park in the company of his girl cousins, Robert found that he no longer needed to keep a diary. We have no direct record, therefore, of the arrival in the attorney James Morrell's household that autumn of his other nephews, the younger brewer Mark and his brother, Robert's future banking partner, James.

CHAPTER TWO

BREWERS AND BANKERS, 1797–1815

Oxford in the late 1790s, the home of Edward Tawney, James Morrell and his nephews Robert, Mark and James, was a largely pre-industrial city, much dominated by the country gentry from round about and by the celibate, clerical fellows of the twenty-five colleges and halls. In the centre of the city, between Magdalen Bridge, the Trill Mill Stream in St Aldate's and the fields at the north end of St Giles, the colleges and university buildings clustered together like groups of greater or lesser country houses, with their newly classical or traditionally gabled, battlemented, crocketed and towered exteriors surrounded by stables, brewhouses, kitchen gardens and groves. To the south, east and west the city was bounded by the rivers Thames and Cherwell; to the north by farmland, market gardens, the flood-prone common grazing land of Port Meadow, and the elm-planted walks of the Parks.

In the main central streets shops were few but inns and alehouses frequent. Banking, as we know it now, had barely begun, and was in the process of evolving out of other branches of trade. Two Oxford banks with premises in High Street, Richard Cox & Co. and Fletcher, Parsons, had both been drapers' or mercers' businesses until the early 1790s. Fletcher, Parsons went over to banking in 1792 and handled the affairs of many prominent local families, including the Tawneys and the Morrells, before becoming Parsons, Thomson & Co., and eventually merging with Barclays Bank.[1] Other banking businesses, such as Tubb, Wootten and Tubb, and Thomas Walker & Co., were apparently begun by attorneys as a way of investing part of their earnings.

In the absence of suburbs most business and professional men lived in the houses in which they had their offices, or close by. James Morrell did business from his house at the south end of St Giles, an ancient, deeply built property with an office, dining room, parlour, kitchen, pantry, larders and wash-house on the ground floor, and two drawing rooms and ten bedrooms on the two floors above.[2] In the early 1780s he had invested in the freehold of the smaller, next-door property to the north, the present 1 St Giles, formerly part of a larger City-owned leasehold property named the Dolphin to whose head-lessee he had previously lent money. Finding nothing that he wished to do with this extra property, James leased it rent-free to the retired Bodley's librarian in exchange for repairs and maintenance. Later his attorney son, Baker, incorporated it into the main family house next door, which he had persuaded his mother and unmarried sisters to vacate in exchange for his own smaller and less distinguished house in Holywell.[3]

Transport in and out of the city was, if not on foot, either water-borne or horse-drawn. Several dozen coaches a day left Oxford's major inns (including the Morrell-owned Three Cups in Queen Street) for London or for destinations in the Midlands, the south or the south-west. Heavy freight still travelled by river, landing from the south at Folly Bridge wharf or being diverted up or down the Trill Mill Stream/Castle Mill Stream. Since 1790 the Oxford Canal, with its basin on the site of the present Nuffield College in New Road, had linked Oxford with the coal- and iron-producing Midlands and brought it one step nearer to becoming an industrial city in its own right. With the new canal came an influx of migrants from northern Oxfordshire, Warwickshire and beyond. Chief among them were members of the complicated coal-dealing dynasty of Ward, who established themselves in Ward's Yard off George Street and later occupied a coalyard and malthouse in Tidmarsh Lane next to Edward Tawney's former malthouse. There came, too, a temporary horde of hard-drinking navvies, some of whom settled permanently in the tenements of St Thomas's Street, and found new employment working the narrow-boats for the fishermen and boatmen of Fisher Row and their families.

Mobility, for those rich enough not to have to travel everywhere on foot or by cart, was by stage-coach, hired post-chaise, private carriage, or (the most usual means for men who were fit and solvent enough) on horseback. All inns and colleges, and many substantial family houses, had their own stables and coach-houses, although horses could also be kept out at livery. When a family travelled together the men would often go on horseback and the women in the carriage, sometimes with a lighter chaise following behind them with the luggage. On one such occasion, when James Morrell and his family were returning from their summer house at Compton, footpads leapt aboard the chaise and stole their trunks on a lonely stretch of the road between the Botley Turnpike and the western outskirts of the city in St Thomas's.[4]

Both Mark and James were accustomed to riding and made full use of the stables attached to the brewery. The Tidmarsh Lane malthouses had their own capacious stables, in which Edward Tawney had probably kept his carriage when in Fisher Row. Across the road from the main brewery premises in St Thomas's Street was another set of stables, now housing the surveyor's office and works yard, on the site of a former dyehouse and brewhouse belonging to Christ Church. Since about the early 1770s the college had leased this property on favourable terms to St Thomas's parish, whose feoffees in 1790 included both Sir Richard and Edward

Tawney, and during the early nineteenth century both Morrell brothers. The brewery paid rent for these stables, using them for its team of dray horses, to the parish until 1923, when Christ Church finally parted with the freehold. In 1772 Edward Tawney owned stables lying immediately behind the brewery stables, when he was still living farther along Fisher Row in his father's former house.[5] It therefore seems likely that the brewery had the use of this property by that time, giving Tawney access from his own stables to St Thomas's Street.

The layout of the brewery itself had changed somewhat during eighty-odd years of occupation by the Kentons and the Tawneys. On the east side of the main yard a range of brewhouse buildings had accumulated along the line of the Back Stream, with space for a small yard immediately next to the stream for unloading and loading water-borne freight. By the late 1820s, when the Morrells had installed a steam engine to power the brewhouse machinery, this had become the coal yard. On the right-hand side of the entrance lay a range of storehouses, incorporating some of the stonework of the long Elizabethan brewhouse that had enclosed the yard to the south. Isaac Taylor's Oxford plan of 1750 shows this building as still substantially intact, with the range of stores continuing behind it on the west side and a narrow way round it to the coalyard, enclosed by other buildings, on the east. Either Richard Tawney or, more probably, his son Sir Richard demolished the central part of this old building to extend the main yard farther to the south. An early nineteenth-century brick building with a modern upper floor, which juts out into the left-hand side of the yard as one enters from the street, may represent a replacement for the east end of the Elizabethan brewhouse. Gradually various workshops such as a cooperage and a smithy were added at the south end of the newer brewhouse, encroaching on the triangle of garden, which by the late nineteenth century had all but disappeared.

The brewery house, which stood just to the left of the entrance with a blank stone end wall facing on to the street, occupied that position until 1896 when it was demolished to make way for the tun room. Throughout much of the nineteenth century it was lived in by brewery employees – first by the clerk, John Webb, his wife and daughters, and then after his death in 1855 by two successive brewers. Although built, like many seventeenth-century houses, of timber and plaster with stone rear and end walls, it does not appear on the Christ Church map of 1782, which shows a narrow entrance to the brewery yard still flanked by the remnants of the row of sixteenth- or seventeenth-century houses that once separated this from the road. With its pitched roof, dormers, and unadorned sash windows set almost flush with the front wall, it gives a superficial impression of being contemporary with these houses, and may indeed

The brewery gates, c. 1895. On the left is the house formerly occupied by John Webb, brewery clerk (d. 1855), then by successive brewers. Later it was used briefly as offices before the block on the right was completed in 1892. Demolished in 1896, it made way for the present tun room

have been built in the early nineteenth century re-using an older timber framework.

Did Mark and James build this house, or had it already been constructed by Sir Richard Tawney for his brewer or managing clerk? In 1812 and 1813 the Morrells were paying 18s. parish poor rate on their brewhouse, storehouse and stables, 12s. on the Tidmarsh Lane malthouse and 5s. on James Morrell's house (1 Fisher Row). In 1814 no rate was levied; and in 1815 they paid £1 2s. 6d. on a house, a brewhouse and additional buildings, 8s. on James Morrell's house and 12s. on the malthouse. In April 1815 a local builder valued the brewery premises for Christ Church, probably as the result of the recent erection of a house, and estimated their total annual rental value to be £70, of which he valued the house at £20, the brewhouse at £15, the yards and coopery at £10, the four storehouses at £20 and the garden at £5. 'The Premis's', he added, were 'for Old Buildings in decent Repair – one store room rebuilding'.[6] The Morrells' bank book for this period gives no clue about the building or rehabilitation of the house, and we can assume only that the year 1814 was one in which they had been generally busy with building, possibly restoring or re-erecting an older house for use by an employee, and at the same time updating or even rebuilding James Morrell's house, 1 Fisher Row.

Brewing for the Kentons and the Tawneys had been virtually unmechanized, and would have required the constant attendance of a skilled brewer to supervise the various operations connected with brewing. These included the grinding of the malted barley, usually with a horse-mill; the mashing or infusion of the malt with water in a mash-tun, using wooden paddles; the pumping of the wort, or malt-infused liquid, from the underback below the mash-tun into a copper, to boil either with or without the addition of hops; the running off of the heated liquid into shallow coolers; and its fermentation in a tun with yeast until clear, before being run or ladled off into casks. If the water-wheel or its precursor existed, as presumably it did from at least the Tawneys' time onwards, this would have powered a pumping mechanism to raise the wort from the underback to the top of the copper. The estimation of correct temperatures, both in boiling and in cooling, depended on the experience of the brewer, since neither thermometers nor refrigerators were used.

Apart from overseeing the brewing and malting processes, Mark and James also had to supervise the sale of beer to private customers and innkeepers (in connection with which a counting house, in a little building on its own, had appeared to the left of the brewery entrance by 1829).[7] They had to concern themselves with the brewery horses, with arrangements for grazing and shoeing and with supplies of hay. They had to purchase barley for malting, which was sometimes done by drawing up a contract with a particular farmer for a specified period. And they had to widen their custom, both by cultivating potential regular customers and by purchasing or leasing convenient public houses either within the city of Oxford or within easy reach of it by horse-drawn or water-borne transport.

Some industries are, and always have been, wholly urban; but brewing, with its dependence on arable farmers for barley and its need for convenient pasture and meadowland, contained a strongly rural element when carried out on a small to medium, not too highly mechanized scale. This remained true of Morrell's Brewery up to the end of the nineteenth century, when brewhouse workers may have turned out in force to help with the haymaking in the Botley Road meadows, and the brewery manager attended Thame and Oxford markets every week with most of the farmers of the district, despite also buying in consignments of Californian or Hungarian barley or Smyrna malt. In St Thomas's, Mark and James lived in the style of country gentlemen surrounded by horses and dogs. Within a few years of arriving in Oxford Mark was hunting regularly with the Old Berkshire Hunt, of which he eventually became Master. Once he needed to kennel foxhounds as well as to stable and pasture hunters, he and James leased Bradley Farm at Cumnor from Merton College. This was Mark's bachelor rural retreat, where he was evidently happier than in the constricting surroundings of St Thomas's. It was also the first of the brewery's many dependent farms, a continuous swathe of which would lie to the east, south-east and south of Oxford, from Garsington and Blackbird Leys to Culham, with outlying leaseholds to the west, by the mid-1860s.

During their first ten years at the brewery, probably for financial reasons above all else, both Morrell brothers remained unmarried. Edward Tawney died in March 1800, followed by their uncle James the attorney in the summer of 1807. Much of their efforts during these years went into paying Tawney (or his executors) the instalments of the £9,975 that they owed him for the various freehold brewery properties; repaying their uncle, in smaller but more regular instalments, a loan of over £10,000 that he had made them to cover the payments to Tawney; and paying Christ Church a small sum (40s. a year with two capons, together with an entry-fine) for the lease of the brewery premises, which they renegotiated in 1803.[8]

On 20 December 1797 Mark and James opened a joint business bank account with Fletcher, Parsons in High Street, Oxford. By early July they had paid in bills totalling nearly £5,000, not quite balancing their withdrawals, which had reached the same figure before the end of May. Their payments to Edward Tawney between February and May 1798 totalled £1,931 16s. 3d., most of this consisting of a single, final instalment in late May. Various other irregular payments to Tawney followed: two at Christmas 1798 and two much larger ones, of £2,660 8s. 6d. and £2,000 (the second sum apparently paid directly by James Morrell) at Christmas 1799. By the time of Tawney's death in March 1800 the two brothers appear to have paid him over £7,000 (although the deed of release of his properties, dated August 1800, states that he had received only £5,494, 10s.) Within the next few months they paid his executors a further £2,638 5s. 6d., including £510 towards the purchase of his house, £13 10s. for a quit-rent and £17 5s. for his wine. Finally, in May 1801 and January 1802, they paid the executors two instalments totalling £2,480 10s. in redemption of a bond.[9]

If somewhat backward in their payments to Tawney during the last two years of his life, Mark and James had other equally pressing obligations to meet. Between October and December 1798 they repaid their uncle a first £1,000 in nine separate instalments. By the end of 1801 they had repaid him nearly £7,000 in all, and between that time and his death in 1807 they made him further payments totalling over £12,000.[10] We must assume, therefore, that James not only lent them the whole of the capital sum that they needed to buy Tawney's freehold properties, but also lent them money on a month-by-month basis to finance the general running of the brewery.

Without this cushion of readily available capital, young men such as Mark and James, with only very modest personal fortunes, would have found it very difficult to cover the deficit in their accounts at times when their income from sales of beer was low and their expenditure on hops, malt and excise duties high. Brewing in the late eighteenth and early nineteenth centuries was not a poor man's occupation, for it was unlikely to start paying for itself until a sizeable amount of capital had been sunk in it. Hence its attraction for the retired, such as Mark and James's uncle Jeremiah Morrell in London, who could invest a life's savings in a business that, once started, would repay them by steadily enriching future generations.

The war with France, however, made this investment more difficult by increasing excise duties on beer, pushing prices up and reducing the certainty of custom. In May 1798, by then clearly in full control of the brewery, Mark and James made their first excise payment of £499 17s. 4¼d. During the next six months they paid further sums of just over £1,500, and in 1799 over £3,600. Thereafter their payments rose steadily to an amazing £8,600-odd in 1804, the year after the resumption of war with France. Not surprisingly, James Morrell's financial backing was insufficient to meet all their needs by 1801, and at the end of that year they borrowed £1,000 from their bank at 1 per cent interest. Excise payments fluctuated throughout the Napoleonic War, £6,000 a year being a fairly average amount to pay, with a seasonal high in June, usually with a charge of well over £1,000 in that month, and another towards the end of the brewing year in September. In September 1811 the two brothers began making additional excise payments for a smaller operation at Wallingford, which suggests that they may have taken over the brewing side of their elder brother Charles's milling and malting business, as bequeathed to their father by their grandfather Jeremiah.[11]

College custom was an important consideration for an Oxford brewing firm; and here Mark and James benefited directly from their uncle's connections. The lawyer Morrells became virtually a university family through marriage, Baker Morrell, the attorney James's son, marrying a daughter of the President of Trinity College, and his grandson Frederick Parker Morrell marrying a daughter of the President of St John's. By then several generations of the family had served as stewards of St John's College, not only because the Morrells lived virtually next door to the college in St Giles, but also no doubt as a result of the marriage of James's daughter Maria, in 1797, to her distant cousin Robert Wintle, a relation of a fellow of the college. Robert was a clergyman at Acton in Middlesex, with a title to the living of Culham and an additional benefice at Compton Beauchamp, both in Berkshire. Thomas Wintle, his exact contemporary and evidently a close friend and kinsman of his, was a fellow and tutor of St John's.[12] In 1799 Mark and James Morrell took out a lease on the St John's College brewhouse to brew exclusively for the college. Similarly at Magdalen College three years later Treacher and Hall were receiving a regular fee for carrying out the college brewing.[13]

In the early 1800s the Morrells owned five pubs in the city centre. These were the sixteenth-century Anchor, New Road; the Wheatsheaf, St Aldate's, with its rustic-sounding 'Skittle Ground, Stables, Pigstyes, Outhouses and Dunghole'; the Jolly Post Boy at the west end of High Street; the Three Cups nearby in Queen Street; and the Red Lion, immediately next to the Jolly Post Boy in High Street, which the Morrells had exchanged for the previously Tawney-owned Boar's Head in Queen's Lane in 1801. Two years later they took on a lease from Christ Church of the Nag's Head in Fisher Row, and the following year they formalized a lease of the City-owned Three Goats' Heads in George Street (later renamed the George Hotel, and unconnected with the present Three Goats' Heads in St Michael's Street), which Edward Tawney had originally leased in 1799. Among the leaseholds that they took over from the Tawneys were two that either contained, or later developed into, public houses – the Paviour's Arms in Castle Street and the Paradise House in Paradise Street, St Ebbe's. If the Tawneys had other leasehold public houses no trace of them has survived, for their history is more ephemeral and difficult to keep track of than that of freeholds. We know, however, that by the 1850s James Morrell and his son James had over seventy tied public houses, of which nearly a third were leasehold, and that, of these, the great majority were in the centre of Oxford rather than in the country or the present outer suburbs.[14]

Being mobile and ambitious, Mark and James began to extend their freehold purchases into the country round Oxford as soon as they had finished paying off their debt to Edward Tawney. Keeping clear of Wells-dominated Wallingford (where Mark, who had apparently inherited the Anchor pub, leased this out in 1800),[15] they turned first to the aged Duke of Marlborough's part of the country, buying the Lamb at Bladon and the Dog and Duck at Woodstock in 1803. During the ten years of the Napoleonic War that followed they bought only six more pubs: the Crown at Charlton on Otmoor; the Three Horse Shoes at Garsington (where their uncle James Morrell had invested in the 1780s in a farm); the Turk's Head in St Thomas's Street, near the brewery; the Chequers at Wheatley; the Cape of Good Hope on the corner of the present Iffley and Cowley Roads, and the Queen's Arms in Park End Street, Oxford. Their most active period of

The Red Lion, Eynsham

The Cape of Good Hope, Cowley and Iffley Roads, Oxford (rebuilt 1893), drawn by Claude De Neuville before its demolition

public-house buying, averaging more than one new freehold a year, followed the peace of 1815, and demonstrated that hard times for the nation generally could be prosperous ones for brewers, especially those with plenty of liquid capital.[16]

To produce enough beer for their expanding custom, the Morrells required a steady supply of malt, which all major breweries with the premises to do so usually processed in their own malthouses from plain unmalted barley. The chief requirement here was space, in the form of a large, oblong building, for the barley was spread out on floors to germinate before drying off in a kiln, curing, dressing and polishing. Most big London breweries preferred to have their barley malted where it was grown, in the dry, chalky areas of Berkshire and Hertfordshire, and transported by river in the form of malt to save bulk transport costs. Millers such as Edward Tawney, Charles Morrell in Wallingford, or the Rowland family with their malthouse in the former Rewley Abbey in St Thomas's, could make a lucrative sideline out of malting for smaller domestic brewers. With the initial bonus of the Tidmarsh Lane malthouse, however, it would have been out of the question for the Morrells to buy malt at a time when only English-grown barley was used for the malt to make English-brewed beer. Their quest for additional malting space led them first, by 1809, to rent a large, semi-dilapidated malthouse from a local builder, Symms, who lived on the corner of St Thomas's Street and The Hamel. The malthouse lay behind Symms's house, and next to another whose tenant was said to let it out to 'travellers of the lowest Description'. Although Mark and James paid out several hundred pounds to Symms this may not have been for improvements to the malthouse, since it lasted them only for about fifteen years and was still in a poor state of repair in 1823. The following year they paid another builder, Fox, to rebuild the Tidmarsh Lane malthouses, which were renamed Fox's Malthouse and uprated from 12s. to 16s. in the church poor rate (as against the mere 2s. 6d. charged for Symms's Malthouse). Still in use in 1825, Symms's Malthouse had been pulled down by 1827; while Fox's Malthouse, refurbished and partly rebuilt in the 1880s, kept most of the dignified Regency character that the surviving buildings, of red brick on a probably older stone base, still have as the storerooms of the University surveyor's office today.[17]

Brewing, hunting and a token amount of public activity in Oxford occupied Mark Morrell, who rapidly established himself as the more retiring of the two brothers, a countryman at heart who could never settle down comfortably to life in the city. In 1799 he became a member of the Twenty-Four, the junior group of city councillors, probably as a necessary result of purchasing the freedom of the city; but he seems never to have proceeded beyond this in public life. The following year the more public-spirited James acquired a chamberlain's position, and later served as a city bailiff, another position of financial responsibility.[18] James, too, was a churchwarden of St Thomas's parish until 1822, and within the next two years had become a vestryman of his new residential parish, St Clement's.

In the various local benefit societies formed to help tradesmen and businessmen to help one another, James also took the more active part. At least three of these, the Unanimous, Useful and Union Societies (the latter unrelated to the Oxford Union Society, which dates only from 1825), overlapped with one another in Oxford at the beginning of the nineteenth century. In addition to pooling financial resources to form a fund for members or their widows in distress or need, the societies existed as clubs for a certain mildly Pickwickian conviviality, with monthly meetings at which members dined or drank together, paying small fines for non-attendance. They were thus of greater benefit to the brewers, innkeepers and bankers than to other members; and the brewing, banking and innkeeping interests joined together to organize them. In the early 1800s the Morrell brothers and their banker John Parsons were jointly responsible for the finances of the Union Society. James Morrell and John Parsons ran the St Thomas's branch of the Useful Society, while James and a Mr Whitefoot, the landlord of the Morrell-owned Anchor Inn in St Peter le Bailey parish, ran the Unanimous Society, which had held most of its meetings there since its foundation in 1770.[19]

On a higher level, too, the connections between brewing and banking were strong, since well-established brewers were accustomed to lending money on mortgages to innkeepers and others, and banks, still in their infancy, always welcomed the security of capital generated by brewing. Several of the great London brewing families such as the Barclays and Whitbreads had banking interests, as had a number of lesser provincial ones. The increase in speculation on land, supported by the enclosure movement, had created a fairly constant demand for loans of capital or low-interest mortgages, which might be of little immediate profit to the lender but were always subject to foreclosure. Provincial banks, still unregulated by statute, could freely issue their own notes for concurrent use with the Bank of England paper money which had been the national currency since 1797, and were well placed to support the development of local industry, landownership and charitable trusts.

The idea of a family-owned bank had first occurred to the young James Morrell in 1805 or 1806, while riding to Wallingford with his cousin Robert, a solicitor in partnership with their Oxford cousin Baker Morrell. 'Jem' (Robert explained in a letter describing their decision to go into partnership together) had been enthusiastic but cautious.[20] Both cousins were unmarried, in their early thirties, with excellent prospects and the potential of plenty of spare investment capital. Government stock in the consolidated fund ('consols') offered only miserly returns, and may have appeared unsafe in view of the huge expense of fighting the Napoleonic War. Buying up odd farms, as their uncle James the attorney had done, was a more satisfying but untidy and inconclusive way of tying up spare money. Canal shares, the Tawney family's favourite investment, were steady but low-yielding. A bank promised untold wealth, but for James at least would be a dangerous liability while he still owed money to their uncle. The cousins agreed, therefore, to wait for an opening in an existing business, then to go into it in partnership when it came.

They had only a short time to wait. In 1807 Richard Cox, the former High Street mercer, who had already run through several other banking partnerships, invited James and Robert to join in a new partnership with him and his son, Richard Ferdinand Cox. James Morrell the attorney had recently died, and Mark and James may have paid off all, or almost all, that they owed him. No doubt James's share of the brewery profits looked attractive to Cox, since he must naturally have hoped to win the brewery account away from Fletcher, Parsons to make it one of the chief assets of Cox, Morrell & Co. Robert, as a solicitor, would also have appeared a potentially useful partner, since he could provide a free conveyancing service together with free advice in any deals that involved putting money into land.

The beginning of the banking partnership, however, was delayed until early in 1808 by James's marriage on 17 December 1807. Now thirty-four, he was marrying a girl half his age for what appear to have been largely dynastic reasons. Jane Wharton, Edward Tawney's half-great-niece, was the nearest possible approximation to the former brewery owner's heiress. Her mother Ann, widow of Theophilus Wharton the Oxford apothecary, had inherited Tawney's house at Headington, and would pass this on at her death to her eldest son Theophilus. Both Theophilus and Brian, Jane's two eldest brothers, were unmarried. Her elder sister Ann had died several years earlier at Brighton, probably of a lingering illness. Although the youngest of several children, Jane seems to have been the only one of her family to marry. If she had children it would therefore be natural for them to inherit the family property from their bachelor uncles. She was also quite comfortably off on her own account, with an income of £400 a year or more derived partly from canal shares and partly from an investment of £10,300 in 3 per cent consols.[21]

James and Jane were married at Headington and settled down to live in Edward Tawney's former town house in Fisher Row. Early in 1808 Robert Morrell broke the news of the impending bank partnership to his cousin and legal partner, Baker Morrell. Suffering, perhaps, from the Morrell-like hot-headedness that Robert had earlier seen in James, Baker sulked and complained at Robert for his secretiveness, and insisted that their own partnership should end. In vain Robert tried to persuade him that there was no need to transfer their firm's account to Cox, Morrell & Co., and that his share in the bank would make no difference to their business. Baker insisted, and the end of their partnership was made public in late March 1808. From then onwards they practised separately, Baker inheriting several of his father's former clients, while Robert acted for his cousins at the brewery and for another family of cousins in complicated financial circumstances, the Dalzells of Wallingford. A lifelong bachelor, Robert lived and had his practice in Turl Street, opposite Lincoln College and a few hundred yards from Cox, Morrell & Co.'s offices in High Street near Carfax. Within a few years he was able to afford to build a house of his own by the river in Wallingford, named The Retreat. Here he happily spent his free time in the company of Jaqueses, Dalzells and assorted Morrells, as if he, too, had been born in Wallingford and had been away from it for only a very short time.[22]

* * *

Jane and James, in Fisher Row, had four children within six years. Jane, the eldest, died as an infant and was buried at St Thomas's church. James, Emily and Mark Theophilus survived into adulthood. Their mother, however, died in 1814 in her early twenties. She, too, was buried at St Thomas's, leaving James to remake his domestic life with a family of children aged between one and four years old.

The Whartons' background in Headington may have suggested to James the answer to the problem of where to bring up his children. St Thomas's was clearly unhealthy, with its low-lying dampness and vulnerability to epidemics. Headington was higher, with better air and open country all around; for it was at that stage a small, detached village with one or two moderately large, gentrified houses, lying back from the main London road beyond the summit of Headington Hill, with its open pastureland descending to the River Cherwell in St Clement's. Edward Tawney's former house, a Magdalen College-owned leasehold, stood near the centre of Headington village; while to the east, in the direction of Headington Quarry, Theophilus and Brian Wharton had bought the freehold of Wick Farm, an important investment costing £9,900, in 1813.[23] Four and a half years later, on 31 December 1817, James made his own investment in a large plot of grazing land on the west side of Headington Hill overlooking Oxford, and set about plans for building himself a country house.[24]

CHAPTER THREE

COUNTRY GENTLEMEN, 1815–34

Headington Hill, where James settled his family in a modestly designed new house in the early 1820s, still presents an imposingly wooded or shrubberied flank to the north-eastern side of Oxford. On bright cold days in early autumn, between three and four in the afternoon, the setting sun flashes multiple reflections from the windows of the house that James's son James built for his wife and daughter in 1856. Across the River Cherwell, over Angel Meadow and the Magdalen College waterwalks and deer park, the Victorian brewer's mansion, Headington Hill Hall, dominates the eastward view from Oxford with its mansard roof, plate-glass windows and surrounding groups of wellingtonias and other exotic trees. The elder James's own house, still attached to the larger one but converted into a back wing, can be seen for what it is only from near at hand. Driving up the sunken hill road from St Clement's to Headington, which for the last two hundred years has been the main road from Oxford to London, one can make out little of the elaborate planting with shrubs and specimen trees which the younger James commissioned at the time when he built on to the house, and nothing of the house itself apart from two lodges. Only South Park, an open expanse of grassland running up from the foot of the hill on the right-hand side of the road, and Headington Hill Park, below the present fenced-off grounds of the Hall on the left, give some idea of the family's possessions and tastes in planting by the end of the nineteenth century. Just below the summit of the hill the road passes under a late Victorian, iron-balustraded bridge, on which travellers a hundred years ago might have caught a glimpse of the Morrells and their visitors in a horse-drawn carriage or buggy driving to inspect the kitchen garden and vinery on the far side of the main road from their house.

When James Morrell bought the land for building from a family of graziers named Savage, Headington Hill was known for its picturesqueness rather than for its residential character. Like Wytham Hill now, it was a popular but secluded place for country walks. Pullen's Elm, at the top of the hill where Pullen's Lane now emerges on to the main road, marked the spot where Josiah Pullen, vice-president of Magdalen Hall and rector of St Peter in the East until his death in 1714, was said to have turned round on his invariable, twice-daily walks up and down the

St Clement's Church, Oxford, with the River Cherwell and (in the background) Headington Hill, showing the house built by James Morrell (1773–1855), brewer, c. 1820

hill. A century after him, the German-born drawing master and musician John Baptist Malchair, who had arrived in Oxford at about the same time as James Morrell the attorney and remained there until he died in 1812, became fond of sketching views on Headington Hill. Like all Malchair's drawings, these are moving in their simplicity: some sweeping views, limited to a few lines, of the hilltop and the distant towers and domes of the city; others, denser studies of farm buildings or of the road tunnelling downhill through trees. One of Malchair's favourite vantage points was the turning into Cheney Lane, until then the main road to London across Shotover. Here he sketched the only two houses of any size on Headington Hill: the tall, gabled house on the lower or west side of Cheney Lane, which had probably been built or rebuilt in the late seventeenth century, and a neat Georgian farmhouse or bailiff's house immediately opposite it on the east side of the lane, which seems to have dated from the early 1770s.[1]

The owners of the main house in Cheney Lane, of the land on either side of the lane and of the smaller house on the east side (built by Thomas Adams, probably a local man)[2] were the Smiths, who ranked as gentleman farmers. In 1771 the rector of St Clement's remarked that there was only one family of note in his parish, that of Mrs Smith, the widow of Thomas Smith, of Headington Hill.[3] In 1780, after her death,

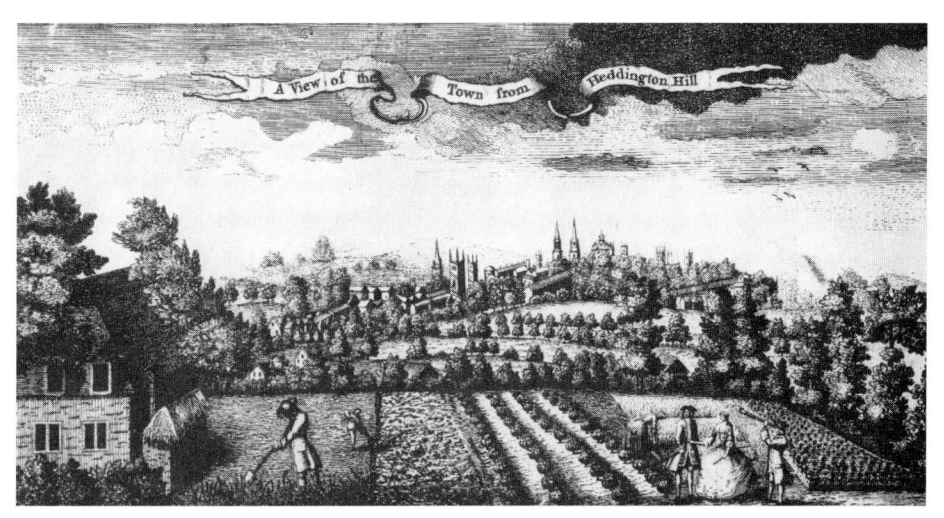

Vignette from Isaac Taylor's Oxford plan, 1750, a westerly view from Headington Hill, with (probably) Cabbage Hall to the left of the picture. Headington Hill Hall now occupies this site

her son William was confirmed in the ownership of the estate, and on his death in 1793 it passed to his spinster sister Elizabeth, who remained there until she died in 1825. In 1780 the house was said to stand in a cherry garden formerly belonging to William Loe, and to have been previously occupied or sublet by Thomas Tagg, perhaps one of the market-gardening Taggs of the Paradise Garden in St Ebbe's.[4]

On the north side of the hill there were two small cottages known as Cabbage Hall and Clay Hall. Cabbage Hall, immediately opposite the turning into Cheney Lane, may explain the vignette in one corner of Isaac Taylor's 1750 plan of Oxford, entitled 'A View of the Town from Heddington Hill', in which the distant city has a foreground of a cottage, a haystack and peasants industriously cultivating rows of cabbages and other crops, while a party of gentry, out for a walk, admire the scene. Clay Hall, slightly farther up the hill, may have been named for the clay-pit across the road on the Smiths' land.[5]

While the Smiths farmed all the land that comprises the present South Park, together with a large arable field on the east side of Cheney Lane, the hillside grazing on the north side of the London Road was not obviously attached to a farmhouse, but may have adjoined Clay Hall or another unknown house, which James Morrell replaced. In the early eighteenth century this land was used for grazing by the well-known London carrier Thomas Godfrey, who lost two successive houses in Headington by fire, and after the first loss set himself up in business plying between Oxford High Street and the Oxford Arms in Warwick

Lane in the City. Godfrey's daughter, Grace Parsons, was the mother of John Parsons, the High Street mercer and banker whose business (incorporating much of the former carrier's business) became Fletcher, Parsons, Oxford's smartest bank. Some time after Godfrey, the land was grazed by another occupant, Savage, whose refusal to pay tithes on part of the land in 1811 led indirectly to a complicated legal case in which James Morrell, attempting to uphold the same right for himself, was defeated by the rector. In 1817, after Savage's death, his widow and daughter sold the land, for an unknown sum, to James Morrell.[6]

Several years seem to have elapsed between James's purchase of the land and the completion of his house, for which he employed a young ecclesiastical architect, Edward William Garbett. Beyond a note of its existence, giving no date, there is no surviving record of his contract with Garbett; but it seems probable that Garbett may have been in Oxford in 1820-2 to help his father William, who was surveyor to the Dean and Chapter of Winchester, design the north and south blocks of the street front of Magdalen Hall, now Hertford College, in Catte Street.[7] Certainly the Hertford College street front, with its rusticated classicism, has a certain amount in common with James's plain and restrained stone house, domesticated though this is by a tiled pitched roof and a possibly later addition, which has made it L-shaped.

Between James's marriage at the end of 1807 and his move to Headington Hill in about 1823, he maintained a separate household from Mark in the Fisher Row house (which the church rate book for St Thomas's designates as Mark's house for the first time in 1824).[8] A nephew from Wallingford, Charles Morrell, who saw a great deal of his uncles in 1820, described dining with one and sleeping at the house of the other, which implies that the two lived close together, probably on opposite sides of St Thomas's Street. We may assume, therefore, that the new or rebuilt house that existed on the brewery premises by 1815 was initially Mark's house. One or both of the brothers' houses were gas-lit by about 1818.[9] James's dogs may have been kennelled at the malthouse stables in Tidmarsh Lane, since an unfortunate incident happened in the summer of 1819 when a favourite, dark-coloured greyhound leapt the wall into the gaol-keeper's garden in the castle precincts, began to steal one of the rank-smelling carcases that hung up there for the gaol-keeper's dogs, and was shot and fatally wounded by an under-keeper.[10]

Living as they did at such close quarters to the brewery and the malthouse, the gaol, and the workshops and disease-ridden tenements of St Thomas's Street, it is not surprising that Mark and James both took time off for hunting, and for planning or enjoying a more spacious country life at Headington Hill or Cumnor. Both, too, kept up their links with Wallingford, where James in particular was a frequent visitor. Some of these visits were social and recreational, to The Retreat, The Wharf, or the home of the one or another of the Wells family, now no longer rivals so much as colleagues in brewing. Charles Morrell records that one day in 1820 both uncles breakfasted at Wallingford before going hunting, and that on another occasion they both attended a birthday breakfast for one of the Wellses. Their joint bank books show that within a few years of beginning to brew at Wallingford they were paying excise charges through Wells & Co., an arrangement which continued into the early 1830s.[11] Later, probably after this joint arrangement had lapsed, they used malthouses at Wallingford, Shillingford, Dorchester and Abingdon to supply the brewery at Oxford. Most of these were leaseholds, apart from the elder Charles Morrell's malthouse of which they had acquired the freehold.[12]

No decade in the nineteenth-century history of brewing at Morrell's could be described as one of loss-making, retrenchment or slump; but the 1820s, an economically unhappy period in England as a whole, with a post-war depression making rents, bread and ale unaffordable for the very poor, seem to have been a particularly successful time at the brewery. It was in this decade that Mark and James amalgamated and rebuilt the Tidmarsh Lane malthouses as a single large one, and may also have altered and enlarged their brewhouse into something approaching its present form. Following the example of other breweries such as Whitbread's, which had been pioneers of steam power in the 1780s, they installed the steam-powered beam engine of 1820s type, which until 1964 supplemented the water-power from the Back Stream to turn the large horizontal drive-wheel in the brewhouse. Still functioning on occasion, this is now in the Leicester City Museum at Coalville. A second, faster engine, the table engine, joined it in the 1840s and remained until both were taken out of the brewhouse to provide additional space.

Brewery profits by the 1820s were such that, in good years, Mark and James managed to pay themselves several thousand pounds a year each from their joint business account. Mark invested mainly in government stock, and James, presumably, in his new house and his children's education. Thus, in 1822, the two brothers took £1,000 each from the business in March, followed by an investment the following month of £1,256 by Mark in consols, and payments of £800 to Mark in July and £2,000 to James in August. In November James took £950 in four instalments, probably to pay builders, and in 1823 took £870 between January and March. The following May Mark invested a further £1,043 5s. in consols, while in September James took an equivalent amount in cash. By 1824 James, too, felt able to spare some of his capital for investment, and in April both brothers spent £965 on consols and £1,086 5s. on 4 per cents. In July James paid himself £1,000 cash, while in August

Mark took £1,070 10s. And so the pattern continued, with the careful Mark continuing to put most of his money at the government's disposal, while James did so only when circumstances permitted.[13]

Investment in land, into which James's banking partner Robert, like their late uncle James the attorney, had begun from quite early on to put much of his spare money, did not immediately appeal to either of the two brothers. Mark, uninterested in making a profit on investments except in the form of government stock, was happy to continue living in Edward Tawney's former house, the joint property of himself and James, and to lease Bradley Farm at Cumnor from Merton College. At no stage in his life did he put a penny into land, or appear to have ambitions to own an estate. James, committed to paying for his new house, began to invest in land only in his mid-fifties, ten years after the purchase of the plot on which he had built on Headington Hill. Then, in 1828, he bought 326 acres at Sandford-on-Thames, the future Rock Farm and nucleus of a future large brewery estate of several linked farms, which cost him £9,400 at auction.[14] This property appeared in various family documents simply as the 'Sandford Farm' until the 1840s and 1850s, when James and his son James entered into further large-scale acquisitions of land in Sandford and nearby in Culham, Littlemore and Blackbird Leys.[15]

Although some barley was grown at Sandford, there is no evidence that this was used for malting at the brewery, or that James had bought the land as anything other than a long-term investment from which to derive rents; and the Morrells continued to buy barley from farther away, for example from a farmer at Crowmarsh, near Wallingford.[16] For grazing and haymaking near the brewery, however, they continued to lease meadowland from large landowners such as Christ Church, University College and the Bishop of Oxford, sometimes on a scale that allowed them to sublet to other users.[17]

Disputes could arise where two powerful and competitive bodies leased grazing side by side, as did Morrell's and Hall's breweries during the first half of the nineteenth century, before the railway arrived to separate the two breweries from the meadowland to the west of Oxford. Along the Botley Road causeway to the south and west of Osney Island, in Osney Meadow, half of which belonged to Christ Church, and beyond it in Oatlands (the site of the present Oatlands Road), nearly half of which belonged to the Bishop of Oxford, lines of demarcation were vague except on paper and physical barriers almost non-existent. In 1831 the Morrells sued their rival the brewer William Hall, the Christ Church tenant of part of Botley Meadow (which lay beyond Oatlands and to the west of the Bulstake stream) in the Exchequer Court for trespass, alleging damage to the land that they leased in Osney Meadow and Oatlands. At the same time they found themselves in trouble with St Thomas's parish for 'impounding the water at their Brewery to the injury of the Land', perhaps also as a result of a disagreement with Hall, who grazed horses in Oxe Close just across the stream or ditch from the southern tip of the brewery premises. Six years later Christ Church instructed them to put up fences round land that they leased in Horse Closes next to St Thomas's churchyard to avoid further boundary disputes.[18] In 1838 they succeeded in buying the freeholds of two portions of meadowland in Oatlands and Osney Meadow from the trustees of Alderman William Fletcher, their former owner, having held these on a lease for many years since his death.[19]

In 1815 the Morrells owned seventeen freehold public houses in all; by the end of 1830 they had almost doubled this number. In the city their acquisitions included the Three Crowns in St Thomas's and the Air Balloon in Queen Street (both 1817), the King's Head in St Martin's parish (1821), the Vulcan in Friar's Entry (1823), the Green Dragon in St Aldate's and the Friars in St Mary Magdalen parish (1825), and the Plasterer's Arms (1827) and Port Mahon (1830) in St Clement's.[20] Among their leaseholds were the Duke of York in Broad Street, a Christ Church property that they held between 1810 and 1838, and the Black Horse in

The Port Mahon, St Clements, Oxford, 1968

St Clement's, the property of the parish feoffees, who had previously leased it to an ironmonger, Thomas Bush, owner of the future Gill & Co. of High Street, before drawing up a new lease in favour of the Morrells in 1826.[21] As James was by then a prominent parishioner of St Clement's, a vestryman and a generous subscriber towards the new parish church, his influence here is fairly evident; and the subsequent purchase of two St Clement's freehold public houses consolidated his already strong social position as the virtual lord of the manor of St Clement's parish.

In the country Mark and James pursued a policy of buying, for the most part, public houses within a 10- or 15-mile radius of the brewery. The King of Prussia, Rose Hill (1816), renamed the Allied Arms for diplomatic reasons in the First World War, and now The Ox, the Crown at Charlton on Otmoor (1817), the Plough at Wheatley (1827), the Golden Ball at Littlemore (1835) and the Swan at Temple Cowley (1835) were all the right distance from central Oxford to be reached without too much difficulty with supplies of beer by dray. The Swan at Sutton Courtenay (1819) could be reached by river, downstream from Oxford, while the Blue Boar at Longworth (1821), although now reached more directly by road through Cumnor and Tubney Wood, was only a mile or two from the river crossing at Newbridge, near Standlake. Gradually, in the 1840s and 1850s, the range of Morrell-owned public houses began to extend

The King of Prussia, Rose Hill, Oxford, *c.* 1910

The Allied Arms, Rose Hill, Oxford (formerly the King of Prussia and now the Ox). The pub was renamed after the outbreak of war in August 1914

farther away from Oxford, to places as far apart as Brookhampton, near Stadhampton, south-east of Oxford, Piddington in north Oxfordshire, Faringdon in Berkshire, and Shillingford, Dorchester and Goring in the lower Thames Valley. Sometimes, however, these acquisitions were half-accidental, as a result of foreclosures on mortgages or other financial complications, and they continued to be accompanied by the acquisition of many other freehold and leasehold houses in the city, its outskirts and the nearby country.[22]

* * *

As a banker and country gentleman, James now divided his time between St Thomas's (where Mark had taken over the Fisher Row house), the bank in High Street, and his mansion, garden and park on Headington Hill. Like Miss Smith's house in Cheney Lane (which was rated as inferior to his in the parish poor rate), James's house came within the parish of St Clement's, which from the foot of the hill to Magdalen Bridge was a depressed, overcrowded area not unlike St Thomas's, full of newly arrived people from the country hoping to find work as town labourers and maidservants, and with a high rate of infant mortality. In the early 1820s the development of a complex of side streets of small, cramped 'artisan dwellings' running down to the River Cherwell more than doubled the number of households in the parish, and nearly trebled its population, in three years.[23] A new church was planned beyond the east end of St Clement's High Street, on the corner of the Marston Road, to replace the old, crumbling parish church on its island site near Magdalen Bridge. As James extended his land with additional purchases downhill to the Marston Road, the church, towards which he had subscribed £100 in 1825, came more and more to resemble a newly rebuilt country church standing near the park gates of the largest landowner in the village.

It was appropriate, then, that James sent his elder son James to Eton in the year that he was building the new house, although he kept him there only until the age of fifteen or sixteen and did not do the same for the more delicate Mark Theophilus. Emily, his cherished only daughter, obligingly remained within the family by marrying a cousin in 1830, at the age of nineteen. William Henry Stone, a London barrister with chambers in the Inns of Court, was the son of James's sister Mary and her husband William Stone of Basildon in Berkshire. At about the time of the couple's marriage, or soon afterwards, William Stone purchased the nearby Streatley House from Mary's second cousin, the bachelor clergyman Deacon Morrell, who had inherited it from his uncle Robert Baker but had no need for such a large country property. This dignified, pleasant, Georgian red brick house became the home of William Henry and Emily Stone, of their only child Jane (who died at the age of sixteen), and eventually of James's granddaughter Emily Alicia Morrell, the child heiress of the brewery and of Headington Hill Hall.

* * *

Meanwhile, at the bank, superficial prosperity concealed a state of corruption which could end only in financial disaster for those who were responsible for it. By 1830 Richard Cox, the senior partner, had been a banker in Oxford for nearly forty years. He had an estate at Tubney in Berkshire, another at Blackthorn near Bicester, leasehold lands held of the Earl of Abingdon at Cumnor, Botley and Binsey on the west side of Oxford and Beckley on the east, and a variety of other investments including canal, railway and turnpike trust shares and a quarrying and coal-mining business in the Forest of Dean. He had been three times Mayor of Oxford, in 1799, 1812 and 1823, and his son and partner Richard Ferdinand was mayor in 1826. Another son, Charles Henry, was a student (fellow) of Christ Church, demonstrating once again the close links between trade and academic life in Oxford before Victorian academic snobbery declared these to be unthinkable.

To finance their various investments and purchases of land, all the partners in the bank borrowed from their joint funds. James and Robert

Morrell took out relatively modest loans of £1,700 and £1,800; Richard Ferdinand Cox borrowed £14,000; and his father, unknown to the Morrells, borrowed something in the region of £60,000. The extent of the Coxes' corruption probably emerged at an accounting session in the spring of 1831, after James and Robert Morrell had discovered that Richard Ferdinand Cox had directly contravened their expressed wishes by lending 'very large sums of money ... from time to time' to a Witney carrier named Richard Parker in addition to the £6,500 loan allowed to Parker by the bank. James and Robert, panic-stricken at the prospect that the bank might run short of funds, expelled Richard Ferdinand from the partnership, and in compensation for the risks that he had made them run took his shares in the bank premises and profits and in a property at Woodstock, which also belonged to the bank.[24]

At this point Baker Morrell's misgivings about associating himself, however indirectly, with the bank might have seemed fully justified. Mark and James had moved the brewery account from Fletcher, Parsons to Cox, Morrell & Co. in 1811, and could have suffered enormous damage, and perhaps the loss of their business, had the Coxes' borrowings led to the collapse of the bank. Richard Cox, in a will drafted in June 1831, three weeks after Richard Ferdinand left the partnership, appointed the two Morrells and his son Charles Henry as his trustees with instructions that they should dispose of his property as they thought fit in order to pay off his own and Richard Ferdinand's debts to the bank, specifically including those incurred by lending money to Parker of Witney and to David Davies, Richard Cox's partner in the colliery business. Possibly, however, this will was a creation of Robert Morrell's to which Cox, finding it too extreme, avoided putting his name. Later documents reveal that Cox kept up some association with the bank until July 1832, and made a final transfer of his freehold and leasehold properties on trust to his two sons, not to the Morrells, before fleeing to Calais in 1833. There, in the traditional refuge of English bankrupts, he made another will confirming the transfer and died on 27 December 1834. The final compensation remained unpaid until 2 October 1841, when Richard Ferdinand and Charles Henry Cox released to the Morrells all their father's former titles to the leasehold farmland in Beckley and Cumnor together with his shares in the colliery in the Forest of Dean, and probably also his freehold estate at Tubney, the future home of the Morrell-owned Old Berkshire Hunt.[25]

CHAPTER FOUR

DEATHS AND GAINS, 1835–56

From the time of the first national census in 1841 we can begin to reconstruct part of the tightly concentrated family and working life that went on in and around the brewery in St Thomas's. Censuses from 1851 onwards give precise details of place of birth and occupation, making it easier still to identify brewery workers and to recognize their origins in parts of the country outside Oxford from which Mark or James, having family, farming or business connections there, may have directly encouraged them to come into St Thomas's to live and work.

St Thomas's, like the other working-class parishes of St Clement's and St Ebbe's, increased hugely in population during the first half of the nineteenth century. In 1802 and 1805 the population of the parish (which then included much of Jericho as well as Osney) was estimated at between 1,100 and 1,200, or about a tenth of the population of the entire city westwards of Magdalen Bridge. By 1808 it was estimated at 1,500.[1] In 1841 the census showed that there were about 700 people living in St Thomas's Street and its courtyards and alleyways alone, and another 225 or so in The Hamel and Paradise Street. Many of these were children born within the parish; but a high proportion of the parents had been born elsewhere and had crowded into the tenements and lodging-houses of St Thomas's to find work. In the 1841 census most of them were described simply as 'labourer', unless they followed specific trades such as shoemaker, butcher, baker, cordwainer, carpenter, coach-trimmer, tallow-chandler, cooper, maltster or brewer. Many trades were carried on in small backyard workshops, and most people lived either directly next to or within a few hundred yards of where they worked. For the brewery workers this meant the small cottages of The Hamel or Abbey Row (a tightly packed row of cottages running back from a narrow opening between 10 and 11 St Thomas's Street, halfway between The Hamel and the original brewery site, built in the mid- to late 1820s to replace Symms's Malthouse[2]), or the equally recent developments of Bookbinder's, Wareham's or Plasterer's Arms Yard on the north side of the street, where former gardens had given way to enclosed, lightless, airless rows of dwellings.

Not surprisingly, in an area with a high population of manual workers engaged in dusty, dirty and thirst-making tasks, St Thomas's contained a large number of public houses. On the north side of St Thomas's Street, the Windsor Castle, the Plasterer's Arms, the Peacock and the Turk's Head operated, at various times in the nineteenth century, within 50 yd of one another. The Shoulder of Mutton, later rebuilt and renamed the Marlborough Arms, was a large lodging-house and public house immediately next to the brewery, notorious by the 1850s or 1860s for badger-baiting on the premises.[3] Round the corner in Paradise Street, by the Castle Mill building that projected across the sluice, stood the Swan, belonging to Hall and Tawney's Brewery. The Nag's Head in Fisher Row, the Albion in Hollybush Row, the Hall and Tawney-owned White Horse on the south side of St Thomas's Street, the Lamb and Flag and the Ox just beyond this in the direction of Hollybush Row, and Hall and Tawney's Chequers on the opposite corner of Hollybush Row, completed the number of pubs and beerhouses within a few hundred yards of the brewery.[4] Various pubs came and went, but in 1913 there were said to be five licensed houses still functioning in the 285-yd stretch of St Thomas's Street, a number that the Chief Constable of Oxford considered to be 'more than was required by the public'.[5]

Until the middle of the nineteenth century it was quite usual for a brewery-owner to live in a moderately grand town house next to his brewery, just as it was for a factory owner to live next to his factory and for a shopkeeper, banker or lawyer to live over the shop, bank or office. In moving away to the country James Morrell was ahead of his time for a provincial brewer, and was perhaps consciously following the example of the fashionable, late eighteenth-century London brewers such as Samuel Whitbread, who had lived at Bedwell Park, Hertfordshire from 1765 until his death in 1790, or Henry Thrale, husband of Dr Samuel Johnson's friend Hester Thrale, with his country villa Streatham Park, several miles to the south-west of the family brewery in Southwark. In the 1850s Charles Tawney, the Halls' successor, was still living in his Brewery House in Paradise Street, sharing his household with three of his most trusted workers, and employing a butler, cook, house servant, lady's maid, dairy-maid, coachman and groom. Only after his death was the house taken over entirely by brewery workers, comprising the head brewer, a carter and five maltmen in 1861, with the maltster in charge of the Paradise Street malthouse sharing the former stable accommodation with a gardener and his wife.[6]

During Mark Morrell's twenty-odd years at 1 Fisher Row no brewery employees shared the house with him, but they were all around in lodgings or rented cottages in St Thomas's Street and The Hamel. John Webb, the brewery clerk, who seems to have been equivalent in importance to a manager, occupied the house just inside the brewery entrance with his wife, daughters and maidservants. The 1851 census tells us that he was born at Sulhamstead in Berkshire, a village a mile or two from Englefield, the earlier home of the Stone family into which James Morrell's sister and daughter married, and from Theale, where Edward William Garbett designed a striking, Regency Gothic church at about the time that he worked on James's house on Headington Hill. Webb was well established at the brewery by 1837, when Mark Morrell left him a bequest of £400 in his will, and remained there until he died in 1855 in his early sixties. In an affectionate caricature of the early 1840s he appears as a rustic, rough-hewn character, more innkeeper than clerk, wearing an enormous apron and a top hat and carrying a jug and key, clearly on his way to draw a quart of ale directly from the stores at the brewery.[7]

Several families worked at the brewery for at least two generations, and cousins, brothers or acquaintances from the same village as a brewery worker might well join the close network of families living round the east end of St Thomas's Street. In 1841, for example, the Morrells' senior brewer was James Fletcher, a married man in his late thirties with three sons. Within the next ten years he had moved away (although he returned to St Thomas's to die in 1864, aged sixty). His successor was his eldest son James, aged twenty-four in 1851, whose two younger brothers, William and Robert, worked with him as brewer's men. James died aged twenty-six, and by the 1861 census the family seems to have left the brewery. The Hearne brothers, Henry and William, a brewer and a maltster, both aged about twenty in 1841, probably also worked for the

John Webb, brewery clerk, *c.* 1842

Joe Hutt, brewery drayman (d. 1842)

Morrells, but had left within the next ten years. Hall and Tawney's senior brewer in 1841, Daniel Faulkner, lived in Paradise Street with Charles Tawney and was assisted by George Talbot, who lived in The Hamel. By 1851 Talbot had succeeded Faulkner and had moved from The Hamel to Paradise Street to take over the senior brewer's quarters on the brewery premises.[8]

Two brewery families who had had some fairly obvious connection with the Morrells outside Oxford were the Clemsons of Cumnor and the Hutts of Warborough, near Wallingford. Jonathan Clemson from Cumnor, a fifty-year-old drayman, was living near the brewery in The Hamel (or just behind it in Abbey Row) by 1851, but in view of his age had probably been attached to the brewery for much longer than that. In 1861, as a brewer, he was listed with his family among the ten households in Abbey Row. In a neighbouring house lived Thomas Clemson from Cumnor, a forty-eight-year-old labourer, and his motherless children, the two elder of whom had been born at Cumnor but the youngest, aged fourteen, in Oxford. As Abbey Row was held on a leasehold by the Morrells, we may assume that any householder there who was described as a labourer probably worked at the brewery. In his will Mark Morrell had left a generous £100 to Ann Clemson, one of the servants at Bradley Farm (while he left only £10 each to two women servants, one of whom had been with him for thirteen years by the time that he made his will, and for nineteen years when he died, at Fisher Row). The Clemsons were evidently a family whom Mark had liked, to the extent of encouraging them to work for him in Oxford; and Jonathan's farm-labouring background must have given him experience of handling the heavy horses that were used for ploughing and for pulling drays. Members of the Becketts family, one of whom was a male farm servant at Bradley in or soon after Ann Clemson's time, occur as kennelmen and a gardener at Headington Hill Hall in the 1850s and 1860s, suggesting that the Morrells liked to take employees from backgrounds that were already known to them even if work at the brewery was not involved.[9]

The Hutts, a still more complicated family, appear in both a brewery and (apparently) a non-brewery context. Joe Hutt, son of Thomas and Martha Hutt of Warborough, a massively barrel-shaped man, was Morrell's drayman until he died in 1842 at the age of thirty-six. The same artist who depicted John Webb also drew Joe Hutt, in smock, apron and leggings with a yoke over one shoulder and two horses partly visible in the background, contemplating a barrel of xxx beer dated with the year of his death. In the census of the previous year he appears simply as 'labourer', as does Thomas, son of Thomas and Sarah Hutt of Warborough (probably Joe's cousin rather than his half-brother), who also lived near the brewery with his family.

By 1851 Thomas Hutt was listed as a drayman, aged thirty-seven, living in The Hamel with his wife, his younger brother Charles, a brewer's labourer, and his children, including a sixteen-year-old son John, also a labourer 'at the brewhouse'. Charles Hutt did well and succeeded the younger James Fletcher as brewer in the 1850s. When John Webb died, Charles and his wife Sarah moved into the house on the brewery premises, where they remained until Charles's death in 1870 at the age of forty-nine. Another Hutt, William, probably the licensee of the Morrell-owned Turk's Head in St Thomas's Street, and perhaps an uncle, was buried in the parish in 1852 at the age of fifty-one. In his will of 1863 the younger James Morrell of Headington Hill Hall awarded a pension to his former lodgekeeper James Hutt and his wife Margaret (probably the couple of that name who were married in St Mary Magdalen parish church in 1820). These, however, may not have been directly related to the Warborough Hutts, since the surname was a common one in Oxfordshire, and other Hutts marrying earlier in the same parish had originated from as far apart as Kidlington, Ascott-under-Wychwood, Sandford, and St Thomas's, Oxford.[10]

Because there are no regular brewery records of nineteenth-century employees, and because the 1841 census lists so many people connected with the brewery simply as 'labourer' with no indication of where they worked, it is difficult to calculate how many people were attached to the brewery before 1850. The 1841 census lists one maltster, the young William Hearne, and six coopers, William and Arthur Hughes, William Bossom, Robert and William Jackson and Henry Jaggar, in St Thomas's Street. The Hughes family may have been independent of any brewery, since Mary Hughes appears to have been carrying on the business alone in 1846. The Jaggars, Henry and his sons Henry and Charles, who were also coopers by 1851, probably worked for Morrell's until the elder Henry Jaggar's death in 1856. William Jackson and a John Coombs were also coopers in St Thomas's Street in 1851, but Robert Jackson, William Bossom and the Hugheses had gone. Other obvious brewery workers listed in the 1851 census of the area included two brewers' clerks (one of them John Webb), four brewers' men, two brewers' draymen, four brewers' labourers and one brewers' storeman, at least some of whom must have worked for Hall and Tawney. In 1861 the Morrells' junior maltster, living in Tidmarsh Lane, was the twenty-three-year-old Richard Stone, who, like the brewer Charles Hutt, originated from Warborough.[11]

Mark Morrell, a jovial but parsimonious figure, remained unmarried until his death in 1843 at the age of seventy-two. One of his Fisher Row servants, Ann Lukerman, who did so poorly out of his will, recorded his characteristically cautious behaviour when adding a codicil to the will eighteen months before he died – how he had sent her to fetch it from a secret drawer in his bedroom bureau, made the alteration when she was out at St Giles's Fair, and then covered it with his hand when asking her to witness his signature on her return. Mark's hoarded wealth was indeed considerable, representing nearly half of the profits of the brewery over a forty-year period. He owned no house of his own, had spent little on himself and indulged himself only in hunting. In all, not counting his share in the brewery and its various properties, he was reckoned on his death to be worth more than £113,000, of which over £95,000 was in consols and the rest invested in stocks or in the bank. Apart from small bequests (£5,000 to one of his sisters, £2,000 each to his elder brother and various nephews, and £200 to his shepherd at Bradley, who predeceased him in 1839), he left the bulk of his estate to his brother James, from whom it would descend in time to the younger James, the inheritor of the brewery.[12]

In his late sixties Mark had narrowly escaped a serious disruption to his life when an illegitimate daughter of the Duke of Marlborough, Georgiana Spencer, the child of a Miss Glover, having scorned a serious proposal of marriage from him a few years earlier, decided to trap him for the sake of his money. A crony of the duke for many years, Mark had often visited him and had once been well on the way to marriage with another illegitimate daughter of his, a Miss Brown, when she had jilted him in order to marry someone more attractive. He had then quarrelled with the duke, possibly after being turned down by Georgiana, Miss Brown's half-sister, then aged about seventeen. On resuming his visits he had made a joke of his earlier proposal to her, had continued to flirt with her amicably, and had probably been treated by the family as a bit of a buffoon. After he had fallen from his gig and been seriously injured, he had received repeated invitations to Blenheim and pointed hints that Georgiana might after all be ready to marry him. On his next visit he had obediently proposed to her; and Georgiana, accepting, had begun to make immediate and expensive plans for a wedding. Within two or three weeks of the engagement, however, he had had cold feet and written to Georgiana's mother to call off the marriage. Georgiana's cold and greedy behaviour, and her mother's evident determination to see him as a supplier of free beer and other luxuries, had perhaps alerted him to the Spencers' and Glovers' poverty, and their obvious hope of diverting his fortune into their own pockets.[13]

None of the embarrassment caused by this episode seems to have affected the friendliness of the more solvent George Spencer, sixth Duke of Marlborough from 1840 to 1857, and his son John Winston Spencer Churchill, the seventh duke, towards Mark's nephew, the younger James Morrell. During the twenty-five years that he spent between leaving Eton and taking control of the brewery, James cultivated the local aristocracy and gentry, such as the Earl of Abingdon, Viscount Valentia of Bletchingdon Park, Sir Henry Dashwood of West Wycombe, and the Duke of Marlborough, officiated as a Justice of the Peace, and hunted. Between 1848 and 1858 he was Master of the Old Berkshire Hunt, which he kennelled lavishly at Tubney, Berkshire, at the house of his father's late disgraced partner, Richard Cox. On his uncle Mark's death he moved out of his father's house and set up his own establishment at 1 Fisher Row, where he replaced the two maids with five servants in all, including two menservants. The elder James was now alone on Headington Hill with his own more modest staff, who in 1851 amounted to a cook from Wallingford, two maids and his young valet, a future Mayor of Oxford and businessman named Jason Saunders. Mark Theophilus, James's younger son, had died early in 1842, leaving Edward Tawney's former house in Headington, which he had inherited from his uncle Theophilus Wharton, back in to the Tawney family in the person of the brewer Charles Tawney, his first cousin once removed.[14]

* * *

The two great breweries in Oxford, Hall and Tawney's and Morrell's, had now survived side by side for about a century since Richard Tawney had taken over the dormant business of the Kentons and Deborah Loader had kept her late husband's brewery functioning until her daughter should marry John Treacher. Many lesser brewing concerns had gone out of business during this time, and most publicans had given up brewing their own beer. At the same time one or two newly opened Oxford breweries offered a degree of rivalry to Hall and Tawney and Morrell's. Hanley's City Brewery of Queen Street and the St Giles Brewery in Observatory Street (whose owner, Daniel George Hall, persuaded the solicitor Frederick Morrell of St Giles to stand godfather to his son Frederick while indebted to him for a £2,700 mortgage)[15] would soon be joined by others, predominantly in St Thomas's, where they took advantage of the opening of the Great Western and London and North-Western Railway stations in the early 1850s, on or near the sites of the former Oseney and Rewley abbeys.

On a national scale the years between 1830 and 1850 had seen important new developments in brewing. As a social class brewers had reached the height of their wealth and influence, and brewing money would remain a solid, dominant sector of the private wealth of the country until the end of the century and beyond. The Beer Act of 1830, which abolished the excise duty of 10s. a barrel on beer, had also seemed at first to threaten the profits made by common brewers from their tied public houses, since it enabled anyone to set up a retail beerhouse provided that he or she could afford the 2 gn. licence and was already paying rates. The price of beer consequently dropped, and within the next eight years there were almost 50,000 new retailers of beer in Britain as a whole. From 1830 the consumption of beer increased among the ever more numerous urban working classes, accompanied at first by an increase in the consumption of gin, which had already done so much damage to the London poor during the eighteenth century. Gradually, however, beer prevailed as the standard working-class drink; and a taste came in for lighter, less alcoholic beers than those traditionally produced by the London porter breweries such at Whitbread's. The newly expanded Burton-on-Trent breweries such as Bass and Worthington, with their lighter, livelier-tasting brew, transported in huge quantities by train to rest in vaults underneath St Pancras station, were the chief ones to profit from the national thirst that resulted from long hours spent in factories, in workshops and on building sites, or in breaking stones for new roads and laying railways.

In vain, then, in the 1830s and 1840s, nutritionists began to argue that beer contained no appreciably nourishing ingredients, and teetotallers like the Oxford Chartist grocer J.J. Faulkner campaigned against alcohol in any form. During the 'hungry Forties', when food was scarce, beer continued to sell chiefly for its mildly narcotic qualities and for the feeling of uplift that it gave at the end of a hard day's work. Although brewing victuallers had fallen hopelessly victims to the economics of production, partly because of the duties on malt, which increased after 1830, and partly because they had been able to make only the most unsophisticated type of ale, the retired farm labourers and market porters who set up as independent beer-sellers usually managed to find a large enough clientele in their immediate neighbourhood to make a modest living retailing the products of their local brewery. Throughout much of England, especially those parts with good railway connections, the Burton ales were gaining in popularity; but traditional local beers such as 'Morrell's entire' (a strong, porter-type beer, made by fermenting the entire unfiltered contents of the cask) could still command loyalty in the region in which they were brewed. Domestic customers buying beer for their servants and others might order 'small beer', a weak brew considered suitable for children and the elderly, and a barrel or two of ordinary ale or the stronger type, graded in different strengths from x to xxxx, as a midday drink for themselves or a dinner-time refreshment for their employees.

We can only guess at the drinking habits of Morrell's private customers; but we know that by the 1850s they included several institutions and many heads of substantial households in Oxford and the country round about. In 1856–7 the Littlemore Asylum owed the brewery £190 5s. 6d. on account, and the bursar of Jesus College £42 10s. 6d. Lesser debtors included members of gentry families such as the Lenthalls; a Lady Churchill; Miss Bandinel of Beaumont Street, probably the sister of Bulkeley Bandinel, who was Bodley's librarian from 1813 to 1860; Baker Morrell's widow in St Giles; John Dalzell, a Wallingford cousin; one of the Mallam family of lawyers and auctioneers; and one of the Hutts, then living at Water Eaton.[16]

During the 1830s, while Mark Morrell was still an active partner in the business, he and James acquired only six new freehold pubs: the Golden Ball at Littlemore, the Swan at Temple Cowley, the Duke of York and the Parrot in St Ebbe's, the Swan at Islip and the Chequers at Cassington. In the 1840s James increased the number of his freehold and copyhold acquisitions to ten. These included a pair of copyhold pubs, the Folly and the Duke of York at Faringdon; the Bear and Ragged Staff at Brookhampton, near Stadhampton; a pair of mortgaged properties, the Plough at Dorchester and the Blue Bell at Shillingford, on which he foreclosed; the Jolly Bargeman in St Ebbe's; and two rural pubs near the Oxford Canal, the Union at Thrupp and the King's Arms at Nethercott, near Tackley. If any pattern is discernible in these acquisitions, it is one of diminished enthusiasm for investment in freehold tied houses in the decade after the 1830 Beer Act, when the burgeoning of small, independent beerhouses threatened to take custom away from these pubs, possibly followed by the realization that, in the long term, the pubs would outlast the beerhouses to remain a sound investment for generations to come.

By the time that he handed over the brewery and all its assets to his son James in 1851, the elder James owned nearly fifty freehold and copyhold public houses. These included one or two oddities such as the Rose and Crown at Blackthorn, near Bicester, whose thousand-year lease, dating from 1777, had come to James as part of Richard Cox's estate. (Another similarly freakish long lease, that of the Seven Stars at Piddington for 1,490 years, was acquired by the younger James in 1853.) Other tied public houses were mortgaged to, rather than owned by, the brewery, such as the Jericho public house (now the Jericho Tavern) in Walton Street and the Bookbinder's Arms in Victor Street, Jericho, near the new home of the University Press.

Increasingly, to compete with the beerhouse trade, the Morrells had also established a foothold in Oxford by acquiring short leases of pubs from the City, the colleges or private individuals. Because the leases were frequently renewed and the earlier leases not always kept, it is often hard to establish when these properties first became attached to the brewery. We know from outside sources, for example, that some of them, such as the Nag's Head, Fisher Row and the Three Goats' Heads (rebuilt as The George in the early 1850s) in Cornmarket Street, had leases in the Morrells' names going back to the very beginning of the century. Other leases dated from the 1820s, 1830s and 1840s, while many were renewed in 1852 as a result of the elder James's transfer of the brewery property to the younger James the previous year. By this time there were at least twenty-six leasehold pubs attached to the brewery, all but a very few of them (the Tree at Iffley, the George at Botley, and the General Elliott and the Cross Keys at South Hinksey) in or near the city or the working-class suburbs of Oxford. These were the Black Horse, St Clement's; the Black Swan, George Lane; the Blue Pig, Gloucester Green; the Coach and Horses, King Street (now Merton Street); the Coach and Horses, St Giles; the Druid's Head, George Street; the George, Cornmarket Street; the Globe, Queen Street; the Grapes, George Street; the Holly Bush, St Thomas's; the Horse and Groom, St Ebbe's; the Horse and Jockey, Woodstock Road; the King's Head, Holywell; the Lamb and Flag, St Thomas's Street; the Nag's Head, Fisher Row; the Oddfellows' Arms, George Street; the Old White House, Grandpont; the Paviours' Arms, St Ebbe's; the Punch Bowl; the Two Hands; the Wagon and Horses, St Giles; and the Windsor Castle, formerly the Three Crowns, St Thomas's Street, which had been in the Morrells' hands since 1818.[17]

By 1851, when the elder James, then aged seventy-eight, transferred the brewery, its freehold and leasehold pubs and premises and its farmland to his son, the younger James was already forty-one.[18] A florid, thick-set

James Morrell (1810–63), brewer, JP and country gentleman, at the time of his retirement as Master of the Old Berkshire Hunt, 1858.

man, he followed the family tendency to corpulence. (His cousin Charles in Wallingford had weighed over fourteen stone as a young man.)[19] In a portrait engraved a few years later, an endearingly chubby face looks out from between the bushy sideburns of the period and from under the tall hat of a gentleman dressed for hunting. He had not yet married; but in late November 1851, three months after succeeding to the ownership of the brewery, he married Alicia Everett, the twenty-nine-year-old daughter of a clergyman's widow whose late husband, the Rev. William Everett, had been vicar of Romford, Essex.

After their society wedding at St George's, Hanover Square, the couple returned to live next to the brewery at 1 Fisher Row. James continued his duties as Master of the Old Berkshire Hunt, probably delegating much of the day-to-day running of the brewery to his experienced old clerk, John Webb. Industry in Britain was expanding fast, as the Great Exhibition of that year had triumphantly shown, but for the time being James was content to keep things at the brewery as he found them. When he did invest capital in new ventures, it would not be in machinery, equipment or new buildings, nor in a vastly enlarged empire of tied public houses in other counties, nor in mergers, branches or subsidiary businesses, nor in trying to break into the nationwide retail trade or the export trade. Temperamentally James was a country gentleman, and his money, when he spent it, would go into the country gentleman's traditional indulgences – private building, planting, and purchases of land.

Emily Alicia, James and Alicia's only child, was born in January 1854 and christened the following month at St Giles' church, Oxford. Her parents' choice of a church for the ceremony may reflect distrust on her mother's side for the flagrantly High Church practices of the vicar of St Thomas's, the Rev. Thomas Chamberlain, one of the leaders of the Ritualist movement, who had introduced surplices, incense, robed choirs, and sisterhoods of celibate ladies who devoted their time to ecclesiastical embroidery and visiting the sick. There can have been little sympathy between Chamberlain and the old-fashioned Morrells, who now lived mainly outside St Thomas's and had done nothing to help promote Chamberlain's missionary activities among the dissolute, badger-baiting, beer-drinking poor of the parish.

This choice may, on the other hand, simply reflect the growing friendship of the younger James Morrell with his solicitor second cousin Frederick Joseph Morrell and his wife Elizabeth, daughter of the bookseller and University printer Joseph Parker. Frederick and Elizabeth had now been married for twenty years, and had taken over Elizabeth's father's former house, Black Hall, a conspicuously tall seventeenth-century stone farmhouse, possibly rebuilt after a fire in the 1660s, on the east side of St Giles near the church. Here Frederick, and later his son Frederick Parker Morrell and daughter-in-law Harriette, daughter of the Rev. Philip Wynter, President of St John's College, kept their collection of books and manuscripts and Harriette's celebrated flower paintings, tapestries and collection of handicrafts. In the country they had a house at Broughton, near Banbury, inherited from an aunt of Frederick Joseph Morrell's on his mother's side, Sarah Chapman.

Like his father, Baker Morrell, Frederick was Steward of St John's College and a respected public figure in Oxford. James evidently trusted him as wholeheartedly as his father had trusted his cousin Robert, at the expense of Baker Morrell, Robert's former partner. When he drew up his will a few years later the younger James placed the entire responsibility for the brewery business in the hands of Frederick and the brewery manager as trustees. As for Frederick's future daughter-in-law, the artistic Harriette Wynter, her own daughter-in-law, Lady Ottoline Morrell, later wrote of her that she was:

a most gifted and unusually charming person, lively, witty, critical. . . . She had been an important figure in Oxford, very much more remarkable in taste and entertaining than any other woman there. She had gathered round her in their beautiful house many interesting people, who found her a delightful and witty friend and hostess. Indeed, Henry James, it is said, took from her the inspiration for *The Spoils of Poynton*.[20]

Robert Morrell, the elder James's partner in the family bank, had died in November 1849 at The Retreat, his house in Wallingford; and with his death, or a year or two before it, the bank had come to an end. (The elder James, in the census of 1841, had described himself as 'banker' rather than 'brewer', but ten years later, despite the imminent transfer of power to his son, had reverted to calling himself 'brewer'.) Much of Robert's estate went to James, his executor; and in 1851 all the Coxes' former landed assets, including their coal-mine in the Forest of Dean, passed to the younger James with the brewery. Also included among the brewery lands were the farmland at Sandford purchased by the elder James in 1828, and a further 250 acres adjoining this that he had bought in 1847 at Thomas Mallam's auction sale of the Duke of Marlborough's Sandford estate.[21]

Emily's life overlapped very briefly with those of the elder James and his cousins, the sons of James Morrell the attorney. Both Deacon and Baker Morrell died in 1854, Deacon having long since parted with Streatley House to the Stones, the family of Emily's aunt and uncle, William and Emily Stone, and Baker having passed on his law practice to his son Frederick. In November 1855 the elder James died, aged eighty-two. Hard work and a certain frugality had allowed him to outlive all his contemporaries in the family; and there can have been none left in Wallingford who remembered the hot-headed, quarrelsome apprentice maltster of sixty years earlier. The younger James, meanwhile, was looking forward to increasing and beautifying his estates, and within a matter of months was buying farmland outside Oxford and levelling, planting and building on a grandiose scale on Headington Hill.

CHAPTER FIVE

THE LANDED MAGNATE, 1856–63

A watercolour painting by John S. Austin exists of James, Alicia and Emily Morrell on the terrace above their new house at Headington Hill in the late 1850s. All three are beautifully and fashionably dressed – James plump and prosperous, Alicia and Emily delicately pretty. While Emily plays behind them, James and Alicia gaze out over the south front of the house with its ground-floor colonnade and balustraded roof, and over lawns and beds of shrubs newly planted with the dwarf shapes of exotic evergreens. The brewer's mansion has taken shape; its grounds have been laid out for decades of prosperity to come. The elder James's house, now demoted to a kitchen and nursery wing, is neatly set back on the north side of the house and echoes the details of the main block in its identical chimneys and rustication.[1]

James's intention in adding a large, square block to the original house was clearly to create a mansion for entertaining. To design this he hired John Thomas, a fashionable Londoner, as well known for his sculptures on the exteriors of buildings and for large public monuments as for country houses. In the 1840s Thomas had designed the heavily Jacobean-cum-Italianate Somerleyton Hall in Suffolk for the railway magnate Sir Morton Peto. He had also worked, and would continue to work, for the Royal Family, designing an elaborate tiled dairy with a coffered ceiling, gothic arches and stained-glass windows for the home farm at Windsor Castle two years after his work on Headington Hill Hall. Here, however, his style was purely Italianate, or Franco-Italianate, with rusticated corners and pilasters, a colonnade reaching right round the south and west fronts of the house, and a mansard roof behind a balustrade. Inside the house was dramatically hollow, with a central staircase ascending past a galleried first floor to a light in the roof. The long ground-floor rooms with their plate glass windows opened into one another, and seemed designed for an existence of parties rather than for ordinary family living.

While the house was being built James had also restructured the grounds and arranged for them to be planted by William Baxter, the curator of the Oxford Botanic Garden. Baxter, an enthusiast for the new discoveries that botanists were making in the Himalayas, China and South America, had little room in his cramped, seventeenth-century garden to plant these, although he did expand outside the walls to put in a wellingtonia, a stone

Headington Hill Hall from the south-west

pine and a pair of monkey-puzzles. On Headington Hill he could spread himself on a grand scale; and he gave James plantations of wellingtonias (newly introduced into England in 1853), Bhutan pines, honey locusts, monkey-puzzles, tulip trees and Atlas cedars. Shrubberies on all sides of the house contained rare specimen plants such as hydrangeas, berberis and Chinese tree peonies, together with trees varied enough to stock an arboretum.[2] In between lay lawns large enough for a wedding party or the opening meet of a hunt. It may have been James's intention, before suddenly retiring from hunting in 1858, to move the Old Berkshire Hunt from its kennels at Tubney to new kennels that he made at King's Mill on the Cherwell, just below Headington Hill off the Marston Road.

Not content with his rebuilding and replanting, James also spent the first six years after his father's death in hugely expanding his ownership of farmland. In 1853 the Sandford Brake Farm, adjoining James's land and previously let out at £80 a year, had been offered at auction in Abingdon by its owner, Richard Faulkner, but had apparently failed to make its reserve. Three years later James bought it by private treaty. The following year he bought Sawpit and Blackbird Leys farms; and in 1861 he bought the farm at Garsington, named Holloway's for its tenant, which lay just to the east of Sawpit and Blackbird Leys farms, and had been inherited by Frederick Joseph Morrell from his father and grandfather. James's aim here was obviously to consolidate; for he now owned a swathe of farms stretching from near the River Thames at Sandford to about 2 miles to the eastward. At the 1847 sale another investor, the Rev. Professor Hussey, had bought the lordship of the manor of Sandford and enough different lots to prevent the elder James's purchases from forming a coherent whole. This state of affairs persisted until 1866, after the younger James's death, when the Husseys were persuaded to exchange certain portions of their lands for others originally bought by the Morrells.

At Culham, meanwhile, in 1856, James had the satisfaction of buying an entire estate of five farms in a single purchase. Two or three miles down the Thames from Sandford, enclosed in a westward loop of the river that divided it from Abingdon, the estate consisted of Rye, Hill, Manor, Zouch and Warren Farms, amounting in all to nearly 1,500 acres. Rye Farm can be easily reached on foot from Abingdon Bridge; Zouch Farm lies to the south of Culham railway station and the main A415 east–west road; and the remaining farms lie roughly in between them. Since the mid-seventeenth century the estate had descended through the Bisshopp family until it devolved on a son-in-law, Sir George Brooke-Pechell. By then the farms were indebted in the region of £40,000, and James bought them for £72,750. What he spent on his other farms is not always clear, but we know from a notebook at the brewery that Blackbird Leys and Sawpit farms had failed to make a reserve of £11,750 at auction in 1856, so James may well have paid less than that when he bought them by private treaty the following year.[3]

For a landowner, buying farms which do not adjoin the property where he lives must always be less satisfactory than buying those that extend his own immediate domain. James, however, with no prospect of extending the Headington Hill estate to give himself a home farm which he could see from his upper windows, settled for second best, extending the Sandford estate that he had taken on with the brewery and buying a second estate that he clearly intended to let out. The annual value of the Culham farms was estimated in 1856 to be £2,833 7s. 6d.; so within his lifetime, if he had lived another twenty-five or thirty years, James could have expected to see his investment pay off.[4]

The Sandford farms, which became the nucleus of a home farm managed directly from the brewery, may always have been intended by the Morrells for a venture of this kind. In Mark and James's joint bank book there is a debit entry for £9, dated 10 October 1829, which reads 'Castle for Pigs'.[5] Castle was an auctioneer, and the pigs may well have been intended for the first Sandford farm that James had bought the previous year. If the area was suitable for barley it may have seemed a potential source of direct supply for the Tidmarsh Lane malthouse, as Bradley Farm was in a small way in the late 1850s. Certainly some barley was grown on the Sandford farms in the 1850s and 1860s; but it was never enough to supply the brewery's needs and was not always of the right quality for malting. Rather, Blackbird Leys, Sandford Brake and Sawpit Farms, run together as one and referred to simply in brewery records as 'the farm', constituted the private home farm that the elder and younger James may always have wished they had nearer at hand on Headington Hill. James's new house now supported seventeen servants, and the amount of produce consumed there suggests almost continuous entertaining when the family were at home. In the brewing year ending October 1859 the farm supplied Headington Hill Hall with 40 ducks, 90 chickens, 31 turkeys, 8,600 eggs, 61 fat sheep and 1 lamb, 37 fat hogs and porkers, 6 sacks of apples, 33 sacks of potatoes, 15 sacks of turnips and 5 sacks of white peas. Labour costs at the farm that year were £935 3s. 1d., or little less than the £1,095 8s. 6d. spent on labour at the brewery. In both places (but less so at the farm than at the brewery, for obvious reasons), wages were supplemented by payments in beer consumed on the establishment. At the brewery that year, the cost of beer consumed at work was estimated at £813 19s. 6d., with an estimated further £1,000 laid out in staff discounts and payments of beer-money.[6]

Although its chief purpose was to supply the family rather than to provide a supply of barley for malting, James Morrell and his successors ran the farm in direct conjunction with the brewery for the best part of forty years. To some extent the relationship was one of mutual convenience, for the farm provided some hay and straw for the brewery horses and a small proportion of the barley needed for malting, while absorbing waste products from the brewery such as malt-dust and manure from the stables. Dray-horses in need of a change could be put to farm-work, and vice versa. The brewery manager, a freer agent than the clerks who spent their day in the counting-house or (later) the offices, led a pleasantly open-air life supervising the farm bailiff and negotiating sales and purchases of stock. The notional costs of brewery waste products used on the farm were duly entered in the accounts, as were the notional annual rents paid for the use of what was in fact freehold land: sums of £500 for Blackbird Leys and over £600 for Sandford, which were periodically entered on the debit side to balance the brewery's books.

From the brewery accounts for 1856–7, the year in which James acquired Sawpit and Blackbird Leys farms, it seems evident that the farms worked from the brewery could have only the narrowest profit-margin and could run, as they often did, at a considerable loss. During a period in which the outgoings at Bradley were £301 16s. 10d. and at Blackbird Leys £1,941 14s. 3½d., the total income from both (excluding just under

£100-worth of barley from Bradley) was £2,584 13s., giving an overall profit of £541 1s. ½d. At Sandford, in the same year, the total outgoings on labour and other expenditures, including payments for sawing, barley hoeing and stone digging, were £2,361 14s. 3d., and the income £966 15s. 11d., excluding barley worth £219 12s. This was in a year in which the brewery paid out a total of £15,742 on purchases of barley, so the contribution of the home farms to the brewery's stocks of barley was negligible. Nevertheless, in 1860 James considered it worthwhile investing £200 in a new chaff-cutter and grinding-mill, and at about that time also bought the farm one of the first ever threshing machines to be manufactured, which by the late 1870s had become quite worn out.[7]

Despite the draining effect of the farming venture on the brewery economy, some investments in property were still paying their way. Rents from farms, including the former Cox-held leaseholds that had not required any capital outlay, totalled £4,788 8s. for the brewing year ending in October 1860 and £4,061 12s. for the following year. Rents from public houses came to £3,359 7s. for the year ending in October 1860 and £3,539 4s. 6d. for the following year (discounting an additional £62 10s. for public houses which had stood vacant for part of the year).[8] Only if James had let out all his farmland and insisted on keeping on the family bank could he have reasonably expected to make a bigger income than he did; and the banking operation had become one so fraught with risks that his father had evidently seen investment in land as a safer option. A sharp recession in 1847–8, following a period of national greed earlier in the 1840s with manias for investing in railway shares and for speculating in corn at the expense of the hungry poor, had caused many provincial banks to close their doors, some permanently. The elder James's purchase of the Sandford land in 1847 may have resulted directly from the freeing of capital which had previously been tied up in the bank; and the younger James's more lavish purchases were only a continuation of the process begun by his father, made in the hope of finding a home for capital that national investment crazes and panics would not be able to undermine.

To compensate his father's former bank clerk, Robert Haines (to whom he also left £100 and a suit of mourning in his will), the younger James had allowed him to move into 1 Fisher Row when he moved out to take possession of the house at Headington on his father's death. Within two years, however, Haines was required to move on, for in October 1857 James gave him notice that he wished to have the house for his new brewery manager.[9] This was Thomas Sherwood, a native of Purley near Reading, and one of the new, mobile, professional class of business managers. To judge from the birthplaces of his three eldest children he had previously worked at Basingstoke, the home of several breweries (chief among them John May's, established in 1750), and before that at

Workington, Cumberland, the home of John Curwen's High Brewery since 1792.[10] Few records survive of Sherwood's seventeen years as manager of Morrell's; but he was evidently held in high esteem by both James Morrell and his trustees, and in James's will received a permanent entitlement to a salary of £1,000 a year, together with free beer and coals and rent-free occupation of his house. When he died this right passed automatically to his widow, a privilege not enjoyed by the widows of the clerk John Webb and the brewer Charles Hutt in the house on the brewery premises. While successive brewery managers came and went, Mrs Sherwood continued to live at the house on the corner of Fisher Row, succeeded by an unmarried daughter who continued living there until early in the Second World War.

Below Sherwood in seniority at the brewery there were now two clerks, George Hill and George Lord. They were responsible for casual and regular sales of beer, for the weekly payments to the fluctuating staff of brewhouse men, and for separate payments to coopers and blacksmiths (£3 to £4 a week for each, probably representing the work of three or four coopers and two or three blacksmiths, or two men and a boy). Annual expenditures on labour at the brewery came to £997 in 1855–6, £1,038 0s. 10d. in 1856–7, and £1,095 8s. 6d. in 1858–9. In the first of these three years the amount spent weekly on wages fluctuated from a low of £17 4s. at the end of the brewing year in late October to a high of £22 12s. 6d. the following February, then to an all-time low of £16 12s. 8d. in June, rising to a steady £19 12s. through late August to mid-September, and then falling again to £18 12s. for the first two weeks of October. Mayhew's *London Labour and the London Poor*, compiled in the 1850s, reveals that £1 a week was a reasonable town labourer's wage during that decade. Different brewhouse workers were obviously paid different amounts, and boys might be paid only half as much as grown men, so it is difficult to calculate even a roughly average number of workers likely to have been employed in the brewhouse, malthouse and yard and in driving drays. Given, however, that the men consumed an estimated £15–16-worth of beer a week between them, and that this would have been counted as part of their pay, it is likely that the total wage-earning labour-force in the late 1850s numbered at least thirty, and possibly nearer forty at the busiest times of the year.[11]

With the addition in the 1840s of the fast-running, steam-operated table engine, augmenting the power of the water wheel and the slower beam engine to turn a horizontal gear wheel which activated the pumps and the other brewhouse machinery, productivity of beer had been considerably speeded up. Using water from the brewery's own well, the mash tun and copper in the brewhouse could take 30–35 quarters of malt at a single brewing and convert these into roughly 120 barrels of (by

The water wheel, 1974

today's standards extremely strong) beer. In the late 1850s the total yearly output was about 32,000 barrels, of which ordinary ale accounted for just over half, the stronger and more expensive x brew for about a third, and porter, small beer and pale ale for the remainder. At this stage pale ale was an experimental novelty, with a single brewing of 160 barrels being produced in 1858–9 and again in 1860–1, but none at all in the intervening year.[12]

While at work the brewhouse men, blacksmiths and other brewery workers probably consumed the relatively innocuous ordinary ale, which was nevertheless stronger than its equivalent today. When, however, James arranged a roof-raising party for the workmen building Headington Hill Hall, on 1 November 1856, in the gas-lit fives court attached to the St Clement's public baths, with catering provided by the landlord of the Coach and Horses in St Clement's, he supplied beef, mutton, veal, pork, fowls, vegetables and an 'unlimited supply of "Morrell's Entire"'.[13] This was the old-fashioned, full-bodied, porter-type brew, famous for its strength and robustness rather than its clarity. At a much more sumptuous dinner that he gave in September 1860 at the Oxford Town Hall to celebrate his connection with the local Volunteer Rifle Corps and his fiftieth birthday the previous spring, James entertained most of the county aristocracy and gentry, the heads of most of the Oxford colleges and halls, the Bishop of Oxford, 'Soapy Sam' Wilberforce, and seventy-nine other clergy and their wives, who, with the other ladies, were segregated in a gallery while the men dined and drank their wine below them. Beer was not, of course, served at this dinner, but at the end an announcement went out that James would distribute the leftovers among the city's poor, with an added bonus of seven fat sheep and 1,500 loaves of bread to be divided between them, and a bottle of beer for every family in receipt of this charity.[14]

* * *

At Headington Hill Hall James, Alicia and Emily enjoyed their new-found status as members of the landed gentry with lavish room in which to entertain. There is no record of any outing of brewery workers to the newly built mansion, as there would be twenty, thirty or forty years later. When members of the newly formed Volunteer Rifle Corps called on James to congratulate him on his fiftieth birthday, he allowed them into the grounds but not into the house as he had a house-party staying there. When planning the subsequent dinner that he held for the Corps in September he originally thought of providing it out of doors, and then changed the location altogether to the Town Hall. Yet, given time and organization, the Morrells could entertain large local parties at their house. Alicia, with only one child of her own to care for, decided soon after moving to Headington Hill to endow a local free school for girls as an alternative to the girls' half of the parochial school, which had been built only twenty years earlier but was already outgrown. This school, originally for thirty children, was built on land belonging to the Morrells near St Clement's church; and Alicia undertook to pay the schoolmistress's salary and the running costs of the school in return for being left free of all interference by the rector and other parochial officials. In early June 1858 she gave a party for the opening of the school, entertaining the children to roast beef and plum pudding at Headington Hill Hall, then inviting them back after the opening ceremony for tea and an uplifting speech by James 'in the presence of Lord Valentia, and other guests'.[15]

James, meanwhile, had been unexpectedly shaken by a fall out hunting, and at the end of the previous season had decided to withdraw from it altogether. The Old Berkshire subscribers presented him with a magnificent, engraved piece of plate, an object which became so dear to him that he directed in his will that it should remain as a family heirloom at Headington Hill Hall, but which now forms part of the collection belonging to the City of Oxford.[16] The organization under his patronage of the Oxford Volunteer Rifle Corps, one of a nationwide network of Yeomanry regiments and volunteer corps which had been allowed to lapse at the end of the Napoleonic War, then, inspired by the fear of Napoleon III, had revived to become a regular feature of life in Victorian England, partly filled the gap in his interests that had been left by the Old Berkshire Hunt. He was clearly unwell, however, and became more corpulent as his life became more sedentary. He spent more and more time in London, where he maintained a permanently hired landau, and at health resorts in the hope of a cure from sea air. At home he could be driven in a loop round the shrubberies, and even round the walks of the fruit and vegetable garden on the other side of the main London road, in a selection of vehicles ranging from a phaeton or chariot to a pony-drawn garden chair or invalid chair.[17]

At Brighton in the autumn of 1862 James's health suffered its final, fatal upset. Seeing an overturned gig he tried to get out of his carriage to help the occupants, fell and injured his leg. By then his constitution was too unhealthy for the injury to heal, and he grew flabbier and more atrophied after taking to his bed. Lung complications set in, bewildering the London specialist and the local doctors who visited him, and he began to lose all appetite for food. Through the spring and summer of 1863 he lingered on at Headington Hill Hall, first making his will under the direction of his solicitor cousin Frederick, then adding codicil after codicil to it, providing now for his greyhounds, now for a former servant or charity. While omitting to make his wife's school a direct charge on his estate, he urged that any future occupants of the house should subscribe £150 a year to clothe the girls and pay the schoolmistress, and that they should choose her without reference to the vicar or any other clergyman. Nine of his close friends received mourning rings – among them the seventh Duke of Marlborough, the Earl of Abingdon, Lord Valentia and the Rev. Philip Wynter, President of St John's College, whose daughter Harriette would later marry his cousin Frederick's son.[18]

James died on 12 September 1863. His funeral at St Clement's parish church was attended (a local paper reported) by 'at least two thousand persons', including the mayor, several aldermen, 'members of the University and County Gentry . . . tenantry and *employés*'. During the week between James's death and the funeral, all the Morrell-owned public houses in Oxford and the neighbourhood had kept their shutters partly closed as a mark of respect, while on the funeral morning the bells of several city churches tolled in unison between eleven in the morning and midday.[19] It was the quietest time of the Oxford year, with undergraduates and many dons away and grass (according to William Sherwood, the brewery manager's son)[20] growing between the cobbles in the streets. Mid-September in Oxford can be a time of brilliant clarity; and on Headington Hill, with the leaves just beginning to turn, the scene of empty grandeur must have been all the more poignant for its beauty.

Alicia Morrell survived her husband by only five months. Grief, worry or some long-standing illness of her own eroded the bonds that held her to Emily and the girl pupils at her school. James had left her only a slender £3,000 annuity, although his Trustees would have met most of the running costs of the Hall, with kennelmen, gardeners, grooms and indoor servants (now increased to nineteen) to be paid, gas-lamps kept burning until dawn in the grounds, glass vineries and peach-houses to heat, and a coachman, postillions and stable-boys divided between Headington Hill and livery stables in Oxford, where James had kept most of his huge collection of horses and carriages.[21]

When Alicia died in February 1864 Emily was aged just ten. In a hasty codicil to his will James had appointed two extra trustees, the Oxford banker Herbert Parsons and an Abingdon solicitor, Thomas Hedges Graham, who now acted for the brewery, to be her guardians. Parsons, however, declined the responsibility for Emily; and in 1864 the senior trustee, one Richard Sneyd Ramsbottom (appointed with Frederick Morrell and Thomas Sherwood to administer the brewery and James's estate, but largely an absentee since he lived in Dover) had her made a Ward of Court to ensure that no unscrupulous suitor should gain possession of her fortune while she was still under age. Her aunt Emily Stone, who had been widowed the previous year, agreed to look after her in return for an allowance from James's trustees, and removed her to the happier surroundings of Streatley House. The Hall was let to a respectable, blind landowner from Shropshire, Richard Corbet, whose standards were considerably less lavish than those of the Morrells, and who within the next few years had reduced the number of living-in servants in the house to ten.[22]

CHAPTER SIX

TRUSTEESHIP, 1863–85

Two years after James, Alicia and Emily Morrell had moved from St Thomas's to Headington Hill, the brewery manager Thomas Sherwood took over the Fisher Row house with his wife and three small children. His eldest son William, at that time an observant five-year-old, grew up to attend Magdalen College School and eventually became Master there, as well as Mayor of Oxford (two years running in 1913 and 1914) and Vicar of Sandford on Thames. Relatively sheltered for a St Thomas's child, but less so than Emily would have had to be had she spent her childhood in Fisher Row rather than surrounded by acres of shrubbery and parkland, William rapidly became aware of the differences between the area round the brewery and the more respectable parts of Oxford, and between his own school-uniformed self and the rougher St Thomas's boys, who began what work they could find at the age of ten or twelve after only the most rudimentary education in the parish school.

The railway, which had cut through St Thomas's a few years before the Sherwood family arrived, now defined the main part of the parish, cutting it off from the grazing lands of Alley Meads, Osney Meadow and Oatlands along the Botley Road. (Much of the Jericho part of the parish, north of Worcester College, had been transferred to St Paul's church, Walton Street in 1837, while the remainder joined St Barnabas' parish in 1869. Osney Town, built to the west of the railway in the early 1850s, formed part of the new St Frideswide's parish once this was created in 1873.) The St Thomas's Street area, long established as an industrial suburb with a shifting, partly migrant population, was now a constricted, densely populated slum, much ravaged by the cholera epidemic in the autumn of 1854, which had killed mainly women and children. Working men had only a short to moderate expectancy of life even when securely employed at Morrell's, as we have seen from the deaths between 1842 and 1870 of James Fletcher at twenty-six, his successor as brewer Charles Hutt at forty-nine, and Joe Hutt the brewery drayman at thirty-six. Those without regular jobs, existing from day to day and hand to mouth in a series of irregular occupations, might be worn out at forty (as an elderly St Thomas's man observed to Mary Prior) 'with worry on how to exist'.[1] The fishermen and boatmen of Upper, Middle and Lower Fisher Row were, as Dr Prior has shown, a distinctive group in the life of the city with

A former lodging-house, St Thomas's Street (partly demolished 1934)

'a reputation for a sort of cheerful violence'.[2] William Sherwood noticed the violence of life in St Thomas's generally: the number of well-known pugilists who came from the area, and the drunken fights after dark as the many public houses emptied.[3]

Since the late eighteenth century, when Park End Street was opened, St Thomas's Street had ceased to be the main road into Oxford from the west. Throughout the nineteenth century, however, it still attracted the drifting, temporary inhabitants whom a surveyor of 1809, finding them renting space in the dilapidated house next to Symms's malthouse on the corner of The Hamel, had called 'travellers of the lowest Description'.[4] Several of its public houses served at various times as lodging-houses, as they had no doubt done since before the Reformation. First the canal and then the railway had brought their temporary populations of navvies, and later the rootless travellers often to be found in the neighbourhood of main-line railway stations. The Shoulder of Mutton pub next to the brewery, formerly the scene of badger-baiting, was established as a lodging-house by 1871, and ten years later housed eight members of a German band. Eight other lodgers also lived at the pub, while five more Germans, apparently the younger members of the group, aged fourteen and upwards, lodged farther down the street below The Hamel. In 1891, now the Marlborough Arms, the pub accommodated an elderly rat-catcher, a female college servant with her two children, a sixteen-year-old girl who sold cress, with her seven-year-old sister, and nine Italian organ-grinders and other musicians, including a mother, daughter and small boy.[5]

The Marlborough Arms, St Thomas's Street, Oxford, with Morrells Brewery in the background, 1968

In the midst of all this impermanence, the brewery stood out as a solid and in many ways benign institution. One small example was the fire-engine, a heavy object like a large hand-cart. According to William Sherwood, this was the biggest non-municipal one in Oxford, and would as a matter of course be used to put out local fires. 'The City had none, I suppose because the University were responsible for us at night. The University had two small hand-worked squirts which were kept in St Mary's church. The Press, I think, had one. . . .'. Even after the formation of the volunteer City Fire Brigade in 1870, the brewery engine could be requisitioned to help with serious fires. Sherwood remembered being called out of bed, probably as an eighteen- or nineteen-year-old, to trundle the brewery engine single-handed up the slope of George Street to a fire in the city centre, only to find that it produced no water and that the volunteer firemen had to put out the fire without his help.[6]

The eleven years of trusteeship between 1863 and 1874, when Thomas Sherwood died, was a period during which the brewery quietly maintained its position, with no notable innovations in technology or expansion of the premises. Encouraged by the railways, new, rival breweries were becoming established in Oxford or (like the Burton

Brewery Company, which had offices in Cornmarket Street by 1872), opening agencies in the city centre, ready to arrange for the transportation of their beer to Oxford by rail. In 1872 there were eighteen breweries or brewery agencies in Oxford, by 1874 twenty-two. In the city centre the premises of Hanley's City Brewery stretched the length of a block from 20 Queen Street to include the present Museum of Modern Art building on the north side of Pembroke Street. Nearby, Edward Le Mills's St Ebbe's Brewery occupied premises in Church Street, where the rear part of Lewis's department store now opens into Pennyfarthing Place. By 1872 the Reading firm of H.G. Simonds had opened a pale ale and porter brewery at 30 Queen Street, almost directly opposite Hanley's, with another branch under a separate manager at 1 Cowley Road, near the Morrells' Cape of Good Hope pub. By 1882 the firm of Phillips had taken over the former Cross Keys pub, also on the Canal Wharf in Park End Street, near the coal wharf on which Nuffield College was subsequently built. Weaving's Eagle Brewery was established in Park End Street by 1867, and celebrated the possession of a modern steam engine by calling itself the Eagle Steam Brewery. Similarly Phillips', adopting the new vertical brewing layout, became Phillips' Tower Brewery. Hall's, no longer with a Tawney as part-owner, still flourished under the ownership of Colonel A.W. Hall, who from 1876 to 1892 (with a very brief interval out of office in 1880) was Conservative Member of Parliament for the City of Oxford.

Given the strength of the competition from other breweries, it would not have been surprising if Frederick Morrell, the absentee Richard Ramsbottom and Thomas Sherwood had decided to sell off the freehold public houses and Fox's Malthouse, hand the lease of the brewery premises back to Christ Church and arrange for Emily to derive her future income from a combination of investments on the Stock Exchange and the rent from Headington Hill Hall. The crucial factor in the brewery's survival during the decade after James Morrell's death was probably the fact that he had appointed Sherwood a trustee, while guaranteeing him a free house and a generous salary of £1,000 a year for continuing in his post as brewery manager and agent for the various farms. Other former senior employees of James's such as William Ward, the head gardener at Headington Hill Hall, might be ditched by the Trustees as part of an economy drive,[7] but it would scarcely have been in Sherwood's interest to encourage the abandonment of his own livelihood. While Emily grew up at Streatley, then, the brewery continued under the official ownership of 'Morrell's Trustees' (or, more cumbersomely, the 'Trustees of the late James Morrell Esq.'), who gave the business the little-used, alternative name of 'Lion Brewery' to simplify and brighten their corporate image.

* * *

Emily grew rapidly. At fourteen she was already mature enough to have attracted the attention of an older cousin, George Herbert Morrell, then aged twenty-three, educated at Rugby and Oxford, and the almost perfect incarnation of mid-Victorian industriousness and manliness. Herbert, Emily's third cousin, belonged to the branch of the family descended from the solicitor Baker Morrell, which had proliferated (mainly with clergymen) while the brewing side of the family had dwindled almost to nothing. Three of Baker's five sons were in Holy Orders, including Herbert's father, the Rev. George Kidd Morrell, vicar of Moulsford, a riverside parish adjoining that of Streatley on the Thames. Herbert was not rich, but he was academic, ambitious and interested in political and social questions. Trained as a scientist, he had a job as an Assistant Demonstrator in Physiology at the University Museum, and hoped for a second career as a Conservative Member of Parliament. In his spare time he devoted himself to shooting, both with the city Volunteer Rifle Corps, which James Morrell had supported, and with its University equivalent.

At Christmas 1868, when Emily was not yet fifteen, the couple seem to have declared their love to one another. Shortly after that a rumour reached Emily's legal guardians, the trustee Ramsbottom and the solicitor Graham, that Herbert and Emily had become engaged. When challenged, Herbert's uncle Frederick Morrell admitted this to be at least implicitly true, but her aunt Emily Stone denied it. While the family closed ranks in an attempt to protect the young couple, Ramsbottom and Graham invoked Emily's status as a Ward of Court and secured an injunction from the Master of the Rolls forbidding Herbert to communicate in any way with Emily until she had ceased to be a minor, in other words for a further six years.[8]

Apart from Emily's youth, which was the insuperable problem as far as Ramsbottom and Graham were concerned, few sensible objections could be made to her marrying Herbert. As a cousin he could not be condemned as an adventurer, since Emily's money would remain within the family if she married him. Now that Emily and her aunt were the only remaining members of the brewing branch of the family, an alliance with the thriving branch of legal and clerical Morrells seemed all the more desirable in order to perpetuate the family name. In addition, the Trustees formed an effective barrier to any husband of Emily's assuming control of the brewery and the estates, since they had not been instructed to hand these over to her (or to her husband) once she was of age. At eighteen, when she had come out, Emily would return to live at Headington Hill Hall and would be one of the richest and most important members of county society. A high-minded, sober protector such as Herbert would be the best possible thing for her at that time, both to bar the way to more unscrupulous suitors and to provide her, in due course, with the brewery's heir.

Such was the family view of things, while, in the best tradition of Victorian fiction, the love affair continued through intermediaries, accidental meetings and glances exchanged across crowded rooms. Emily took up archery, while Herbert continued rifle-shooting. In 1870 he published a two-part textbook, *The Student's Manual of Comparative Anatomy and Guide to Dissection*, which expounded the classification of mammals laid down by his professor, T.H. Huxley, but was slated by a reviewer for its timidity in omitting any mention of the sex organs of mammals. Even before he had declared his love to Emily, he had also contrived to have himself made a manager of the St Clement's parish schools, having gained a seat on the Oxford School Board of which his uncle, Frederick Morrell, was clerk. In 1870 Parliament passed Forster's Education Act, which, while providing for universal primary school education, imposed new rules on the established parochial schools by forbidding parish clergy to teach Scripture in the schools within normal teaching hours, and parents to remove their children from school before the age of twelve. As a Conservative, Herbert threw his energies into opposing Forster's Act and campaigning for Church schools to have the right to opt out of state control, thus going directly against the example set by Emily's father James Morrell in protecting his wife's school from interference by the clergy.[9]

As Emily grew older and began (although not yet 'out') to go to parties and other gatherings, the difficulty for Herbert of meeting and ignoring her seemed all the greater. Herbert's cousin Fred, the young solicitor, married since 1867 to Harriette Wynter, took his part in trying to explain to Emily's guardians that it could not be helped if the couple sometimes met socially, as they may have done at Black Hall, Fred's parental home in St Giles. Once Emily was eighteen, Herbert tried directly petitioning the Master of the Rolls to allow her to marry early, only to be opposed in the courts by Ramsbottom and subjected to long delays. He, meanwhile, had taken a second degree in Law and in 1871 was called to the Bar, probably as the time-honoured way of furthering his political ambitions rather than from any desire to practise in the Law Courts.[10]

Emily was presented at Court by the Duchess of Marlborough at a drawing room at Buckingham Palace in April 1872. Two months later, by long-standing arrangement, Emily and her aunt moved back into Headington Hill Hall, which the Corbets had vacated after an eight-year stay. It was now almost Emily's official duty to give parties, in the grounds of the Hall (as usually happened) if not in the house. By the following summer she and her aunt were well established enough to give one of the grandest summer garden parties in Oxford, attended by various Morrell relatives, city notables and county landowners, the Marquess of Tavistock, and several heads of colleges, including the Vice-

Chancellor, Dean Liddell of Christ Church, his wife and his daughters, of whom Alice was only a year or two older than Emily.[11]

Herbert's exclusion from gatherings of this kind would have been a social absurdity, whatever Emily's guardians might privately think of a man who could bring himself to declare his love to a girl of only fourteen. In an attempt to reinforce the Master of the Rolls's instructions to him they had warned him solemnly, if he happened to meet her on social occasions, to stand back and let other young men have a chance of finding favour with her; but both Herbert and Emily were obstinately single-minded. Realizing that he would have to petition the Master of the Rolls directly to be allowed to propose to Emily before she was twenty-one, Herbert did so, and eventually received permission in November 1873. Emily accepted at once, and by Christmas, shortly before her twentieth birthday, the couple were given official leave to marry. Six weeks later, on 4 February 1874, they were married at Streatley as lavishly as circumstances would permit, while in Oxford separate dinners were given for the brewery workers, the gardeners and servants at Headington Hill Hall, and the girls who attended Emily's mother's (now Miss Morrell's) school. After a short, wintry honeymoon at Hastings, the couple returned to Headington Hill Hall to live there permanently, and to benefit from all the efforts that the brewery Trustees could make to provide them with an income suitable for their position in life.[12]

The marriage of Herbert and Emily made copious work for lawyers, and eventually affected the running of the brewery by precipitating a complete overhaul of the trusteeship arrangements. Instead of James's will, Herbert and Emily's marriage settlement was the document on which the organization of the Trustees depended. The funds that they administered were no longer treated as a single entity, but were divided into a number of different settlement funds to be used for brewery, estate or family purposes. This new dispensation did not come into force immediately, but had effect from January 1875, once Emily had turned twenty-one. Until that time the Trustees granted Emily an income of £1,000 a month from her parents' settlement funds, while Herbert's father increased his allowance from £400 to £600 a year. After Emily's twenty-first birthday she received her income from the new private settlement fund, while Herbert received an allowance of £2,000 a year, with the promise of the income from half the estate should Emily happen to predecease him.[13]

Natural wastage from death or retirement had also led to a change in the body of Trustees. Thomas Sherwood died in 1874, and was not replaced as a Trustee by his successor as brewery manager, Arthur Jorden, who had already been working at the brewery for some years and clearly occupied an inferior place in the Trustees' estimation to the privileged position enjoyed by Sherwood. Jorden's basic salary, from February 1876, was only £600, augmented by bonuses of £50 or £100 but still several hundred pounds less than Sherwood's had been. Mrs Sherwood continued to occupy 1 Fisher Row, while Jorden settled with his wife in the Banbury Road, in an area chiefly occupied by successful tradesmen. Sherwood's carriage was sold by order of the Trustees in April 1875, while Jorden apparently walked to work in the mornings, and when he drove may have done so in some all-purpose horse-drawn vehicle belonging to the brewery.[14]

Frederick Morrell the solicitor, who was in his early sixties at the time when Herbert and Emily married, chose that moment for his retirement and gave his place as a Trustee to a fellow Oxford solicitor, William Blagden Gamlen. His son Fred had now been married for some years; and this may have seemed an appropriate moment for his father to hand over the business to him and retire from Black Hall to the family's country estate at Broughton. Gamlen was now the chief local Trustee, with the advantage of being unrelated to the Morrell family, and with the ability to speak the same professional language as at least two of the other Trustees, the Lincoln's Inn barrister Richard Randall and the Reading solicitor Henry Collins. In 1875-6, for example, Randall wrote him a revealing series of letters criticizing Jorden for his intractability but concluding regretfully that he was too old to be expected to change his ways.[15] Although careful of their resources, the new board of Trustees were by no means opposed to progress, and achieved an important expansion of the brewery's premises, the family's landed estates and their holdings of tied public houses during the last quarter of the nineteenth century.

While Queen Victoria's reign also entered its last quarter century, Emily and Herbert lived in state in their hilltop mansion like a latter-day Victoria and Albert, distributing charity among the poor as it seemed fit to them to do so. In the General Election of 1874 Herbert might have offered himself as a Conservative candidate in another constituency, but instead, with Emily's active support, canvassed for the rival brewery owner A.W. Hall, who was duly returned as Member for the City of Oxford. Herbert's political enemies attacked the young couple's gift of coals to the poor of St Clement's on the occasion of their wedding as an election bribe on Hall's behalf, and this had to be hastily excused as an act of pure benevolence. The Halls, meanwhile, had become friends of the young Morrells, and in the summer of 1874 gave a joint dinner for the employees of their own and Morrell's Brewery. Emily and Herbert, who could entertain large numbers easily in the grounds of Headington Hill Hall, returned the invitation the following summer, when about 120 brewery workers and members of their families dined in a marquee and watched or joined in a cricket match between the teams of the two breweries.[16]

At the managerial level relations between the two breweries were not always so harmonious. In both firms the maltsters could be difficult, perhaps because the separateness of malting from the main brewing process, and the maltsters' undoubted skill, encouraged them to feel independent or indispensable. (In the 1880s Jorden more than once reported trouble with the maltsters: once when they went on strike during difficult, snowbound conditions when the barley proved more than usually unwilling to germinate; on another occasion when unspecified trouble led him to consider sacking all of them.)[17] In 1877 Hall's manager, Evetts, had been successfully poaching maltsters with offers of higher wages until Morrell's raised all their men's wages to 1s. a week above the level paid by Hall's. When this news reached Hall's their men struck for higher wages, whereupon Evetts went to Jorden with a proposal for a maximum wages agreement between the two firms. Predictably the Trustees refused to entertain this idea; but the fact that Evetts felt able to suggest such terms at all points to a certain degree of habitual friendliness between the two firms.[18]

As well as strikes by the work-force or by mutinous sections of it, drunkenness was a frequent cause of time lost to work or of dismissals. This is hardly surprising in a work-place where the pay was heavily supplemented by beer drunk on the premises, and where (for example) Jorden could provide Scotch whisky as a reward for men whom he had set to clear snowdrifts from one side of the malt and hop stores late one December.[19] In 1875 Jorden told the Trustees that he had sacked the two brewery blacksmiths after cautioning them several times for absenting themselves and getting drunk. In 1879 he reported on a sadder case – that of Mr Burrows, a clerk in the counting-house, whom the brewery had employed for the past ten years to take and execute orders for beer, and who had taken to drink. After many complaints from customers Jorden recommended that Burrows should be dismissed. The Trustees, however, were merciful, and simply cautioned Burrows once he admitted that the complaints were well founded.[20]

Discharged workmen and widows of workmen who had been attached to the brewery could receive allowances from the Trustees, but this was very much a discretionary matter. Retirement was almost non-existent, since most men worked until illness carried them off, and the friendly societies, which they were encouraged to join, made very basic provision for their widows and for incapacitating periods of sickness. When in 1878 the brewery night-watchman Paine, who had done the job for twenty years, felt unable to continue, being over sixty, he merely asked to be transferred to 'some light employment'. Six years later another employee reported that his doctor had declared him unfit for any form of work, and asked the Trustees for a pension. They instructed Jorden to

'Ascertain his circumstances whether a member of any society'. An employee's widow, in 1879, was found to have two small children, the younger a two-month-old baby, and no means of subsistence, whereupon Jorden 'gave her cheque for £10'.[21] Pensions and allowances, then, were effectively means-tested rather than bestowed as a matter of right, at least in the decade or two after 1875 when they were first recorded. Sometimes a widow might receive a benefit in kind, like Sarah Hutt, widow of the head brewer Charles Hutt who died in 1870. Within a year of being widowed Sarah had vacated the house on the brewery premises to her husband's successor, and was keeping a small general grocery store at 11 St Thomas's Street between the brewery and The Hamel, as a sub-tenant (possibly rent-free) of the brewery.[22]

Another category of widows who could create problems for the Trustees was that of public-house tenants, who had sometimes to be evicted if they proved reluctant to leave. Some were considered to be suitable replacements for their husbands, others (or their adolescent children) less so. A deserted wife, like that of the landlord of the Royal Blenheim in Little Clarendon Street, whose husband eloped with his maidservant in 1884 after only three weeks' occupancy of the pub, could also be evicted once the brewery had obtained a holding period from the licensing magistrates.[23] A landlord served with notice by the Trustees for keeping a disorderly house might appeal against this with evidence to the contrary, like the licensee of the Anchor in Cornmarket Street, who in 1883 was accused of encouraging prostitution on the premises. This particular accusation was evidently part of a personal vendetta; and although the landlord persuaded both his regular customers and the police to confirm that the prostitutes who drank regularly at the Anchor were not in the habit of plying their trade there, he too suddenly left, having apparently succumbed to a campaign of persecution. On that occasion Jorden told the Trustees that he had 'put one of the Brewery men in'.[24]

* * *

At Headington Hill Hall, or in London or Brighton, Emily and Herbert lived remote from the minor details of brewery administration. Childless and carefree for the first eight years of her marriage, Emily continued to give balls and parties, first at home, then (from 1879) in hired rooms in the Royal Pavilion at Brighton. Herbert's interests, meanwhile, had moved away from the unpromising area of opposing educational reform at a local level. His attendance as a member of the Oxford School Board dwindled, then died out altogether. Instead he began to develop an interest in farming, and in 1876 was elected a vice-president of the Oxfordshire Agricultural Society. In that year he also acquired a farm of

The Rise, Cheney Lane, Headington Hill, home of J.H. Morrell from 1926

his own when the Trustees purchased the land on the south-west flank of Headington Hill, formerly the property of the elder James Morrell's neighbour Miss Smith and later of a large family named Knapp, who, but for the Trustees' intervention, might well have sold their land to a developer for building.[25]

South Park, as the nucleus of the Knapps' former land is now known, rises up as a continuous, grassy slope on the south side of Headington Hill, bounded on the south and west by Morrell Avenue, on the north by the London road, and on the east by Cheney Lane. Below the junction of Headington Hill and Cheney Lane, where several blocks of expensive, picture-windowed flats now stand, the Knapps' and Smiths' stone-built, gabled house, later known as The Rise, stood in its large, private garden until demolished by a building speculator in about 1970. Miss Smith's neat Georgian farm bailiff's house on the east side of Cheney Lane, directly opposite her own house, seems to have disappeared by the 1830s, perhaps because her successors found it irritating to have the bailiff's family so close at hand. Later bailiffs seem to have lived at Cheney Farm, a more distant farmhouse at the south end of Cheney Lane near the Warneford Hospital.[26]

After Miss Smith's death in 1825 the property had passed by inheritance to a Miss Ann Knapp of Abingdon and her nephew, Tyrrell Knapp of Hampton Poyle. Tyrrell Knapp had eventually succeeded his aunt and had lived a long, prosperous life at the house until he died in 1869, leaving a widow and seven children. In 1876 Knapp's widow sold her late husband's furniture and books and moved away; and her children, having previously planned to sell off the present South Park as fourteen separate building lots linked by a network of residential roads, finally agreed to part with the whole property to Morrell's Trustees for £26,000.[27] This purchase, financed out of one of the private settlement funds, saved Emily and Herbert from disagreeable proximity to a large, late-Victorian suburban development, gave Herbert some nearby acreage to play with, and in the long term preserved the area to become one of Oxford's more strikingly green open spaces. In 1878 Herbert celebrated his new standing as an agriculturalist by acting as host to the Bath and West Show, which was held in a large field off the London road below the Knapps' former house. This he separated from its land, naming it Headington Rise, and let it to a military family with eight children and nine servants.[28]

The year after the purchase of the Knapps' house and farm, Herbert linked his possessions on both sides of Headington Hill by commissioning William Wilkinson, one of the most High Gothic of Oxford architects, to design a private bridge for foot and carriage passengers between the grounds adjoining the house and the fruit and vegetable garden that lay uphill from the Knapps' former land. In the same year he began to cast about for further farmland to experiment with. Emily's aunt, Mrs Stone, had inherited the important Wick Farm in Headington from her uncles, Theophilus and Brian Wharton. Knowing that the farm would almost certainly pass to Emily on her aunt's death, and hearing that the current tenant was about to leave, Herbert asked his cousin Fred to look up the terms of the elder James Morrell's will (assuming, wrongly, that the farm had come originally from him), and expressed his urgent desire to take over the farm directly rather than let another tenant in.[29]

Given Herbert's energy in agricultural matters, it was quite logical that he should in time assume much of the responsibility for running the brewery's home farm at Blackbird Leys. This constant drain on the brewery's finances, and on the time and energy of the brewery manager Jorden, had been aggravated during the late 1870s by the persistent mismanagement of the farm by an ill-chosen bailiff. As Jorden pointed out to the Trustees in 1877, the farm bailiff must be one who 'would . . . be likely to obey' him, since 'the farm must be worked in conjunction with the Brewery if kept in hand'.[30] Eventually Jorden chose a more satisfactory bailiff, John Gilkes, a member of a farming family from north Oxfordshire, who was paid £100 a year for his services by 1886 and remained at Blackbird Leys until the 1890s. (Gilkes's wooden chest, the inside of the lid ornamented with penny stamps, and with small possessions of his such as combs and toothpicks still intact in their leather cases, together with some early Victorian family correspondence, survives at the brewery.)[31] Jorden supervised Gilkes as he had his predecessor, and rode out to the farm at least once a week to keep an eye on things there. Herbert, however, had shooting rights over the farm, and seems to have secured part of it to farm directly on his own account during the last ten years before the Trustees sold Blackbird Leys in 1896.

As far as the brewery was concerned, Herbert took it upon himself, Prince Albert-like, to advise the Trustees on a number of matters, in particular those concerned with building design. Any major decision had, as a matter of courtesy, to be referred to Herbert and Emily, but the Trustees evidently did this for form's sake rather than from any particular willingness to be corrected. Occasionally, therefore, they had to go to some lengths to convince Herbert of the rightness of their decisions. There was, for example, the matter of the brewery gates, which still stand with their rampant lion motifs surmounting the open ironwork gate-piers as Messrs Lucy's men erected them in 1877. The conversion of the house on the brewery premises into offices, and the consequent abolition of the separate counting-house that had previously stood at the brewery's street entrance, seemed to call for a suitably grand pair of gates to close off this entrance from the street. Herbert argued in favour of wooden gates, which he thought would make the yard more private than see-through iron ones. Jorden, however, consulted 'three practical men (two of them builders)', all of whom came out in favour of iron, with iron plates for privacy, and Herbert was overruled. After some delays on the part of Lucy's, the gates, with their distinctive arch containing the name 'Morrells Brewery', were erected, and the bill (for £124 12s.) paid out in October 1877.[32]

Although the brewery profits had reached £20,000 a year by 1875–6 (offsetting an annual loss of £2–3,000 on the farm), the settlement fund which was available to the Trustees to use for brewery purposes did not contain any large reserves of capital. When, therefore, the Trustees heard that Christ Church was anxious to sell them the freehold of the brewery premises in 1877, they had to turn to Herbert for the money with which to buy it. In June 1863, three months before he died, the younger James Morrell had had the brewery valued in the hope of bequeathing the freehold to his Trustees, and had been told that its net annual value was £157 17s. 3d. and the fee simple value £1,993 16s. 4d. Since then the estimated net annual value had risen to £526 3s. 3d. and the fee simple value to £10,520. The Trustees, seizing the opportunity to secure not only their own freehold but that of the group of four decrepit houses and gardens,

7–10 St Thomas's Street, immediately to the west, declared themselves willing to pay £15,000 for the pair of freeholds, even though the fee simple value of 7–10 St Thomas's Street (previously leased to the Rowland family) was estimated at only £1,320. In return they asked that Christ Church should pay them £360 a year until their lease expired in 1897, less £2 5s. fixed ground rent, which was already paid.[33]

For both the Trustees and Christ Church (as the agents, Field and Castle, pointed out to them), the sale was an opportunity not to be missed. If the Trustees turned this down they might well be unable to renew their forty-year lease when the time came to do so, should Christ Church (for example) decide to use the area for housing. In 1866 the Dean and Chapter had already pulled down a row of houses between The Hamel and Woodbine Place to erect their Model Dwellings, a block of thirty tenement flats reached by outside staircases. In 1893 the New Buildings, a similar but less attractive block in Hollybush Row, would follow. Castle, on the other hand, urged Christ Church to take advantage of the Trustees' offer, writing:

> I am quite certain that nothing like this sum could be obtained for the Property from any other purchaser and if the Trustees do not purchase the Property and are consequently compelled to remove their Brewery the value of the Premises would be reduced at once to less than half the sum which they now offer for it. An additional reason is that the Property is in the poorest part of Oxford, and is never likely to be required or saleable for any other than Trade purposes or for Houses and Shops of the smallest and poorest description.[34]

The purchase of the brewery premises duly took place on 1 April 1878, a year in which the Trustees also sold the lease of Whitley Farm at Cumnor, one of the properties that had come to the Morrells from the Coxes. They were still, however, short of the major part of the sum that they needed to pay to Christ Church, and consequently persuaded Herbert and Emily to allow £15,250 to be taken out of Settlement No. 5 (a fund designated for family purposes), with no obligation on the Trustees' part to repay this out of the income from the brewery, but with a guarantee from Herbert that he would take out an insurance policy sufficient to cover its repayment out of his own resources. Eight years later Herbert tried to persuade the Trustees to reimburse Settlement No. 5 out of the capital that they had released by selling the brewery's portion of Blackbird Leys, and thus allow him to discontinue his policy. The solicitor Graham and the brewery manager Dowson pointed out, however, that the deed of covenant signed by Herbert and Emily in November 1878 specifically exonerated the Trustees from repaying this sum to

Settlement No. 5, and that Herbert remained personally liable to keep up the policy covering it unless he could find £15,250 in cash to repay it himself.[35]

A year or two before purchasing the freehold of their premises, the Trustees had already invested much of their available capital in overhauling the brewing plant, initially increasing its output from 32,000 to 35,000 barrels a year.[36] The beam and table engines installed in the 1820s and 1840s still worked well, and by the early 1880s had a full-time employee, William Dry (described in the census as 'brewery engine driver') devoted to running them. His pay may have accounted for part, but by no means all, of the 16s. 6d. a day that engine for 'pumping cleansing &c' was estimated to cost the brewery in 1877.[37] Linked with these was the horizontal driving-wheel or horse-wheel, which also derived power from the water wheel, the running costs of which were roughly 3s. a day. In place of the former mash tun, which had taken only about 30 quarters of malt at a single brewing, Ramsdens of London installed a new 50-quarter tun, with associated pumping machinery dependent on the existing horse-wheel. The estimated cost of this, including mashing-machine, 70-barrel cast iron under-back, two grain traps, and alterations to deepen the existing malt hopper and lengthen the worm that delivered malt to the tun, was £820. In addition, Ramsdens enlarged or replaced the fermenting squares at a cost (including extras) of nearly £1,700, converting the three squares under the coolers from 100-barrel to 155-barrel capacity, and replacing the square at the end of the hop back with a larger one, also of 155-barrel capacity.[38]

Not all the vital parts of the brewhouse equipment were replaced, for in 1877 Jorden reported that the wort pumps were very old and only half the size of the other pumps. 'When using them we have to drive the machinery very fast & I fear we shall have something break unless new pumps are put down.'[39] He also had reason to be anxious about the horse-wheel, on which everything in the brewhouse depended. Accidents were occasionally reported, for example to the two smaller driving wheels connected with the horse-wheel; and in 1889 he predicted that an accident to the horse-wheel could hold up production at the brewery for a fortnight.[40] Other considerations, however, claimed priority over the renewal of the machinery. Chief among them was a large-scale building programme, which began in the late 1870s after the purchase of the freehold and continued into the early years of this century, giving the present brewery buildings their overwhelmingly red-brick, late Victorian and Edwardian character.

On the west side of the brewery yard, where the offices now stand, the old storehouses dating from the Tawneys' day and from the early years of the Morrells were now inadequate. The demolition of 7–10 St Thomas's

Street allowed room for new stores to be built, with space for beer below and for malt and hops above. In January 1879 Jorden and the brewery architect, H.G.W. Drinkwater, inspected a concrete store that had been built for Simonds' Brewery, either behind their Queen Street premises or in some outlying area. Jorden reported enthusiastically on the advantages of concrete: 'Not a flaw to be seen anywhere . . . one third less cost in erecting, and more effective in excluding heat and cold. . . .' Of concrete, then, the new store on the east side of the western yard was built, at a cost of £750 including paving. As so often happens when limited building works are undertaken, one thing led to another, and within a year, for an additional outlay of £500, the brewery had acquired a new blacksmith's shop, engine house, bridge across the yard from stores to brewhouse, rear boundary wall and well.[41] Still proudly independent of the City's water supply, the brewery, like Hall's and many others, relied entirely on its own supplies of well water, and in 1878 had turned down an approach from the City inviting it to come on the mains.[42]

In the early 1880s, as in the 1820s, a period of growth at the brewery meant that the malthouses also needed to be overhauled. For years Jorden had coped with a rotting and subsiding building in Tidmarsh Lane, where rats had undermined the foundations, causing sudden collapses. Evidently wishing to avoid making too many complaints to the Trustees, Jorden had not mentioned the condition of Fox's Malthouse for several years when the Trustees commissioned a report on it in 1883. This concluded that the building was dangerous, and the Trustees decided to employ the specialist firm of Stopes & Co. of Southwark to remodel, although not wholly to rebuild it. By September 1883 they had accepted a tender for £2,500 from Stopes for the work, and another from Lucy's of Oxford for £1,000 for the ironwork. They had also decided to get rid of all the country malt-houses, most of which were in poor repair, saving £600 a year on the rented ones and selling those at Shillingford and Wallingford after giving notice to their tenants.[43] In Oxford they kept on two additional malthouses: Ward's in Tidmarsh Lane, an adjunct to the former Ward's coal-yard near the corner of Park End Street, which Jorden had urged the Trustees to acquire in 1879 on giving up one of the Wallingford malthouses, and Goundrey's at Marston, where a separate staff of maltmen worked with daily visits from the head maltster, Whittle.[44]

Stopes's steep-roofed tower at the Tidmarsh Lane malthouse remained a striking feature of the St Thomas's skyline until a fire in one of the kilns gutted it in 1956. Above the tower were two cowls to assist the drying process (which at first gave great trouble, needing to be drastically adjusted a year after they were installed), and within it were three floors for the malt, reached by outside staircases and connected with pressurized cisterns outside and below the tower, with two kilns side by side immediately below the malting floors. The malt and barley stores occupied a new part of the building adjoining the kilns, while in the older part of the building, towards the south end of Tidmarsh Lane, the germination floors of the 1820s remained.[45]

Predictably the new building caused some friction between the maltsters and Mr Whittle, who received a bonus of £8 early in 1885 after a disagreement with his men the previous autumn about the proper protection of the machinery. (That autumn a retiring maltster, Mr Harvey, was given a pension of 5s. a week for one year – only half the amount awarded in 1883 to the new night-watchman's widow, who must have been left with a family of children to support.) Meanwhile the Shillingford and Wallingford malthouses were auctioned in October 1885, cutting the last link between Morrell's Brewery and the family's original home town. Charles Morrell's fine, early Victorian Bridge House still stands beside the bridge, near St Peter's church, as a replacement for his humbler, earlier Wharf House; but the Morrell family were no longer milling and malting in the town, and it was a member of the Wells family who leased the malthouse for a final year's production before the Trustees sold it.[46]

In July 1882, at Headington Hill Hall, Emily Morrell gave birth to her first child, a boy whom she named, with due respect for his forebears, James Herbert. ('I quite expected a girl,' her aunt Emily wrote in a jubilant note of congratulation to the father.)[47] In time this representative of the fourth generation of brewing Morrells would take his place in the firm as an employee of the Trustees, and later, in his sixties, as a director of a limited company. Born in the century of Mark and James Morrell, and within thirty years of his great-grandfather's death, the young James Herbert would live through both world wars and become the leading figure in the brewery of the 1950s, many features of which can still be seen in the thriving but traditionally based business of today.

CHAPTER SEVEN

EXPANSION, 1885–1906

Arthur Jorden, brewery manager at Morrell's from 1874 until early in 1891, compiled the first existing sets of Trustees' minutes (rough and fair-copy) from January 1875 onwards, and also kept a work diary from at least the middle of the 1880s. Several volumes of this diary, in large quarto size, the pages interleaved with blotting-paper, and with entries in blue-black ink in Jorden's regular, sloping hand, have survived.[1] Sometimes more impersonal than Jorden's entries in the Trustees' minutes, these diaries of his are in no sense private. They chronicle a regular, partly open-air life, with a range of duties whose present-day equivalents could not conceivably be carried out by one person. These included secretarial, clerical and accountancy work (writing letters, making up the books for the Trustees, taking cash to the bank); purchasing raw materials (including hops and barley) and new equipment; buying and selling horses, and overseeing the health of those that were kept in the brewery stables; dealing with customers who came to the brewery or who met him elsewhere; visiting any of a hundred-odd public houses to negotiate with tenants and see about necessary repair-work or rebuilding; consulting with the brewery architect, Drinkwater, about these projects, and with the Trustees' solicitor, Graham of Abingdon, about a variety of financial and legal matters; making daily inspections of the brewery and malthouse to check on the condition of the beer, the malt, the buildings and the machinery; hiring and firing less important members of staff, dealing (often brusquely) with their grievances, sending them meat and wine when they were sick, and assessing the need to provide support for their dependents when they died; reporting weekly to the Trustees and drawing up agenda for their meetings; and overseeing not only the Blackbird Leys farm but other outlying properties belonging to the brewery, such as meadowland or extra stabling for brewery or farm horses.

Like many other late Victorian businessmen, Jorden seems to have taken no holiday apart from a few odd days' shooting in September or October. On Christmas Day, as on Sundays, he visited the brewery to open and answer letters and check up on the horses and the state of affairs at the malthouse. On Saturdays he was usually at the office in the morning and the Oxford market in the afternoon. (He also attended Thame market every Tuesday, either driving himself through the open country in a gig or dog-cart or travelling there and back by train; while on Wednesday afternoons he was often at the Oxford cattle-market.) On Sundays, after calling at the brewery and walking ritually on Port Meadow, he might spend the afternoon at home or going for a further walk with his wife; but in 1886, when the Trustees rented stables at Red House Farm along the Botley Road, and later when they did the same at Osney Wharf, he regularly inspected these every Sunday before lunch. One week in June 1887 he varied his usual routine of a Sunday visit to the office by walking with Drinkwater over Shotover Hill to Garsington on brewery business, to inspect a well. When haymaking time came round, in the summer of 1886, he spent almost every day in the hayfield during the second week of mowing, and much of a Wednesday and Saturday during the first week. This hay-harvest may have taken place at Blackbird Leys, or at Red House, or in Oatlands Meadow on the west side of the Botley Road, a piece of freehold land of which the Trustees sold the greater part in 1886. After that summer Jorden confined himself to buying hay, and no further mention of haymaking occurs in any subsequent volumes of his diary.

For, gradually, the Trustees were rationalizing the huge complex of landed estates that James Morrell had left to them. The great agricultural depression of the late nineteenth century, which had begun in 1874 and would continue unabated until 1918, was eroding the value of James's former land, acquired so perserveringly and with such evident hopes of future profit. When the leases of two of the farms that belonged to the Coxes, Owlington and Beckley, expired in 1875 and 1876, they were not renewed. The lease of Whitley Farm, as we have seen, was sold in 1878.[2] The huge white elephant, Blackbird Leys and its associated farms, had already diminished considerably in size in the late 1870s, when the City of Oxford purchased land at Sandford to create a sewage farm. In 1886-7 Blackbird Leys Farm finally ceased to depend directly on the brewery when Herbert Morrell took over the responsibility for running part of it, and the remainder was let to a Mr Parker.[3]

To administer this farm (together with the Culham estate, which was let, and various other family-owned properties such as the Wick Farm at Headington and another at Ashampstead, near Streatley), Herbert appointed an agent, Major Drage, giving him an estate office at Headington Hill Hall and leaving him to settle the various accounts between himself and the Trustees. Jorden described in his diary how he had met, and snubbed, Drage at Oxford Market in August 1887: 'He asked how Trustees were going to let him out of the valuation of farming stock. Told him I knew nothing about the farming business & was very glad to be out of it. My impression is that his a/c will not prove as good as he anticipated.'[4] On inspecting the farm with the valuer in October, Jorden found, indeed, that things had not gone well at the farm since the brewery had given up control of it: 'We discovered that the implements have been used on other farms – that very little has been done in the way of repairs & some have had bad usage – Especially Engine & Thres[hin]g M[a]ch[ine]. Exchanges of horses Cattle & implements have taken place from Garsington & Sandford Farms which will materially reduce the valuation.'[5] The farm was finally sold by the Trustees in May 1896, after Herbert had become absorbed in a new career as a Member of Parliament.[6]

While brewing itself caused Jorden relatively little worry, malting was full of pitfalls. There was the ungovernable behaviour of the maltsters, who, like all other workers outside the brewhouse, were more prone than the brewers to be dismissed for drunkenness. (Two maltsters and a blacksmith were discharged for this offence in May 1883, and a cooper in November 1887, while 'Williams and his mate' were sacked for fighting on duty in February 1887.)[7] There was the danger of fire, which eventually destroyed the main part of Fox's Malthouse sixty-five years after Jorden's death. On 8 July 1886 a fire broke out at eight o'clock in the morning in the grinding-room, where the malt being ground for the next day's brewing exploded as a result of friction by the worm against the malt grist-case. Happily the brewery fire brigade put out the fire within five minutes, by which time damage costing £105 had been done to the building and £48 6s. worth of malt had been destroyed. This was not the first small fire to have taken place on the brewery premises in Jorden's time; but in both cases speedy action saved the brewery from a serious conflagration. The fire engine was no longer the cumbersome hand-pumped object that William Sherwood had manhandled up George Street in the dead of night, but a steam-operated pump, first seen on the premises in 1877. Two years later this seems to have been replaced by another one, since Jorden offered to have the 'present engine' converted to steam at a cost of £95, not only to use in case of fire but to pump out the foundations of the storehouse being built in the newly acquired yard to the west.[8]

Most problematical of all, by the mid-1880s, was the nature of English barley, which no longer seemed reliably fit to malt. At the end of his diary for 1886 (having bought what he thought were good samples of barley in Oxford market on 20 November, then having had to reconsign the purchase), Jorden wrote with uncharacteristic vehemence:

> This was a very bad season for malting barley. The greater portion would not germinate and the best samples had to be sweated on the Kilns. This put off the steeping till the last week in Dec[embe]r consequently we shall not be able to make our usual quantity this season. The Sâale and Danish Barl[e]ys were very good. Tried some Danish Malt[.] It gave an Ext[ract per quarter, i.e. 336 lb] of 90 [lb] & splendid wort for Stock Beers.[9]

During the next few years, the quality of British barley continued to vary. In February 1887 Jorden thought that he had found some good Scotch barley, and in September he bought barley from Woosters of Bledlow, Buckinghamshire. By late October he felt able to exclaim that that year's barley was better than any in the last ten years. He was also, however, buying foreign malt on trips to London: 100 quarters of Algerian in the spring, fifty quarters of pale and another 100 of Algerian in the autumn.[10]

In 1888 things were worse again, with slight mouldiness reported from the malthouse floor in May, and very bad mould resulting from warm weather in the autumn. In late October (he noted twice) the kilns had to be stoked up at midnight because of the onset of mould. That season English barley refused to germinate, and Hughes (apparently a dealer) recommended Californian barley. After various purchases in London (100 quarters of malt in late August, 500 quarters of barley in mid-September), Jorden accepted the advice of a representative of Spillers, the Cardiff-based milling and corn-dealing firm, and met him at Paddington station to conclude a deal whereby he bought 127 quarters of Smyrna malt.[11]

When inspecting the brewhouse it was customary for Jorden to be taken round by the head brewer, Heritage. In the summer of 1887 he suggested that Heritage should take a pupil, and two months later, just before the beginning of the new brewing season, Haslett joined the brewery. It was a mark of the new professionalism of Morrell's that assistant brewers were no longer untrained local boys who mastered the trade through a kind of unofficial apprenticeship. Harry Haslett came from Winch & Co. of Chatham, and was initially taken on trial at £50 a year. By Christmas he was confirmed in his appointment as under-brewer, and a year later he was earning £300 a year with a £50 bonus.[12] An eager, innovative worker, Haslett brought about changes at the brewery within a few months of arriving there. In the spring of 1888, for example, he suggested reducing the gravity of running beers during the summer months. Morrell's brew had always been heavy with a concentration of malt sugars, and even in the lighter form proposed by Haslett was still heavier than other local brews. Herbert, always a devout traditionalist, tried to intervene to stop the change, but (as in so many other matters, from the design of the brewery gates to the type of bricks used in rebuilding Fox's Malthouse) was tactfully outmanoeuvred.[13]

Haslett's arrival also came at an opportune time for him to recommend certain alterations to the brewery plant. This was gradually being updated after the partial refit of 1875–6. By now, for example, all modern breweries cooled their beer by refrigeration rather than allowing it to lie open to the air, and to airborne infections, in shallow open coolers. In 1885 Ramsdens of London supplied refrigerating equipment at a cost of

£153 10s.; but this proved unreliable and needed repairing within three years. The brewery eventually acquired a completely new Morton's horizontal patent refrigerator, with a 60-barrel capacity, in 1893 at a cost of £355.[14] On Haslett's advice a leaking mash tun was replaced in April 1888. New bottle-washing machinery was installed the following year for £106, since the demand for bottled beer for sale in off-licences and shops was increasing steadily. (Its popularity in the brewery itself is shown by the fact that, in 1888, Jorden had to reprimand the clerks for drinking the bottled beer rather than drawing supplies directly and more messily from the barrel.)[15] Scouring out the casks proved more difficult than keeping bottles clean, and in 1885 there were complaints that the foreman cooper had allowed beer to go out to customers in foul casks. The problem of 'stinkers' persisted for several years, despite the appointment of a professional head cooper, Campbell, who arrived in the autumn of 1887; and early the following year the brewery was frustrated in its attempt to sell the foul casks to a vinegar factory.[16]

As more highly trained members of staff joined the brewery, there are signs that Jorden began to relax his tight and comprehensive grip on the running of its affairs. As the equivalent of chief clerk or company secretary, he had always considered himself responsible for balancing the

Brewery workers, *c.* 1885

books; and when (for example) he found a 10s. cash deficit in gold at the end of the day, he made this up out of his own pocket.[17] By 1890, on the other hand, he had begun to delegate responsibility for minor matters such as personally taking cash to the bank, employing Whittle the maltster to do this for him, as, on occasion, he also sent him to attend the market at Thame. (The band of clerks, lowly figures subsisting on £60–80 a year, rarely stirred out of the ramshackle offices in the former house on the east side of the brewery gates.)

In the summer of 1890 Jorden began to arrive at the brewery several hours earlier than had previously been his habit. Instead of breakfasting at home and arriving at 9.00 or 9.30, he would arrive at 6.15 or 6.30, go home to breakfast at eight and resume work at nine. This routine continued unexplained until 18 February 1891. An entry for that day in his diary, not in Jorden's hand but in that of the Trustee W.B. Gamlen, describes his last day at work:

Mr Jorden was at the Brewery early in the morning and saw Mr Haslett. On his way home to breakfast, soon after 8 a.m. he felt violent pain, and returned to his house in a cab. Sent for Dr Gray, who found him vomiting violently. Dr G. attended him at intervals throughout the day. At 8.25 in the evening he expired. Dr G. thinks the cause of death must have been the rupture of an artery.'[18]

Within a few weeks of Jorden's death the Trustees appointed a new brewery manager, Henry M. Dowson. Married in the year of his appointment, Dowson remained in charge of the brewery until his sudden death thirty-five years later, when James Herbert Morrell, Emily and Herbert's son, then aged forty-four, succeeded him as manager.

* * *

No major building alterations, apart from the development of the yard to the west, had taken place at the brewery in the years before Jorden's death. In 1887 the Trustees renewed a lease of the Shoulder of Mutton, now the Marlborough Arms, and its adjacent cottages from the City of Oxford, and within the next two years they had pulled down the cottages and converted them into a hospital for sick horses. This, Jorden had argued, would isolate infectious horses from the fit ones in the brewery stables (where he had lost three horses and had fourteen ill in the winter of 1886), and would save the trouble of sending them out to Red House farm, which the brewery held only on a short-term tenancy.[19] The pub continued for the time being as a lodging-house, with the horse hospital on one side and the Back Stream and brewery offices on the other.

Major changes, however, were soon to take place. Drinkwater condemned the offices, which had rotting floors and only a crumbling, timber-framed front; and in 1892 new offices were built to Drinkwater's solid but outwardly domestic design in place of the former beer stores on the west side of the main yard. This left a gap immediately opposite the new offices, which in 1896 Drinkwater filled with the new, red-brick tun room. Haslett's report on the layout of the brewery had exposed deficiencies in the system of cleansing the beer, which involved the movement of the wort between several vessels during fermentation in order to allow it to be separated from the yeast. In place of this traditional method he recommended skimming, in which beer remained throughout fermentation in a single, large vessel from which the yeast was skimmed through an opening in the side. This he preferred, not only because it was cleaner and less wasteful than the older method, but because the fermentation remained under control from beginning to end. It would require, however, at least two additional tuns, which could be accommodated only if the brewhouse floor-space was enlarged. After negotiations with the Thames Conservancy, who objected to a proposal to build over the Back Stream, the new tun room was built with space for four fermenting tuns and a cooler, for which Ramsden sent in a tender for £1,540.[20]

The 1890s were also a period of intensive rebuilding and enlargement of public houses. Of the 300-odd fully licensed houses, beerhouses and other houses licensed to retail beer on the premises in Oxford (excluding Cowley and Headington, but including the western suburbs and peripheral villages), Morrell's had control over nearly a hundred at the height of its tied-house empire before the First World War. Outside Oxford its sphere of influence extended as far as Swindon (although the Trustees had turned down the White Horse at Cricklade, in 1884, as being too far from the brewery).[21] Railway connections clearly helped; and by the 1890s, in addition to four or five pubs at Swindon, Morrell's had acquired the Railway Hotel and the Jolly Porter at Culham and the Great Western Hotel in Hythe Bridge Street, near both Oxford railway stations.

Drinkwater, a part-time ecclesiastical architect whose work includes St Margaret's church in North Oxford and the transepts of SS Teulon's and St Frideswide's church in the Botley Road, had been carrying out bread-and-butter jobs for the brewery since at least the mid-1870s, earning nearly £5,000 gross in fees in 1876–7.[22] In 1896, a typically busy year, we find the brewery rebuilding, repairing or extending the Welsh Pony at Gloucester Green, the Globe in Queen Street, the Old White House in the Abingdon Road, the Wheatsheaf in High Street, the King's Arms at Banbury, the Crown at Bicester and several other pubs.[23] As health regulations became more stringent, some required the demolition of crowded and insanitary cottages, outbuildings or privies that hemmed them in. A typical example of this was the Blue Pig in Gloucester Green, a rough market pub on a congested site, which Jorden had been instructed to alter in 1883. He told the Trustees: 'We shall get no better terms from the City[;] they have reduced the fine in consequence of the stable &c being taken away. I think Drinkwater had better re-arrange the house & sanitary part of premises instead of spending the amount required by the City.'[24]

While the number of pubs per head of population in England and Wales was continually decreasing (from one to 168 in 1831 to one to 375 in 1909), sales of beer were holding steady through advertising, off-licences, the use of commercial travellers, and an emphasis on competition between breweries to produce a high-quality range of different beers. In an age of fervent striving for national or international gold medals among producers of almost any commodity on the market, Morrell's did not rise to the challenge of Hall's, who could claim to have won gold medals for both pale ale and English malt at the Paris Exhibition of 1889. Nor did they claim, like Hanley's City Brewery, to be 'The Largest Brewers of Family Ales in the County'.[25] Their price lists and labels, however, reveal that they were keeping level with other breweries in offering the beers which were fashionable in late Victorian England (India pale ale, invalid stout), while specializing in strong ales such as 'Brown Oxford Ale', 'Light Oxford Ale' and 'Castle Ale'. A Morrell's price list of about 1890 shows a wide difference in price between strong ale (xx), stout and the best India pale ale at 53s. a 36-gallon barrel, less strong ale (x) at 42s. a barrel, mild ale at 32s. a barrel, and stock dinner ale at 30s. a barrel. Hall's charged roughly similar prices in 1892 (50s. a barrel for East India pale ale. 54s. for stock pale ale, and 50s. for double invalid stout), and Simonds of Queen Street charged 29s. a half-barrel for India pale ale, 22s. for 'season-brewed' ale and 18s. for light bitter. Phillips' Tower Brewery in Park End Street specialized in xxx and xxxx ales ('mild', 'strong' and 'extra "stingo"'), costing between 1s. 4d. and 2s. a gallon, while Hanley's City Brewery offered a 'delicate and sound' light dinner ale at 1s. a gallon.[26]

As breweries grew more competitive, the age of take-overs began. In the early 1890s Morrell's, with an estimated working capital of £760,000, came high in the second rank of registered English brewing companies, and was therefore a tempting proposition to anyone hoping to take it over. The top sixteen, with working capital of over £1m each, included most of the best-known names in brewing today, such as Allsopp, Courage, Ind Coope, Whitbread and Younger. One or two other companies of similar standing remained unregistered and therefore could not be included in the count. The second rank of registered brewing companies, with authorized capital of between £100,000 and £1m, numbered 197; the third, with authorized capital of less than £100,000, 192.[27] Altogether, in the British Isles, 8,863 licences were issued in 1894–5 to brewers for sale, including a vast majority of obviously very humble concerns; a number which had diminished to 3,746 by 1914 and to 1,772, excluding the Irish Free State, by 1927.[28]

Unfortunately we know little of the various approaches that were made to Herbert Morrell or to the Trustees with a view to purchasing the brewery. We know only that one such application was made to the Trustees in 1890 and another to Herbert in 1899. On the second occasion the Trustees requested Herbert to send on any future applications to them.[29] Since the brewery was run by a trust, not a public limited company, there could of course be no question of a take-over bid by shareholders in the modern sense. The Trustees were themselves not averse to the idea of a modest take-over, provided that it did not stretch their resources too far; and in 1898 they were prepared to bid up to £6,700 for the St Giles Brewery in Observatory Street and its four tied public houses. They were outdone, however, by the Northampton Brewery Company, who put up £9,000 (and suffered a delayed revenge when, in 1916, Morrell's decided not to supply any pubs in Oxford that were owned by the Northampton Company). In 1897 Herbert and Emily were asked to consider a possible purchase of Hanley's City Brewery, for which the Trustees had begun negotiations; but they turned this down in view of Hanley's retail business, not wishing to become associated with the wine and spirit trade.[30]

Conservatism, however, did not enjoy an entirely free hand at the brewery, for the 1890s were too much of an innovatory decade for Morrell's to remain entirely untouched. In 1893 the Trustees acquired a half-yearly lease of a city-centre office at 142 High Street (formerly the University typewriting office) in order to compete with the other local brewery companies whose offices were concentrated in the Queen Street and New Inn Hall Street area. This had a short life, however, and was given up in 1912. In 1894 the Trustees agreed to pay 12 gns a year for inclusion in the Oxford area telephone system, with the subscribers' numbers 13 and 13a (for Dowson's office). In 1900 Dowson bought the brewery's first typewriter.[31] The Trustees, on the other hand, shunned advertising, agreed specifically in 1894 not to advertise on tram-cars, and opposed the use of motorized vehicles at the brewery until after the outbreak of the First World War. An exception occurred in 1907 when the new licensee of the King of Prussia at Rose Hill needed a replacement for a worn-out horse and cart, and Dowson agreed to look into the cost and running expenses of a motor-car.[32]

The fresh-air-loving 1890s saw a great increase in the consumption of commercially bottled soft drinks such as ginger beer and lemonade. Promoted partly by the temperance movement, partly by manufacturers who took advantage of the continuing Victorian taste for spicy stimulants such as pickles, raspberry vinegar and ginger, the soft drink trade was greatly helped by the importation of cheap sugar, either from Continental sugar-beet or from the West Indies. (Sugar imports into the United Kingdom increased from nearly 17,000 cwt in 1871–5 to over 28,000 cwt in 1891–5, rising to a record figure of over 37,000 cwt in 1911–13.)[33] Naturally, the craze for ginger beer and similar drinks directly threatened the brewing industry; and in 1898, in order to cash in on this new trend, Morrell's Brewery opened its own mineral-water manufacturing and bottling plant in a two-storeyed building on the east side of the stable yard. Despite the reluctance of the Morrells to become involved in selling wines and spirits, the brewery also undertook the following year to supply its public houses with the hugely popular, sweet and moderately alcoholic Stone's Ginger Wine.[34]

The use of sugar in brewing had been legal in England since 1847, but had not become widespread until after 1880, when Gladstone's Finance Act (or Free Mash-Tun Act) had removed the obligatory duty charged per barrel of beer on the malt used in its manufacture, and transferred it instead to the product of brewing. One result of this act was that brewers were no longer effectively coerced into using malt by having to pay the duty on it, and so had a free choice of substitutes for it if they wished. (Saccharin was banned as a substitute in 1888, since it gave the beer an apparently greater gravity than in fact it had.) Many brewers continued to use only hops and malt, and to regard the addition of sugar to the brew as adulteration. In a circular letter dated 1901, Dowson proclaimed his opposition to brewing with cheap sugars, since this involved the risk of using sugar that had been adulterated with arsenic, such as had been discovered in a recent poisoning case in the Midlands. 'Old fashioned people', he wrote, 'still think that the sugar contained in malted barley is the only proper sugar for brewing purposes. . . . If every brewer gave up the use of substitutes, the benefit to the British farmer w[oul]d be great, as the competition for the best malting barley would become keener.' By 1920 Morrell's was to use sugar regularly in brewing, but for the time being the brewery advertised its beers as being made with 'the very finest Malt & Hops only. No sugar or raw grain being employed in their production.'[35]

In the 1890s, too, the social atmosphere of the brewery was changing. After Jorden's death only one man, a blacksmith, was sacked for habitual drunkenness at work, in 1901. Early in 1895 Herbert carried out a formal inspection of the brewery accompanied by his two young sons, James Herbert, aged twelve, and George Mark. In his letter of thanks to the Trustees he wrote: 'I would . . . like to congratulate you on the tone prevailing throughout the place as far as we could judge in the two hours spent in the works which seemed to indicate a general mutual support in every department.'[36] The growing emphasis on co-operation between staff and management, rather than on the disciplining of a sullen work-force, can be seen in various ways in the 1890s and early 1900s. There was, for example, the Brewery Cricket Club, to which the Trustees agreed to pay a £2 subscription in 1901 (although some years previously they had refused support to the newly formed brewery band). There was the help that they guaranteed to Weller, a maltster, when he went off to fight in the Boer War, promising to pay half his wages to his wife during his absence and to keep his job open for him until he returned. And there were the brewery summer outings, which as a regular institution may be attributed to Dowson, since they began in July 1891 during his first summer with the firm.

Works outings, often by train (or, from industrial riverside cities, by boat), were by no means a novelty by the 1890s. Some more enlightened firms had been giving their workers an annual summer treat since the beginning of Victoria's reign, or in exceptional cases even earlier.[37] Paid summer holidays for workers were as yet unheard-of; so the institutional summer outing, taking them to the coast, to some country spot for picnicking and boating, or to London for sightseeing and cultural purposes, encapsulated a holiday in a single, long day. Otherwise most workers had only Sunday free, and (from 1871, after the Bank Holidays Act), the four annual Bank Holidays on Easter Monday, Whit Monday, the first Monday in August and Boxing Day.

Discounting earlier summer visits to Headington Hill Hall (which were repeated in 1898 and 1903 in lieu of an expedition farther afield), the first brewery outing took place on 22 July 1891, to the Tower of London. Cultural considerations evidently counted for more with Dowson than the pleasures of the seaside, for London remained a favourite destination until the outbreak of the First World War. In 1899 the brewery employees visited Madame Tussaud's and the 'Savage South Africa' exhibition at Earl's Court (which perhaps inspired Weller to enlist for the South African War the following December). In 1904 they visited the Italian Exhibition, and in 1906 the Austrian Exhibition. In other years they visited Portsmouth, Southampton and Windsor, and even (in 1905) Folkestone and Boulogne. In 1902, Coronation Year, they had no outing; and in 1903 they were entertained to a sumptuous fête at Headington Hill Hall to celebrate the twenty-first birthday of the heir to the brewery, James Morrell.[38]

Emily and Herbert, the once romantic couple of thirty years earlier, were now middle-aged. Herbert, in his fifties, had achieved his ambition of becoming a Conservative Member of Parliament, representing Mid-Oxfordshire since 1895. (His earlier victory, at a by-election there in

> **MORRELL'S TRUSTEES' BREWERY EXCURSION,**
>
> Monday, July 18th, 1904.
>
> ....
>
> The party will assemble at the Oxford G.W.R. Station at **8.40** a.m., and will leave by the **8.55** Train for Paddington (carriages will be reserved, and both Railway and Orange-coloured Tickets must be shewn). The Train will stop at Goring at **9.15** to take up the party from Streatley House and Hawtridge Farm, and will arrive at Paddington at **10.25**. In the Station, Pleasure Brakes will be found waiting to convey the party to
>
> ### THE ZOOLOGICAL GARDENS.
>
> About two hours will be allowed inside, and at 1 o'clock punctually the Brakes will leave and proceed by way of Albany Street and Great Portland Street, down Regent Street, Pall Mall, past Whitehall and the Horse Guards to the Houses of Parliament and
>
> ### WESTMINSTER ABBEY.
>
> The Brakes will set down the party here in the Square in front of the Abbey, and time will be allowed for those who wish to obtain some dinner in any of the numerous refreshment houses in the neighbourhood. An excellent Dinner for 1/- can be obtained at the A.B.C. Shop opposite the Clock Tower. The party can also visit Westminster Abbey, but must be careful to be ready to remount the Pleasure Brakes in time to leave at **3.30** o'clock precisely, and drive by way of Grosvenor Road and Chelsea Embankment past Chelsea Hospital to Earls Court to the Warwick Road Entrance to the
>
> ### ROYAL ITALIAN EXHIBITION
>
> where there is plenty of amusement provided. Each person will have a ticket for "Venice by Night" and a Gondola Ride through the Canals, also a Ticket for either the Water Chute, Sir Hiram Maxim's Flying Machine, or the Blue Grotto of Capri. But in addition to this, on payment of a small sum, the following can be seen—Venetian Glass Blowing, Wax Works Exhibition, St. Peter's at Rome, Crater of Vesuvius, Electric Butterflies, Topsy-Turvy House, Farthest North, &c., &c. There are also beautiful collections of Lace, Furniture, Mosaics, Gold and Silver Work, &c., and the Art Galleries are occupied by the Paintings of many leading modern Italian Painters.
>
> The party must re-assemble outside the Warwick Road Entrance at **10.15** o'clock, where the Brakes will be found in readiness to convey them to Paddington Station to catch the **10.55** p.m. Train back, stopping at Goring **12** midnight, and reaching Oxford at **12.30**.
>
> N.B.—Each person will have Five Tickets, viz.:— An Orange-coloured "Morrell's Trustees' Excursion" Ticket. A Railway Ticket. An Entrance Ticket for the Exhibition. A Ticket for Venice and the Gondola Ride. And a Ticket for the Chute, or the Flying Machine, or Blue Grotto.

A brewery outing to London

1891, had lasted only until the General Election the following year.) He had been High Sheriff of Oxfordshire in 1885, at the height of his landowning and farming phase, and had enjoyed allowing his land in South Park to be used for great local spectacles such as the National Fire Brigades' demonstration in 1887. Latterly, as parliamentary work absorbed him, he had lost his enthusiasm for farming; and, having tried and failed to let out the former brewery farm since the early 1890s, he had been happy to see it sold to Oxford Corporation in 1896 for £22,000.[39]

Herbert Morrell, in the uniform of the 1st (University) Volunteer Battalion, Oxfordshire Light Infantry, at Headington Hill Hall, probably in the 1880s

Three years after that, in early February, he and Emily had revisited the scene of their honeymoon at Hastings to celebrate their twenty-fifth wedding anniversary. Thinking it appropriate that the brewery staff should remember them in their happiness, he wrote to Dowson:

> Mrs Morrell & I have for some time past had under consideration how best we might associate ourselves with you all on this Feb 4th (1899) at the conclusion of a period of some 25 years of our more intimate association with the Lion Brewery and have come to the conclusion that there is at all events one simple method by which we may hope to associate ourselves with our friends in their homes on that day, & that is by asking all those engaged on the works of the Lion Brewery on that day to accept from us a small honorarium with our heartiest good wishes for their welfare, & most grateful thanks for their long continued co-operation contributing to success attained.
>
> I should be much obliged if you would arrange that each may receive a sum equal to two weeks of his pay on Feb 4th. This of course entirely apart from the regular pay sheet.
>
> Yours very truly,
George Herbert Morrell.[40]

Coming-of-age of J.H. Morrell, Headington Hill Hall, 9 July 1903. In this group of family and retainers H.M. Dowson, Brewery Manager, is third from left, back row; J.H. Morrell (evidently tired from rowing in the victorious Magdalen College Eight at Henley regatta) is fourth from left; his mother Emily fifth from left, front row

By 1903 Herbert had even more reason to feel contented with life. He had been returned unopposed in his constituency at the General Election of 1900. His son James, an undergraduate reading physics at Magdalen College, promised to repeat the athletic prowess in running and rowing which he himself had shown as an Exeter College undergraduate in the 1860s. Energetically involved with the University branch of the Oxford Rifle Volunteers, in the tradition created by his father and grandfather, James had forged a long-term connection with this body that would survive its change of name into the University Officer Training Corps and continue into the First World War. As a member of the University Athletic Club, he won the quarter-mile in 1902, the half-mile the following year, and the hundred yards in 1904 and 1905. In rowing he was a member of the Magdalen College eight who won the Ladies' Plate at Henley on his twenty-first birthday in July 1903. Athletically inclined undergraduates of James's type were not expected to work particularly hard; and it is not surprising that James took four years to complete his degree, or that,

Herbert and Emily Morrell, their two sons and family properties, against a 'tree' background, *c.* 1905. Properties pictured are (from top) Headington Hill Hall, Culham, Streatley House, the Lion Brewery, Wick Farm, Headington, and Hawtridge Farm, Ashampstead, near Streatley when he did so, he was awarded a Third. A report on his progress at the Clarendon Laboratory at the end of the Michaelmas Term of his third year concluded that 'his advance would be at a quicker rate if he had not so many calls upon his time in connection with boating, athletics &c', but praised him for a good term's work despite interruptions, and commended his experimental skill and his apparent understanding of the work in spite of a 'somewhat slender knowledge of Mathematics.'[41]

In his early sixties, then, Herbert had the satisfaction of seeing his elder son beginning to grow up into a more carefree, Edwardian version of the public-spirited, athletic, Victorian scientist and sportsman that he himself had been in his early twenties. James did not appear to have inherited Herbert's political interests, nor his insensitivity to what employees and others thought of him. (Before he entered Parliament, Herbert had been notorious at the brewery for his sudden, unannounced visits of inspection, and for giving the clerks a 'warm time', as Jorden once noted in his diary, in the manager's absence.) Like his father, James qualified as a barrister after leaving Oxford with his Physics degree, but there is no indication that he did this in the hope of becoming a politician, or indeed for any other reason than that residence in the Inns of Court was still accepted as part of the education of a gentleman. He did not immediately show any sign of wishing to become involved in the running of the brewery, and was in his early thirties before he began to join unofficially in the weekly Trustees' meetings. By then Herbert had been dead for several years, for he did not long survive the fall of Balfour's government in December 1905 (weakened by the issues of Irish Home Rule and Imperial preference for home-produced goods) and his own failure, in the General Election of the following month, to keep his Mid-Oxfordshire seat.

Perhaps ironically, it was on a brewing issue that Balfour's government had initially become unpopular with certain of its powerful Conservative supporters. The Licensing Act of 1904, an attempt to placate the radical, teetotal element in Parliament, had transferred the licensing authority from the JPs (many of whom were brewers) to the Quarter Sessions, and had encouraged the regular withdrawal of pub licences by the Quarter Sessions, arranging for them to pay compensation to the owners (and, on a much smaller scale, the licensees) of pubs where no known misconduct in the running of them had taken place. Reasons that could now be given for closing down pubs included a too great density of them in any given area, or insanitary and run-down premises, or both together.

In Oxford, in the General Election, the Conservative Lord Valentia, the successor to the Morrells' friend and brewing rival Colonel A.W. Hall (who had survived accusations of electoral bribery in 1880 and continued to represent the city until 1892), held his seat despite the formation of a

Liberal government under Campbell-Bannerman. Herbert, however, lost his by a narrow margin of 441 votes. Almost immediately his health began to decline. Like Emily's father James he was a big, florid man, and he had shown no loss of energy until suddenly brought to a halt in his career by the election result. Then heart trouble and dropsy between them transformed him from an active sixty-year-old into an invalid. In a respite from his illness he travelled with Emily and James to Bad Nauheim in Germany to take the waters, but died there quite suddenly on 30 September 1906.

Herbert's funeral took place at Streatley, now effectively the family home since Emily had inherited the house (which she clearly preferred to Headington) from her aunt Emily Stone. Fifteen members of the brewery staff attended, among them Haslett, head brewer since 1892; the maltster Weller, safely back from the South African War; the head cooper, Campbell; a father and son named Haines, probably related to the former clerk in James and Robert Morrell's bank; and all the clerical staff. A local newspaper reported that 'A special train from Oxford carried nearly 200 gentlemen to Streatley, and other trains from Reading and several places between that town and Oxford carried large numbers in addition, who all wended their way to the churchyard, and the large assemblage awaited in solemn silence the arrival of the funeral procession.' The Mayor and Deputy Mayor of Oxford and half a dozen aldermen and city councillors, including the Brewery Trustee Alderman W.B. Gamlen, were among the 200-strong contingent from Oxford. Of Herbert's friends from among the local aristocracy and gentry, the Earl of Abingdon, Lord Sale and Sele of Broughton Castle and Sir George Dashwood of West Wycombe were present at the funeral, while the Duke of Marlborough, Lord and Lady Jersey, Lord and Lady Valentia and the Dillons of Ditchley Park sent wreaths. The brewery's tribute, 'In respectful remembrance of our kind and generous employer, Mr George Herbert Morrell', came from the 'Staff, Employees and Pensioners at the Lion Brewery, Oxford'. Emily's wreath, of red and white roses, bore the message 'In fondest loving remembrance. Mizpah. February 4th, 1874 – September 30th, 1906.[42] Like Queen Victoria she would outlive her spouse by several decades, but with the death of Herbert, who had in some ways personified the late Victorian age, it could be said that that era in the history of the brewery and its estates had finally ended.

CHAPTER EIGHT

PRE-WAR AND WARTIME, 1906–18

Balfour's Licensing Act of 1904 had accelerated, but not to any drastic extent, the process by which public houses and beerhouses were already decreasing in number. Morrell's Trustees' Minutes now contained a regular series of items headed 'Brewster Sessions', detailing the threats to, or actual losses of, pub licenses as a result of proceedings by the licensing authorities. This injury to the brewing industry as a whole, together with the threat created by the unsuccessful Licensing Bill of 1907, which proposed to limit the life of a public house to fourteen years by reducing the right of renewal of licences to that period, brought the brewing firms together on the defensive. A general economic depression had followed the end of the Boer War; and the Liberal government's attempts to cope with this, and with the growing threat of war with Germany, also involved designs on the capital tied up in the brewing interest. Lloyd George's budget of 1909–10, which was principally directed against the beneficiaries of unearned income, proposed to extract part of the government's revenue for its war on poverty and unemployment from hugely increased duties on liquor licence and spirits. Such budgetary measures, and the resulting inflation from increased prices, are a commonplace of late twentieth-century economics; but to the brewers of Edwardian England, who had barely been saved in 1907 by the Lords' rejection of the Licensing Bill, the prospect of having to raise the price of beer by 1d. a quart to pay the increased licence duties seemed a drastic one. Although less severely threatened than the major London brewers by the proposed increase in licence duties, Morrell's Trustees were still concerned about a necessary rise in prices, which (it seemed) could take place only after thorough consultation between the brewing firms. For many years Morrell's had subscribed to the Oxfordshire Brewers' Association; but now Dowson attached himself to the more vocal Berkshire Brewers' Union, and attended a meeting in London in May 1909 at which the brewers agreed to try to create a consensus on beer prices within the twelve counties closest to London in the hope of persuading the London brewers to fall in with it.[1]

In the autumn of 1909 the House of Lords defeated Lloyd George's Budget, precipitating the constitutional crisis which eventually destroyed their power to throw out finance bills, and beer prices fell again. In the election of January 1910 the Liberals were returned as a minority government, with 274 members to 273 Conservatives, 41 Labour members and 82 Irish, who, as a group, were hostile to Lloyd George's liquor duties, and who held the balance between the two main parties. Life remained uneasy for the brewing interest, however; for the Prime Minister Asquith, determined to carry the budget through, introduced the Parliament Act (eventually passed in May 1911), which provided that bills certified as money bills by the Speaker could not be rejected by the Lords, and that any bill rejected by the Lords but passed by the Commons in three successive sessions should become law within two years of first being introduced. This neatly placated the Irish by holding out a firm possibility of Home Rule, and thus bought their consent to the increase in licence duties. Meanwhile in 1910 the Licensing (Consolidation) Act codified existing legislation about pub licensing, making it clear that this area would remain under searching governmental scrutiny in the future.

Suffering as they already were from a drop in sales resulting from the depression (for the working man's pint was often necessarily sacrificed in times of unemployment), the brewers could be forgiven at this point for feeling under threat. Morrell's decision to give up their High Street office in 1912 may have been taken as an economy measure, while the

Wedding of J.H. Morrell and Julia Denton, Torquay, 16 April 1913. Emily Morrell is seated on the far left

appointment in the same year of a second commercial traveller for the Oxford area, with a much lower guaranteed salary (£50 a year with 5 per cent commission on sales) than the existing traveller, suggests a sense of the growing need to sell beer through off-licenses and clubs. Nevertheless, in December 1912 the Trustees reported that the decrease in their profits was smaller than they had feared it might be. In February 1912 they permitted the sale of £12,000-worth of consols in order to give a lump sum to James Morrell and in April 1913, when he had announced at the age of thirty that he was about to marry Julia Denton, the daughter of Sir George Denton, a former Governor-General of The Gambia, they released another £15,000-worth.[2] Emily still continued to keep up two households, at Streatley and Headington Hill Hall (from which, in addition to the girls' charity school on the Marston Road, she supported a private local training-school for girls going into domestic service). James lived for the time being at the Hall, moving out to a separate house on Headington Hill only towards the end of the First World War.

* * *

By the middle of the Edwardian decade the main complex of brewery buildings looked very much from the outside as it does today. From the corner of Paradise Street and St Thomas's Street, the continuous street frontage of warm red brick now ran from the single-storey Horse Hospital through the rebuilt Marlborough Arms to the end of the tun room. The yard had recently been paved, and in 1901 the conspicuous, tall chimney had been erected towards the rear of the site. This funnelled out steam

Architect's drawings for the refurbishment of the Windsor Castle, St Thomas's, 1903

from a new, powerful steam-main, connected with new boilers that Ramsden of London had fitted as part of the same system. Ramsden's estimate for new boilers and coppers had come to the high figure (in comparison with previous installations) of £2,478 18s., but the Trustees had cannily requested a £90 reduction on condition that the boiler pressure was reduced from 100lb to 80lb.[3] These investments for the future must have sharpened their determination to keep the business going, however great the Liberal government's apparent dedication to eliminating part of the brewing interest altogether.

King Edward VII died on 6 May 1910. For the next six months the government postponed the question of enforcing the 1909 Budget and reforming the House of Lords; but a General Election in November returned the parties again with a narrow Liberal lead. Asquith's government would now remain in power, with a House of Lords very largely deprived of its powers of veto, until the post-war election of November 1918.

In Oxford, as elsewhere, the Quarter Sessions continued to condemn public houses, sometimes making it clear to a group of breweries with houses close together in a single area that they could choose between them which ones were to go. Early in 1913 Morrell's lost one of its original public houses, the Old Wheatsheaf in St Aldate's, which Sir Richard Tawney had bought in 1782, and which had come to him detached from its next-door malthouse but with a rural-sounding 'Skittle Ground Stables Pigstyes Outhouse and Dunghole'. The compensation offered to the tenant for withdrawal of the licence was £150, while the brewery received £915 together with the pub fixtures, and remained in possession of the freehold. After plans had been considered for turning the front of the building into two shops and selling off the back premises, the whole building was converted into a Labour Exchange in the tasteful, late arts and crafts style of 1914.[4]

More interesting was the story of the closure of the Windsor Castle in St Thomas's Street in the summer of 1913. The Quarter Sessions had simultaneously withdrawn Hall's licence for the neighbouring Peacock; and the breweries initially made a joint appeal against the decisions in the Oxford magistrates' court. In his evidence the Chief Constable said that the Windsor Castle:

> was a full-licensed house belonging to Morrell's Trustees, and under the tenancy of George Longshaw. There was a bar, tap-room, and a room for lodgers. There were four bedrooms, containing 12 beds and let to casual lodgers. The sanitary arrangements were fair. He said they were fair, because the structure was quite good enough, but it was not properly supplied with water, the tenant having to do his own flushing. The private departments were fair. It was eight yards from the Peacock,

27 from the Turk's Head, 83 from the Marlborough Arms, 90 from the Chequers, and 132 from the Albion. The Peacock was a beer-house in High-street, St Thomas', the tenant being Henry James Cudd, and the owners Hall's Oxford Brewery. It contained a large bar, a private bar, and seven bedrooms containing 23 beds, which were let more or less to casual lodgers. The sanitary arrangements were satisfactory, and the private departments fair. The house had been in the occupation of father and son for over 20 years. High Street, St Thomas' was 285 yards long, and contained five licensed houses, and he considered that was more than was required by the public. The neighbourhood contained a moving population, together with a residential population. There were several common lodging-houses, which accounted for the travelling population.

The Clerk: – It is densely populated. – Yes. There is lodging-house accommodation apart from the public-houses for a hundred people, who were made up of what was generally termed tramping classes.

Mr Grimsdale (assistant to the Magistrates' Clerk) deposed to viewing the houses with magistrates on February 5. The tenants of the Windsor Castle told him that the rent was £10 per year and the trade four barrels a week. No spirit trade was done at the house because there was no demand for it. At the Peacock he was told the rental was £15 14s. excluding 5s. 6d. per week for the lodging rooms. The trade was four barrels a week. The rental of the Turk's Head was £10, and the trade was two barrels and a gallon and a half of spirits a week. The Albion was rented for £30 and the trade was three and a half barrels per week.

Further evidence concerning the Peacock revealed that the tenant was an ex-naval man who had taken over the running of the pub from his uncle: 'He accommodated mostly for the working-class, and was particular about the class of man he admitted, taking no foreigners or dirty people. There was a common kitchen in the house for lodgers, and anyone could cook their own food, or have it cooked for them.'[5]

Not surprisingly, both Hall's and Morrell's failed in their appeal to have the licences for these public houses reinstated. A week after the hearing they considered taking their appeal to the High Court, but the Oxford solicitor Wootten, who had appeared for Hall's in the magistrates' court, advised against this since they were certain to lose.[6] The Turk's Head, alone of the former row of pubs on the north side of St Thomas's Street, survived for several decades longer, while the Marlborough Arms still flourishes next to the brewery today.

Three of the original four brewery Trustees appointed early in 1875, Charles Mortimer of Surrey, Henry Collins of Reading and W.B. Gamlen of Oxford, had now served for nearly forty years each when Collins died at his residence, Leopold House, Reading, on 4 May 1914.[7] All three had sons who would inherit their salaries and duties – Bernard Collins and Leonard Mortimer the following October, and John Charles Gamlen a few years later. Before James Morrell and the elder Gamlen, however, could welcome the new Trustees to their inaugural meeting, war had broken out in Europe, on a scale of ferocity that neither Lloyd George and his colleagues nor the governments of the German and Austrian empires could have foreseen.

* * *

For some years after Herbert's death in 1906, Jimmy Morrell (as James was widely and familiarly known) had maintained his distance from the running of the family business. As both he and his younger brother Mark may have been aware, on the ceremonial visits to the brewery that Herbert had arranged when they were boys to give the workers and clerical staff a chance to see the younger generation of the family, the brewery functioned perfectly adequately on a day-to-day basis without intervention from the Morrells; and Herbert's descents into St Thomas's, whether formal or unannounced, had not always been comfortable occasions.

As a product of Eton and Magdalen College, at a time when young men who were supported by the proceeds from family businesses often did all that they could to disassociate themselves from such businesses, Jimmy might well have remained aloof from the running of the brewery for the rest of his life. Long after his undergraduate days were over he kept up the interests which had sustained him then: sport, the Officers' Training Corps, and physics, in particular work on the electron, which was then at a very early stage. Twenty-two years after taking his not conspicuously impressive degree he was officially appointed a University demonstrator in physics; but he seems to have been a member of the physics faculty in some semi-official capacity since the early 1920s, and may have carried out unpaid research work in the laboratories for even longer than that.[8]

When war broke out Jimmy naturally offered himself for enlistment and was turned down on health grounds. By that time he had begun to attend regularly at the weekly Trustees' meetings, not (like Herbert) attempting to impose his own ideas about the running of the brewery on the Trustees, but quietly listening, learning and providing moral support. He did not officially rank as a Trustee, and was almost certainly not paid as they were. As Emily's elder son, however, in his early thirties, married and settled, he was in a position to contribute usefully to financial

The Queen's Arms, Park End Street, Oxford, c. 1910

discussions, and had undoubtedly expressed a wish to become more closely involved with the business, without demanding that a specific position should be created for him to fill. His presence in Oxford throughout the war, coinciding with the first years in office of the new Trustees, gave an added stability to the brewery administration at a time when the disruptiveness of wartime conditions might have shaken it quite badly.

At first, in August 1914, most people believed that the war would be over by Christmas. In the Morrell's Trustees' minutes, Dowson wrote in red ink across the page between two entries '[WAR declared between ENGLAND + GERMANY August 4th]';[9] but this unprecedentedly dramatic note has the appearance of a later insertion, as if the full seriousness of the war had taken time to sink in. Like the rest of England, Morrell's Brewery felt the effects of the war gradually: in losses of men, in trade and manufacturing restrictions, and finally in the post-war economic slump with its particularly cruel and long drawn-out effects.

Despite the notoriously poor physique of a high proportion of her men of fighting age, due to generations of undernourishment among both rural and urban working classes, Britain in 1914 was a militaristic nation whose common, masculine culture in religion, schooling and recreation was based on the idea of fighting, either as a form of healthy exercise for boys and young men or as a fully justifiable way of imposing right by means of might. Herbert Morrell, at first as a member of the university and city detachments of the Volunteer Rifle Corps, and afterwards as a colonel in the volunteer corps of the Oxfordshire and Buckinghamshire Light Infantry, had typified the late Victorian amateur soldier who was never called upon, in the event, to defend his country. Jimmy, who had kept up his association with the University OTC as it evolved out of the University Rifle Corps, found himself in the position of a senior officer helping to direct and train eighteen-year-olds for serious warfare after August 1914. There is a family belief that he instructed the young officers in the rudiments of electronics, or in the practical applications of physics to their training in the use of artillery. Whether or not this was so, he was certainly attached to the OTC in the capacity of acting adjutant in late 1915 and early 1916, as a substitute for the permanent adjutant, Captain Whatley. Jimmy himself was promoted from lieutenant to captain in mid-February 1916, and at about that time was confirmed in the position of adjutant, replacing Whatley. Unfortunately, however, OTC records beyond this date have not survived, so that we cannot tell whether he remained as adjutant throughout the rest of the war.[10]

Because a number of brewery workers were already enrolled among the volunteer forces, Morrell's Trustees (the by now quite elderly Mortimer and Gamlen) accepted that they might lose men through a general mobilization of reservists, and agreed within two days of the declaration of war to pay 10s. a week to the wives of men who were called up.[11] Single men volunteering for service presumably received no inducements to go, unlike (for example) the brewery employees of Whitbread & Co., whose directors offered one month's full pay and three (later six) months' half-pay to unmarried men joining up in 1914.[12]

In all fifty-six employees of Morrell's served in the First World War, just under half of them in the Oxfordshire and Buckinghamshire Light Infantry, a regiment distinguished for many acts of extreme bravery. Nine men were killed and seven wounded, a disproportionately large number in both cases (six and five) being members of the local regiment, and some of these almost certainly trained volunteer reservists.

Initially, however, the government requisitioned horses rather than men. Morrell's teams of dray-horses were still doing all the work that would later be transferred to lorries, for in 1912 the Trustees had flatly turned down the idea of purchasing 'Motor Lorrys', and the following year they had relented only to the extent of allowing Dowson to buy himself a BSA car.[13] In 1914 the war-machine was run on similarly antiquated lines, with draught horses in great demand for hauling gun-carriages at the Front as well as for less dangerous work. On 14 August Dowson recorded that he had been paid £526 for seven horses, five (horse-drawn) vans and six sets of harness, and on 2 October that he had received £225 for four more horses. This severely depleted the brewery teams, which usually consisted of about two dozen working horses. Later in the first year of the war the Army made some recompense to the brewery by boarding out six heavy draught horses there, paying 14s. each a week for their keep and presumably allowing them to work; but by September 1915 these had gone, and there was no likelihood that they would be replaced. Instead, Dowson spoke of hiring four more with the option of eventually buying them, in order to bring the numbers in the stable up to twenty.[14]

Even after the Second World War brewery dray-horses continued in some places to deliver beer to pubs and clubs. For relatively short journeys this was an economical and clean, if slow, means of delivery yet the lorry or motor-van effectively replaced the horse-drawn delivery vehicle in most areas of life during the First World War. Despite earlier intractability on the subject of motor lorries, the Trustees (two of them now younger men) agreed in November 1915 to the purchase of a second-hand 2½-ton lorry, and within the next six months had acquired two more, a 2-ton 'Seabrook' lorry costing £500 and a 30-cwt Garford costing £450, to which they proposed to fit a purpose-built platform.[15]

Even before the arrival of the motor lorries Dowson had been busy in the countryside around Oxford. At army encampments at Bletchingdon, Somerton, Kidlington, Culham and Botley, he erected movable canteens for soldiers and secured the sole right to provide these with Morrell's beer and mineral waters. The following year, in 1916, the Trustees closed down the mineral water factory, perhaps for want of manpower to keep it going; and after the war they did not reopen it.[16] Meanwhile the beer trade had undergone the harsh cuts, followed by minor fluctuations, experienced by breweries all over Britain since 1914.

The first financial effect of the war on the brewing trade was an increase by the government in the duty on beer, from 7s. 9d. a barrel, a figure which had remained constant since 1900, to 23s. (The duty then continued to increase steadily, rising to £5 a barrel by 1928.) In common with other breweries, as Dowson pointed out to the Trustees four months after the outbreak of war, Morrell's had managed to pass on the effects of the 'war tax' to its tenants, causing an increase in the retail price of beer from 2d. to 3d. a pint. The wholesale trade had dropped sharply at the beginning of the war, but had recovered slightly before the end of 1914 to over 70 per cent of its pre-war volume.[17] As Morrell's and other breweries would discover in both world wars, the price and strength of beer made little difference to the public's willingness to drink it when other circumstances were sufficiently dire. Although government directives caused the national production of beer to drop to a third of its pre-war figure in 1917, the breweries continued to make modest profits, economizing in outlay on raw materials, equipment and the modernization of pub premises (since little building took place once war had been declared) to balance the drop in their incomes from the wholesale trade.

Rationing of foodstuffs to individuals began early in 1918, but the government's restrictions on the purchase of sugar by households and manufacturing industries had already come into effect by the middle of 1917. Industrial consumers were restricted to 50 per cent of the amount that they had had in 1915; and, as Morrell's had used no sugar in brewing that year, the authorities informed them that they would not be entitled to use any while restrictions lasted. Given the uncertain supplies of malt, with an interruption in imports of Hungarian and Russian barley, this ruling alarmed the Trustees enough to send Dowson to protest to the district Food Controller.[18] Actual restrictions on brewing also applied, with the object of saving national stocks of fuel. Having kept the brewery's output well below the limit set by the government (in March 1917, for example, Dowson reported surplus barrelage amounting to 798 barrels less than the number permitted to be brewed), Morrell's volunteered that spring to join an Oxford brewers' scheme for temporary public-house closure, choosing the Ancient Briton and the Gamecock in Blackfriars Road, St Ebbe's, the Gardener's Arms in North Parade and the Coach and Horses in St Clement's. The following summer, however, the government increased the permitted barrelage by a third, stipulating at the same time that a third of this extra allowance could be brewed to a low to moderate gravity of 1036° ('standard' gravity of 1055° being unattainable in wartime) for sale directly to farmers as harvest beer. For this the Trustees proposed to charge the equivalent of pre-war prices for high-quality beer: 48s. a barrel at the brewery, or 54s. if delivered.[20]

The loss of men to the Front, especially poignant in a firm that employed fathers, brothers and sons (two Fillmores, one killed, one wounded; two Frenches, one killed; two Haineses, one killed), led to a breach in the all-male solidarity of the brewery staff. Brewing itself has remained very much a masculine profession; but in 1916 Morrell's employed its first women members of staff, sixteen-year-old Violet Cousins from St Thomas's Street and a Scottish forewoman, to tidy away the mineral-water bottles and their cases, wash out casks and do other minor jobs about the place. By 1918 there were at least five girls at the brewery (photographed one summer day in a smiling group, most with hair bobbed short in the new fashion to keep it clear of their work, and the expressions of a privileged rather than an oppressed minority).[21] By the 1930s, according to Olive Gibbs, who grew up in Christ Church Model

Violet Cousins (later Mrs Hounslow) and other women brewery workers, c. 1918

Buildings, just off The Hamel, 'most' local girls worked at Morrell's, 'where I should have to wear clogs!', usually in the bottling department in the former stables.[22]

Violet Cousins (later Mrs Hounslow) remained at the brewery until her forties, then worked for a time in East Oxford until she bought a lodging-house in the Iffley Road. Her account of her early years at the brewery, written in old age in a letter to Jimmy's son, Colonel Bill Morrell (who was a year old when she went to work at Morrell's) deserves quoting for its spontaneity and for her lively recollections of her work and impressions as a young girl:

> Next job to bottle wash. I remember you came one afternoon to watch, with your mother and sister Marjorie [probably Mary, the eldest of Jimmy's children, later Mrs Luard]. You were wearing a brace on your

teeth. . . . Mr Dowson was manager then, and Mr Haslett with Mr Philips from Philips brewery Park End St were brewers at the time. Ralph Green, also a brewer had gone into the army. Soon we went into the scalding shed to clean casks also from Queens College who brewed their own beer xxxx what lovely beer it was. We never mentioned water then, only liquor or beer. They were the days of drays and Staffordshire horses. Cricket was played in the Oxpens at the back in the evenings Morrell's had a team of their own. The Oxpens was also used for ram fairs and Morrell's beer was drunk in a big markquee by farmers.

Next move, to clean tuns upstairs with powdered pumice and small brooms. I loved to poke my nose through the latch to smell the beer fermenting. Next move was to truck casks, 10 kilns 20 firkins 5 barrels, into the filling room run by Mr Cox from Wolvercote. He walked every morning at 6 o'clock with Walter Dicks to Morrell's brewery. Sometimes I would help to put handfuls of hops into each one, before beer was put in. At Christmas we were given 7 lb of English beef, 10 lb for men, from Morrell's own cows. Headington Hall, Mrs Morrell had her home for young girls there, and packed a tin trunk of clothes for them when they left for jobs.

It was rumoured Mark Morrell [who had died in 1843] had a few bastards about Oxford, a Don Juan I may say. Mrs Morrell opened fetes and Town Hall do's. Sat you would see her with the reins in her brougham visiting Mrs Sherwoods in the large house the bottom of Fisher Row. . . .

However I was moved into bottling room to build up stocks. I had an increase of 5/- a week, to me, a princely sum. There was little thieving in those days, checks were made at the front office by J. Mundy and Mr Crozier.

One year we went to Wembley for [the] annual outing. It was a big exhibition for all nationalities, 1923. . . .

Your father James Morrell had built a boat at Harrow and it was in Morrell's builders yard. . . . His last words to me was, Can you find me someone as good as yourself!'[23]

For by then, in the Second World War period to which Mrs Hounslow's memory had transported her forwards, Jimmy Morrell was no longer a supernumerary Trustee, but had been managing the brewery for nearly two decades and, in a new age of burgeoning big business, was determinedly upholding its survival as a family concern against the takeover bids proffered by larger and more powerful companies.

CHAPTER NINE

MORRELL'S TRUSTEES, 1918–43

To the general public, the most striking change imposed on Morrell's Brewery by the First World War was probably the disappearance of the horse-drawn drays and their replacement by motor lorries. Other breweries, in smaller towns, continued using horse-drawn transport into the 1950s; while in London brewery shire horses have remained a much-loved part of the city scene until the present. At Morrell's, the closure of the stables and the nearby horse hospital in the building adjoining the Marlborough Arms, and the relinquishment of the ever-scarcer pastures behind the Botley Road, severed one more link between the brewery and the country immediately outside Oxford. Supplies of beer still reached one or two pubs by water (notably the Isis at Iffley Lock, which had its own punt), but were otherwise transported about the county by lorry or by rail.

More important to the brewery management itself were the changes in beer production imposed first by rationing, then by the cessation of restrictions on raw materials. Before the outbreak of war, the beers most frequently brewed had been pale ale, stock ale, best bitter, table beer, small beer and stout. Only malt and hops were used (pale malt only for best bitter, pale with the addition of a small amount of black malt for ale, and of a larger amount, in the proportions of sixteen quarters of pale to five of black, for stout). The average boiling time was four hours, allowing the maximum possible goodness to be extracted from the hops and malt. In wartime these brews were reduced to best bitter, (ordinary) ale and stout. Pale ale, table beer and small beer were discontinued, and it was not until November 1920 that the brewery began once again to produce its former characteristic strong ale, named, as before the War, xxxx.[1]

By this time sugar had become available once more for brewing, and for the first time appeared as a regular constituent of Morrell's beer. Cane, invert and glucose sugar were all used, either directly in the brew in place of a proportion of the malt that had previously been used or in a special, high-sugar, low-gravity brew that was added to the beer to help secondary fermentation. Boiling times for most brews were reduced to three hours. Thus a brew of ninety-two barrels of best bitter, in 1915, used 18 quarters (18 x 336 lb) of pale malt and 168 lb of hops, giving an original gravity of 1049°, whereas a brew of 128 barrels of best bitter in 1919 used proportionately less malt (21 quarters), proportionately the same amount of hops (224 lb) and 8 cwt of glucose, giving a reduced original gravity of 1045°. Generally, the strength of beer declined as tastes changed, so that, whereas in 1919 the original gravity of stout was 1057°, of best bitter 1045° and of ale 1036°, in 1947 Morrell's dark and light ale had an original gravity of only 1029°.[2] The use of sugar continued steadily for several decades; but since the late 1970s all Morrell's beers have once again been made without sugar, since improvements in malts of different kinds mean that these provide all the sugars that are needed for traditional methods of fermentation.

The initial impetus for the use of sugar was undoubtedly created by the rationing of malt, which continued into 1919 when sugar first began to be used. To cover the costs of immediate post-war production, Dowson proposed to act in co-operation with Hall's to raise the price of ale to 72s. a barrel, while keeping the prices of best bitter and stout at 108s. (£5 8s.) a barrel, roughly twice what they had cost in the 1890s. With prices raised but consumers still buying, 1919–20 was a buoyant financial year; and at the end of it the Trustees awarded their first performance bonuses, £250 to Dowson, £100 to Haslett and £10 each to the remaining brewery staff. They also fixed new salary levels for the senior staff: £1,000 a year for Dowson (the same amount that the younger James Morrell had ordained as a salary for Thomas Sherwood in 1863), £675 for Haslett and smaller sums, between £375 and £275, for members of the clerical staff.[3]

The immediately postwar years were inflationary, with a wages/prices spiral, high income tax, high unemployment resulting from the overcrowding of certain industries at the end of the war, an uncertain balance of trade and a greatly increased national debt. Although the fall of Lloyd George's coalition government marked a return to relative economic normality (with four alternating Conservative and Labour governments, under Stanley Baldwin and Ramsay Macdonald, in the eight years between 1923 and 1931), the depression created by a reduction in wages and prices had a worrying effect on some areas of industry. Hall's Brewery, which had taken on extra men after the war, dismissed several of its more recent recruits in an economy drive at the end of 1921. Two months before this, on 20 October, fire had gutted a malthouse of Hall's in Becket Street, near the GWR station, doing £40,000-worth of damage.[4]

More active than Morrell's had been in the past few decades, Hall's was still, in the early 1920s, in an expansionist phase; for Colonel Hall, after retiring from Parliament, had built up his firm into a private limited company, and had acquired four other Oxford breweries, the Eagle and

St Clement's breweries in 1897, Hanley's City Brewery in Pembroke Street in 1898, and Phillips' Tower Brewery in 1910. (Weaving's Eagle Brewery had been in existence on the south side of Park End Street, just east of Hollybush Row, since the late 1860s. Phillips's Tower Brewery had moved to new premises nearby, next door but one to the corner of Tidmarsh Lane on the south side of Park End Street, in 1889.) Brewing for Hall's was done at the City Brewery until about 1922, and bottling continued to be done at the former Eagle premises for several decades longer. In 1925 Hall's took over Blencowe's Brewery at Brackley; but in 1926 it was itself taken over by Allsopp's of Burton-on-Trent (absorbed soon afterwards by Ind Coope), and only the bottling operation continued to function in Oxford.

Morrell's Trustees, with a more compact operation than Hall's, had worries of a slightly different kind. Resisting any temptation to take over other breweries, they had pared down their commitments still further after the First World War, and in 1920 had given up the malting side of the business when they let out Fox's Malthouse on a yearly tenancy to G.W.E. Downing and his associates.[5] This arrangement continued, with Morrell's remaining responsible for the upkeep of the fabric of the building, and buying some English malt from Downing to mix with a percentage of Smyrna, Californian or other foreign malt, until the fire of 1956 that brought malting at Fox's to an end.

The steep rise in direct taxation, meanwhile, which had increased sixfold between 1915 and 1921, had only been slightly mitigated by subsequent reductions in income tax to 5s. in the pound in 1923 and to 4s. in 1925. Unproductive landed estates were becoming steadily more expensive to maintain, while even agriculturally productive ones (once the immediate post-war farming boom was over) were suffering from the renewed effects of a depression in farming. Although they had disposed of most of the land accumulated by the first two James Morrells, the Trustees were still responsible for the upkeep of Headington Hill Hall, its lavish acreage of shrubbery and kitchen garden (to which they had added a small, final purchase of a hilltop shrubbery from the Davenport family in 1920),[6] and the grazing in South Park below The Rise on Headington Hill and to the south of this in the direction of the Warneford Hospital, where the Morrells kept their cattle for the brewery workers' Christmas gifts of beef.

With new social initiatives beginning for the provision of cheaply rented, decent public housing, and with Oxford itself growing in population as industry increased, the City Council was by now anxious to acquire tracts of potential building land within walking or cycling distance of the city centre. Approaches were evidently made to the Trustees to see if they would part with South Park for building; but they replied that the

Morrells had always kept this open for shows and fêtes, and that only dire need on the Council's part would allow them to give up any part of it for housing, and then only a small fraction of it.[7] The outcome of this was the Council's purchase of the site of the present Morrell Avenue, as far away as possible from both Headington Hill Hall and The Rise, and the building on it in 1929–31 of a small estate of council houses, happily in the generous good taste that prevailed in such projects before the imposition of government economies of the mid-1930s. The year after these were finished the Trustees sold most of the remaining 60-odd acres of land for £25,000 to the Oxford Preservation Trust, keeping back a 5-acre paddock attached to The Rise and stipulating that no building should be done on the remaining land, and that Emily should be allowed to keep it in her possession for a nominal rent for the rest of her lifetime. Cattle therefore continued to graze in South Park until after the Second World War, when the Preservation Trust handed it over to the City Council, retaining discretionary powers over the use of the land to keep it free from building and excessive public wear and tear and to maintain it, as it is today, a dramatically open green space in an otherwise congested part of East Oxford.[8]

* * *

By the mid-1920s the Morrell family in Oxford again numbered three generations. The legal branch of the family, once so prolific of mid-Victorian solicitors and clergymen, had ceased to take an active part in the affairs of the St Giles' law firm and was now represented in Oxford only by the Liberal, pacifist Member of Parliament Philip Morrell, educated at the Dragon School, Eton and Oxford, and his flamboyant wife Lady Ottoline. The close friendship that had existed between Philip's father Fred, the fourth and last in succession of the family line of solicitors, and his first cousin Herbert does not appear to have repeated itself between members of the next generation. At Garsington Manor (which they held on a short-term lease, unconnected with the family's previous ownership of a farm in Garsington parish), Philip, and more particularly Lady Ottoline, kept open house to the notoriously bohemian gathering of artists, writers, rich undergraduates and eccentrics which has been so copiously described in literary biographies of members of the Bloomsbury Group. Not far away, at Headington Hill Hall, Emily Morrell continued the life of a Victorian *châtelaine*, driving out with her coachman among the burgeoning motor traffic of Oxford, and maintaining a rigidly disciplinarian attitude towards her grandchildren. Since Herbert's funeral little or no communication had existed between Headington Hall and the Philip Morrells, or between Jimmy, with his

James Herbert (Jimmy) Morrell

military sympathies and straightforward scientific preoccupations, and his literary, aesthetic and slightly shocking cousins. Between the Philip Morrells and the brewery there existed no connection at all, and they may even have been unaware of the key role played by Philip's grandfather, Frederick Joseph Morrell, in keeping the business in existence during the decade between the younger James's death and Herbert and Emily's marriage.

Jimmy, however, as the heir apparent to the brewery business, was a man of wide enough interests and sympathies to combine a keen concern for the proper running of the brewery with a range of different activities outside it. Like Herbert he was much involved in local affairs, serving as a County Councillor and being largely responsible for the introduction of the first roundabouts at busy crossroads in the county. Like Herbert he served as High Sheriff in the county, and was popular with local landowners. Yet his comparatively modest style of life on Headington Hill (initially, for the first few years of his marriage, in part of the Hall, then across the road at The Firs, and from 1926 onwards at The Rise, overlooking South Park, which until then had been let to a prominent local figure, Judge Radcliff) had freed him from the worries of looking after a landed estate and the obligation to entertain on the kind of scale that his parents had done. Once the war was over he had therefore been free to divide his time between the Clarendon Laboratory, local affairs, and attendance at the weekly Trustees' meetings at the brewery.

On 31 October 1926, after thirty-five and a half years at his post and a few weeks' illness in the Acland Home, Harry Dowson, the brewery manager, died. This was Jimmy's chance to put his organizational skills

Leonard Mortimer: Morrell's Brewery Trustee 1914–43; Director, Morrells Brewery Ltd, September 1943–January 1944

and a dozen years' experience as an interested observer into effect; and before the end of November the Trustees had appointed him acting manager with a suitably moderate salary of £750 a year.⁹ Perhaps because the Trustees felt diffident about giving a permanent appointment to the member of the family who was the chief indirect beneficiary of the Trust, or because they envisaged imminent administrative changes at the brewery once Emily died and the Trust became obsolete, or because he himself had specifically asked for a temporary position, they did not officially confirm Jimmy as manager, and he was still signing himself 'acting manager' in the late 1930s. He was on good terms, however, with the new generation of Trustees: John Charles Gamlen, a partner in the solicitors' firm of Morrell, Peel and Gamlen, Bernard Collins of Reading, whose firm acted for the brewery, and Leonard Mortimer. In 1934 they raised his salary to £1,000, with an annual bonus of £450 for the previous financial year, and sanctioned the purchase for him of a new, 16-hp Wolseley car.¹⁰

The Trust, based on Emily's marriage settlement, and created nearly a decade before the first Married Woman's Property Act of 1882, had existed primarily for her benefit and only secondarily for that of her children. Such trusts are usually broken when the main beneficiary from the income dies. When this happened ownership of the brewery could pass directly to Jimmy (in which case, as part of his estate, it would become subject to death-duties), or it could be shared between members of the family and others as a private limited company. In 1933 a deed of appointment signed by Emily in Jimmy's favour guaranteed him the residue of funds accruing from the winding-up of the Trust, including any proceeds from the possible sale of Headington Hill Hall and the brewery – an indirect way of willing him both these properties, neither of which was hers directly to give away.[11] Emily was then seventy-nine, and lived to be eighty-four. The eventual winding-up of the various Trusts took a further five years, most of it in wartime, before Morrell's Brewery Ltd could be set up in the form in which it has existed for the past half-century.

Thanks to the flourishing state of both the motor industry and the University, neither of which was seriously affected by the Depression, trade in Oxford remained relatively buoyant during the years 1929–37. As the only surviving commercial brewing operation in the city, Morrell's was in a strong position to command local custom, especially now that all but one of the colleges had ceased to brew their own beer. Five colleges, Queen's, Oriel, Magdalen, Corpus Christi and New College, had continued brewing until the 1890s; but by the period between the wars only Queen's College, which claimed to have had a continuous tradition of brewing since its foundation in 1341, was still producing a token thirty barrels a year of College Ale, and a smaller quantity, brewed only in October, of a special, ceremonial beer with an original gravity of 1100°, known as Chancellor's Ale. After the retirement of the Queen's College brewer in the late 1920s Morrell's supervised, and provided materials for, the twice-yearly college brewing in March and October. This took place virtually in museum conditions in the antiquated college brewhouse, with the wort cooled in open, unrefrigerated coolers, then boiled with the hops before entering on a twenty-four hour fermentation period with the yeast in a wooden vessel whose temperature could not be controlled. After this the wort was ladled into casks from which the yeast worked its own way out through an open bung-hole into a wooden trough beneath, where it was skimmed from the accompanying beer, and the beer returned to the casks for eventual racking. Louis Gunter, Morrell's second brewer, inherited the responsibility for overseeing the brewing at Queen's College when he first took on his job, and was once again briefly associated with it when the college partially refitted its brewhouse after the Second World War, before abandoning the six-hundred-year-old tradition of domestic brewing altogether.[12]

It was during the inter-war years, when a high proportion of a predominantly male Oxford undergraduate population spent part at least of its free time drinking beer in the college buttery or in pubs, that the brewery began to identify and target a specifically University element among its customers. Jimmy Morrell's standing as an Oxford graduate and former faculty member, and the ease with which he could identify himself with a potential University market, may have helped him to take up the challenge of cultivating undergraduate custom. Early in 1938, in response

The Black Boy, Headington, Oxford, early 1930s

to an approach from the President of the Oxford University Boat Club, Morrell's agreed to supply the (happily victorious) University Eight with free beer during its month of pre-Boat Race training at Barnes. By that time they were brewing three kinds of expensive, traditional ale: Buttery Ale, which was not available in bottled form, and at £13 4s. a barrel cost nearly twice as much as ordinary ale (then £6 18s. a barrel), and the strong, heavy College Ale (as supplied to the Boat Race crew) and Proctor Ale, which at £16 4s. a barrel cost nearly two and a half times as much as ordinary ale, and were retailed in nips rather than in large or small bottles.[13]

While traditional ales maintained a high level of gravity to match their high price, Morrell's ordinary beer had become lighter to suit changing tastes. A comparison with Allsopp's beers between January and December 1928, of immediate relevance to Morrell's, since Allsopp now owned some 300 pubs which had formerly belonged to Hall's, revealed that Morrell's ordinary ale now had a consistent original gravity of only 1027° (as against 1036° in 1919), whereas Allsopp's varied between 1032° and 1031°. Morrell's best bitter and stout had a consistent original gravity of 1039° (as against 1057° and 1045° in 1919), while Allsopp's best bitter varied between 1042° and 1041°, and their stout between 1039° and 1049.4°. A comparison of xxxx, made on 10 December 1928, showed an original gravity of 1065° for Allsopp's and only 1055° for Morrell's.[14] At the same time, while generally reducing the proportion of malt which went into their beers, Morrell's did their best to cater for the 1930s taste for nourishing-seeming drinks, exemplified by the success during that decade of Ovaltine,

The Fox, Barton, Oxford, 1930s (rebuilt 1967)

Horlicks and other milky beverages, not only as sleep-inducers but as liquid snacks in the middle of the day. Their contribution to this craze was the popular oat-malt stout, which they began to brew in the early 1930s but abandoned during the Second World War.

While the key figure on the production side at Morrell's was unquestionably the head brewer, it had been customary, since Haslett's appointment in the early 1890s, for the brewer to take on a pupil, who might then stay for a few years as second brewer or move on almost immediately to another firm. In this way technical knowledge and ideas were disseminated between one brewery and another, and a range of contacts set up between the larger breweries and the smaller and more traditional ones such as Morrell's. Increasingly brewers and their pupils tended to move back and forth between the larger and smaller firms. John Tremlett, for example, who was taken on as a pupil by Ralph Green, then brewer, in 1931, remained at Morrell's for a few years as second brewer, then moved to another brewery at Wolverhampton. His successor, Brian Achurch, who had come to Morrell's from Bristol, moved back there to join Bristol United in 1938, and after the war moved again to take charge of brewing operations at the small firm of Starkey, Knight and Ford at Tiverton, Devon. Ralph Green died in 1943 and was replaced as head

Ralph Green, under-brewer 1912–14, 1919–29, head brewer 1929–43, in First World War uniform

brewer at Morrell's by Gordon Cunliffe, formerly of Watney's Mortlake brewery, assisted by an elderly retired brewer, Charles Tisdell, from Oswestry, Shropshire. The system of pupillage, and the supply of younger men ready for employment as under-brewers, had been temporarily disrupted by the war; but in the summer of 1946 Morrell's welcomed back Louis Gunter, Brian Achurch's successor as second brewer, who had first arrived at Morrell's in 1937 as a pupil of twenty-one. Louis (as he is affectionately known to most of the present staff of Morrell's) returned to the brewery after war service, followed by a year at Birmingham University. He became head brewer in 1959 in succession to Gordon Cunliffe, and retired in 1983. His career at the brewery represented a valuable element of continuity in the history of Morrell's as it faced up to the challenges of maintaining its position as an independent concern, competing, or co-operating, increasingly with the largest brewing firms as dozens of other small family-run breweries were taken over and shut down.

* * *

At the end of September 1938 Emily Morrell died at the age of eighty-four. A year later, on the declaration of war, the government requisitioned Headington Hill Hall for military use, and a hasty sale was held of the Hall's contents in order to make room for the incoming tenants. As with so many other families whose possessions were dispersed or packed away in those first months of the 'phoney war', the younger Morrells (Jimmy now in his fifties, his children in their twenties) experienced a sudden adjustment to a world in which solid Victorian comforts could no longer be taken for granted. Nearly all the furniture amassed by Emily and Herbert was sold: in the entrance hall a collection of specimen cabinets, including a walnut and laburnum-wood William and Mary inlaid panelled cabinet with twenty-seven drawers, together with five glass cases of stuffed birds and two of foxes' masks; in the great drawing-room the satinwood furniture, Axminster carpet, grand piano and oriental china; in the smaller drawing-room the Indian carved teak furniture and Benares brass vases; in the billiard-room the long table sunk in its slate bed, and the seventeen oil-paintings of hounds and eleven of horses which hung on the walls around it. In the library a collection of racing calendars spanned the years from 1727 to 1863, the year of Emily's father's death. Most evocative of all of the already antiquated way of life that had vanished with Emily was the collection of carriages and other horse-drawn vehicles, which she had either driven herself or been driven in by a coachman: a barouche, a landau, a town brougham and a double town brougham, a four-wheeled bus, a victoria, a hooded phaeton, a two-wheeled dogcart, a governess cart and (for invalids) a four-wheeled Bath chair.[15]

Apart from the changes at Headington Hill Hall, where the family had gathered for the last time at Christmas 1938, a few months after Emily's death, and which none of them would ever again be able to regard as a permanent home, the Second World War had a minor impact on the brewery and other areas of life which concerned the Trustees. Throughout the war the brewery was physically protected by the absence of bombing in Oxford, just as it had been cocooned throughout the Depression by the relative prosperity of trade there. Price, a lorry driver, was called up in September 1939, and was acknowledged to be the brewery's first casualty when reported missing in the summer of 1941.[16] Louis Gunter, who applied for permission to join the Navy as soon as war broke out, eventually joined the Air Force and survived, against great odds, as a bomber pilot. Many of the brewery staff were over-age for the military call-up, having already served in the First World War and then returned to their jobs. Not all continued working at the brewery for as long as J. Edwards, an employee from the age of fifteen or sixteen, in 1876, to the age of seventy-two, when he retired after suffering a stroke and was awarded a discretionary pension of £1 15s. a week by the Trustees with Emily Morrell's consent.[17] Generally, however, the stability of the work-force was one of Morrell's great assets, perpetuating the family feeling, which, extraordinarily in modern business, still survives at the brewery today.

* * *

With wartime shortages (beginning, this time, on the outbreak of war rather than half-way through it, as in 1916), and with increases in duties on beer, the price of beer rose steadily through the first years of the war from April 1940 onwards. In May 1933, in the depths of the Depression, Morrell's had acted in concert with the association of Berkshire Brewers to reduce the wholesale price of beer to the levels that had obtained in 1931. Now, with unemployment virtually non-existent and the duty on beer raised from April 1940 by 17s. a barrel for beers up to an original gravity of 1027° (and an additional 6d. per degree for beers of a higher gravity than this), Morrell's passed on the increases to their tenants at the rate of 20s. (£1) a barrel for lower-gravity beers, and 24s. for those of higher gravity. To the customer, ordinary ales and bitters then cost an additional 1d. a pint, and heavier beers 2d. Further increases occurred in the desperate summer of 1940, and (most stringently) in the spring of 1942, when an increase of 46s. a barrel in duty put the price of all beer up to the customer by a further 2d. a pint.[18]

Because of the expense of malt and the shortages of sugar (for which barley was used in small quantities as a substitute), strong beer went out of production at Morrell's for the wartime and immediately post-war period. Instead the brewery concentrated much of its efforts on producing two brews of beer, dark and light, of a uniform original gravity of 1029°,

Morrell's Trustees
LION BREWERY

Minimum Public Bar Price List

Oat Malt Stout, large bottle	1/1
„ „ small bottle	7½d.
Brown Stout, large bottle	11d.
„ „ small bottle	6d.
Original Oxford Bitter, large bottle	11d.
„ „ „ small bottle	6d.
Brown Ale, large bottle	11d.
„ small bottle	6d.
Proctor, nips	8d.
College Ale, nips	8d.
Bass, small bottle	9½d.
Guinness, large bottle	1/5
„ small bottle	9½d.

Published by the Oxfordshire Licensed Victuallers' Central Protection Society.

August 20th, 1940.   J. B. A. WILEY, Secretary.

Price list of beers, 1940

brewing a parti-gyle with the light (an arrangement whereby part of a brew could be fermented separately from the rest to produce a higher original gravity) to produce small quantities of College Ale. Of the two kinds the dark demanded a richer blend of ingredients (more malt, both pale and black, more hops, more sugar substitute) than the light, but was boiled for only three hours as against three and a half for the light. In a wartime context of increasingly appalling food, long, cold hours of waiting, and the tendency of members of the armed forces to crowd out all available pubs when they could, the diminished strength of the beer went virtually unnoticed. At the end of the brewing year in September 1942 Jimmy Morrell reported to his Trustee, Leonard Mortimer, that sales for the year had reached a record figure of over 39,000 barrels, 9 per cent more than the figure for the previous year, which had itself been a record:

> I hardly know how it was done, but the Beer is very weak, and a large proportion of the Sales are Ale. However the public lap it down and ask for more. There is hardly one of our houses that can keep its sales going for more than 28 hours a week.
>
> The Gross profit is only slightly up, owing to the fancy prices that had to be given for Malt, and any grain in this direction is offset by additional wages and other overheads. After allowing for Taxation, I expect the divisible profit will come pretty nearly up to that of last year. . . .[19]

He went on to report the year's losses from enemy action (a few quarters of malt destroyed in Suffolk, which he had permission to replace from the new season's malt, and slight damage to the Oxford Hotel in Swindon when a bomb fell at a bus-stop, unfortunately killing ten people nearby). He also commented that the executor's accounts and some of the trusts connected with the Morrell estate could soon be closed, since agreement had finally been reached on the amount of estate duty payable, but that the main brewery trust would have to remain open for some time longer.

News and gossip travel rapidly in the small world of English brewing, and the impending break-up of Morrell's Trust must have been common knowledge among the more powerful brewing companies as soon as Emily had died, or indeed before that. Not long before the outbreak of war in 1939, Ushers' Brewery of Trowbridge made an approach through an intermediary to Leonard Mortimer, the senior Trustee, proposing amalgamation with Morrell's. Since the late nineteenth century Ushers had already taken over some fourteen country breweries, mainly in Wiltshire and nearby parts of Berkshire, culminating in the acquisition and closure of the Wells family's former Wallingford Brewery Ltd with its seventy-seven licensed houses in 1928. Had Morrell's followed the long-established Wallingford Brewery into oblivion, two centuries after the Wells family's power and success in Wallingford had effectively prevented large-scale brewing there by any member of the Morrell family, history might have appeared to be pursuing its normal, relentless course.

Jimmy, however, was clearly determined to save his family business, comfortably though he might have lived on his share of a pay-out to the Trustees by Ushers. For much of the past twenty-five years he had watched the brewery struggling against the difficulties imposed on it by the licensing laws, by wartime restrictions and by post-war inflation followed by depression; and for twelve years he had been paid to promote and protect its interests. Of his four children (two sons and two daughters), three survived to participate actively in the running of the brewery. George, the second son, a midshipman, had been killed in a motor accident at the age of only eighteen in 1936. Mary Luard, the eldest child, was married before the outbreak of the Second World War, and joined the Board of Morrells Brewery Ltd only in 1965, as a replacement for her father, after he had died and her children had grown up. Margaret Eld, on the other hand, who lived at home during the war and married her ex-officer husband in 1946, became involved in brewery affairs while still in her twenties when, in February 1944, she was co-opted on to the Board of Directors of Morrells Brewery Ltd to replace a former director, Leonard Mortimer, who had died. In February 1994 she thus celebrates half a century on the Board. Finally the surviving son, Bill (Colonel Bill Morrell), an officer in the Royal Artillery, was understood, if he lived through the war, to be ready to go into the family business in a full-time capacity. Without their father's driving determination, Jimmy's children might well have acceded to outside pressure to let the brewery go; but, as it was, family cohesion kept intending purchasers at bay, not only on this but on several subsequent occasions.[20]

CHAPTER TEN

MORRELLS BREWERY LIMITED, 1943–65

The formal dissolution of the main Brewery Trust, the last of a complex of trusts created under the terms of Emily and Herbert's marriage settlement, took place in September 1943. Jimmy, at the age of sixty-one, finally assumed responsibility for his own capital resources, and in April 1943 became life chairman and managing director of a limited company, Morrells Brewery Ltd, with a Board initially composed of himself and his former Trustees, Leonard Mortimer and J.C.B. Gamlen. Two senior company employees, the brewer Ralph Green and the company secretary John Mundy, were allocated a hundred £1 shares each, but were not invited to sit on the Board. (The first Morrells employee, A.G.C. Worth, assistant managing director, was elected to the Board in 1970, followed six years later by the company secretary Charles Smith and the head brewer, Louis Gunter.) In effect, as Jimmy's daughters have admitted, the Board was initially very much a one-man concern, for which he made most of the policy decisions before instructing his fellow-members, especially when these were his children, which way they should vote.[1]

No sooner was the end of the Trust a foregone conclusion than Ushers closed in again, with a proposal for amalgamation addressed directly to Jimmy himself. In 1945 they made a renewed and more aggressive approach, this time with a view to a complete buy-out of ordinary shares by an unnamed consortium.[2] Although small in comparison with (say) the former Hall's Brewery complex which had been swallowed up by Allsopp's in 1926, Morrells Brewery was still a compact and tempting concern, with its hundred-odd pubs and its unrivalled position as the sole surviving brewery in a thirsty industrial and university city. Profits, which had dipped from £22,195 in September 1937 to only £18,131 in September 1938, had recovered by the outbreak of war a year later to £22,547, and had remained buoyant through the war years. Having sacrificed a part-time academic career in physics early in the 1930s to see the firm through the financially unstable period of the Depression, Jimmy was by now a practised enough industrial tactician to face up to the stringencies of post-war austerity. In 1948 he was joined on the staff of the brewery by his surviving son, Colonel Bill Morrell, who had served with the Royal Artillery throughout the war, in France, Belgium, Madagascar, India and Burma, and had spent the past two years training gunners at a School of Artillery in West Germany. Having resigned his commission in the Regular Army, Colonel Morrell spent six months learning the trade of brewing, then joined his father on the administrative side of the business as assistant managing director. For the next decade father and son ran the brewery together, with Jimmy, in his seventies, remaining firmly in control. An accident in his later years, resulting in a broken hip and thigh, confined him to a wheelchair, and for a time Charles Smith, the company secretary, had to take the necessary office paperwork to Jimmy's home at The Rise on Headington Hill. Abandoning his spacious first-floor office at the brewery, Jimmy had a ground-floor office made for him out of the former watchmen's room (now the receptionists' office), and continued to spend as much time at the brewery as his limited mobility allowed him.

Colonel Morrell, while preparing for the time when his father would eventually give up all responsibilities at the brewery, used the relative freedom of his period as assistant managing director to cultivate the various outside interests which had by then become traditional in his family. Still strongly attached to the army, he joined the Territorials, and in 1959 became Deputy Commander of the 43rd Wessex Infantry Division (Territorial Army) of the Royal Artillery. He hunted, occasionally shot, and from 1959 sat as a magistrate on the Banbury and Bloxham magistrates' bench. From 1960 he was, like Jimmy before him, High Sheriff of Oxfordshire. More outward-looking than his father in making contact with other brewers, he represented Oxfordshire at the Brewers' Society, of which he was a Council member, and contributed to several brewing and bottling committees. Eventually he also became a non-executive director of the Friary Meux Brewery at Guildford and the Aylesbury Brewery, and later of Whitbread Wessex Ltd.

* * *

After the Second World War, and throughout the years in which sugar remained rationed, Morrells continued to brew its two basic kinds of austerity beer, dark and light, with an original gravity of 1029°. The first post-war brewing of ten barrels of stout took place on 23 November 1948, in a parti-gyle with the light ale, and was followed by regular, larger brewings thereafter. On 4 October 1950, for the first time since the war, the brewery produced 10½ barrels of xxxx draught beer, the strong, heavy beer that had been popular before the war as a superior public-house tipple, but was now brewed at an original gravity of 1041° rather than the pre-war gravity of 1055°. (Before the First World War, 'Old

Strong XXXX' had also been sold in bottle, together with stout, light dinner ale, cooper and India pale ale, but this practice had ceased with the austerities of wartime.) Several more small brews of xxxx followed that October; but, increasingly, customers were demanding strong beer in bottles rather than in draught. From 1 November 1950, therefore, xxxx reappeared as Castle Ale, a bottled beer, named (on the initiative of a brewery worker, after Jimmy had invited suggestions from his staff) for the nearby Castle Mound overlooking the brewery from inside the grounds of Oxford Prison. Brown and Light Oxford Ales and stout were also available in bottles, but Castle, with its distinctive light colour, dryness, hop character and clean 'palate', became one of Morrells' most popular and lastingly successful beers.

Introduced less tentatively than the first few post-war brews of nine or ten barrels of draught xxxx, Castle rapidly gained in popularity. That first brew, on 1 November, had produced 21¾ barrels of Castle, in a parti-gyle with 120 barrels of light at an original gravity of 1031°, just above the basic wartime strength, and 10½ barrels of College at an original gravity of 1074°. On 14 and 26 November (for at that time Castle and

Looking up the mill stream towards the water wheel, 1920

College Ales were produced only three or four times a month), 22 barrels of Castle were brewed. On 4 December, 39¼ barrels were brewed; and this figure remained more or less constant for several years, until in November 1956 production shot up from 40¾ barrels on the 7th to 50 barrels on the 14th and 60 on the 28th.[3]

Sugar-rationing, which had led to the use of barley to encourage fermentation, also brought about the post-war use of glucose derived from flaked maize. It had long been customary to make a special, low-gravity, high-sugar brew, always referred to as 'NA', to blend with the beer in the racking vessel in order to stimulate the yeast during fermentation. This continued to be brewed from time to time, using sugar or glucose, even during the working life of the present head brewer – an indication of the relative recentness of Morrells' return to using only the completely traditional, real ale ingredients of hops, malt and water.

Even before the increase in sales of Morrells' bottled beer after the introduction of Castle Ale in 1950, it had been necessary to renew the bottling plant, which gradually became more automated. Bottling took place in a two-storeyed building in the south-east corner of the main brewery yard, where a semi-mechanized system had made it possible for the brewery to undertake contract bottling between the wars. Sedimented beers, such as Guinness and Bass Red Triangle, had been brought in in hogsheads and bottled by hand from beer in troughs. Other beers were bottled mechanically from a conveyor belt using a twelve-head filling machine, then mechanically labelled. The work done by the women in their distinctive clogs was less labour-intensive than it had been in Violet Cousin's early days. Bottle-washing, for example, was now largely done by a succession of machines that soaked, brushed and rinsed the bottles before the women transferred them on to the conveyor. Crating, however, was still done by hand, and the crates of bottles were still stacked up manually, a job of questionable suitability for women.

In April 1948, in response to a clear demand for more bottled beer, the brewery acquired a second-hand eighteen-head Pontefract bottle filler, which was replaced only two years later by a new thirty-head filler. Renewal of the bottling equipment continued steadily through the 1960s and 1970s; and in 1961, after the installation of a new stainless steel receiving main, the brewery began bottling the popular Harp Lager, a product of the Guinness brewing firm and their German brewmaster, Dr Munde, in response to the demand for light, continental-style beers with a medium original gravity of 1041°. This anticipated by twenty-five years Morrells' eventual negotiation with the Harp Lager Company to brew Harp lagers under licence, ironically on the site of the former bottling plant, which was no longer able to justify the expense of its upkeep.

Ralph Green, head brewer until 1943, had been succeeded by Gordon

Cunliffe, formerly of Watneys. He was joined as second brewer in 1946 by the returned Louis Gunter, back from distinguished service in the RAF as a bomber pilot followed by a year at university. During the whole of Cunliffe's career at the brewery, until his death early in 1959, the basic brewing technology was Victorian or earlier, powered by the water-wheel of 1820 or thereabouts, the two steam engines which supplemented it, the antiquated wort-pumps, and the coal furnaces which heated the two boiling coppers. Modernization was mainly peripheral, in such areas as the bottling line, the change from horse-drawn to motorized transport, and the abandonment of the brewery's own well-water (now murkily unappetizing) for mains water, which had happened between the two world wars. Only in the mid-1960s, with Louis as head brewer and after Jimmy Morrell's death, did a major technological renovation take place in the brewhouse, sweeping away the last remnants of nineteenth-century machinery with a drastic fervour that some, at least, subsequently regretted.

Improvements in home-grown malting barley have, conversely, allowed a return to traditionally home-grown ingredients, without recourse to the foreign barley which dominated the brewing scene in England for nearly a hundred years. Just as better-tasting malt and hops now make it possible to brew without sugar, and with a third to a quarter of the boiling time that was necessary thirty or forty years ago, so the improvements in malting performance of home-grown barley have ended decades of experimentation with Hungarian, Danubian, Smyrna or Californian imports. British two-rowed barley, virtually abandoned by Morrell's in the 1880s for its chanciness in malting (largely due to its occasional quality of steeliness, that is non-mealiness, which retarded modification and could lower the eventual gravity of the brew for which it was used), began to make a come-back in quality in the 1920s when two hybrid forms, Sprat-Archer and Plumage-Archer, were developed, combining the traditional malting qualities of one sub-race with the high yield and good straw of another. At that time an admixture of imported six-rowed barley was usually added to help with mash-tun run-off, but improved varieties in the last decades now make this unnecessary.

The brewery's connection with malting, tenuous since 1920 when the Trustees had let out Fox's Malthouse to Messrs Downing (but still maintained to the extent that trainee brewers spent some time there learning the malting process) ended suddenly in the spring of 1956. By then Downing had relinquished the use of the malthouse to the Birmingham-based firm of Samuel Thompson and Sons. On 21 March 1956, nearly seventy years after the lesser fire caused by an explosion of malt during grinding in July 1886, a kiln went up in flames after the malthouse staff had banked up the fires before leaving the building at the end of the day. A police constable in the then county police headquarters in New Road

Fox's Malthouse, Tidmarsh Lane, after the fire of 1956

happened to notice a glow in the sky and called the fire brigade. As the *Oxford Times* reported:

> In a few minutes smoke was coming through the roof and the two cowls, and firemen had forced an entrance into the building and reached the kilns themselves. They were able to find where the outbreak had occurred and attacked it from inside before increasing dense smoke drove them back despite the use of oxygen masks. Flames had now appeared round the cowl at the western end in isolated parts of the roof, and firemen clambered over adjoining roofs to hack away slates from the roof so that water could be poured on the flames. One fireman hacked a foothold to the ridge near the cowl at the other end of the building, and broke the tiles surrounding it so that other firemen could direct hoses at the seat of the flames. Among hazards for the firemen was molten lead dropping from the roof, but no one was injured, though one or two were splashed with it. By this time the malt in the kilns had caught fire and was smouldering, but by 8.30 p.m. [nearly three hours after its outbreak] the fire was under control and the danger of its spreading to the rest of the building or to other buildings in the vicinity was over. However it was far from finished, and for some hours more hoses were played on the burning roof.[4]

While the 12 tons of malt in the kilns were destroyed, another 500 tons of barley in store in Tidmarsh Lane escaped the fire unharmed. The kilns and cowls, however, were wrecked, together with a substantial central part of the roof. Although insured, the building did not seem worth restoring as a malthouse; and on 18 June 1957 Morrells Brewery Ltd sold the freehold (including the former stables, then leased out to the proprietors of a car showroom, King's Motors) to the University of Oxford for £17,000.[5] Three hundred years or so of malting on the Tidmarsh Lane site thus came to an end; and the rebuilt central part of the former malthouse buildings is now the University surveyor's offices, with the older, mainly early nineteenth-century section at the south end in use as stores.

In the fire a long-established but unofficial family of sub-tenants at the malthouse had found themselves evicted. Several of these were given a home by a local lady, Miss Cockburn, and one, a twenty-year-old tortoise-shell named Malthouse Gran, proved unusually domesticated, winning joint first prize at the Oxford Cat Club show on 1 December 1956.[6]

* * *

The loss of malthouse staff, draymen and blacksmiths during the First World War and the years immediately after it had diminished the number of male brewery workers on and near the St Thomas's site. The great influx of female manual workers, mostly employed in bottling, which had begun in 1916, dwindled as the bottling operation began to run down, and ended altogether in 1985 when bottling ceased on Morrells' site. In all, Morrells employed about eighty people in brewing, bottling, administration, clerical work, driving, and repair and maintenance work by the mid-1970s.[7]

Socially the immediately post-war years saw many changes in the relationship between the brewery workers and the senior staff and employers. The winding up of the Trust and creation of a limited company made little difference to the ordinary brewery workers, since shares were not distributed among the work-force. If anything, Jimmy Morrell's change of status from brewery manager to managing director may have slightly increased the paternalistic atmosphere at the brewery, despite the gradual introduction of governmentally imposed benefits (national insurance, State pensions, guaranteed sick pay and paid holidays), which made the workers less dependent than before on the goodwill of the management for their well-being. Happily Jimmy was an authoritative figure whose standing outside the brewery (as a county councillor since 1925, Deputy Lieutenant and High Sheriff in 1930 and a city alderman since 1940) kept him generally respected within it. Increasingly, too, Morrells drew on a work-force from all over the city rather than simply from within the cramped and depressed residential area of St Thomas's.

Some of the tenement courtyards on the north side of St Thomas's Street had been pulled down in the late 1930s, while others on the south side followed in the 1950s. New housing estates to the south, east and north of the city, from Donnington Bridge to Rose Hill and Cowley and from there to Headington, New Marston, Cutteslowe and Wolvercote, had begun, before the Second World War, to accommodate a population of families many of whom had moved outwards from the city centre. From being a tightly populated hotchpotch of residential and industrial uses, the area of St Thomas's round the brewery became virtually empty of young families, with few children growing up locally to assume automatically that they would go into the brewery when they left school at fifteen.

One element of continuity, however, survived from the beginning of Dowson's period as brewery manager in the early 1890s. Despite the introduction of paid holidays, the annual brewery staff outing, suspended during the Second World War, was revived once again in peacetime. The destination was now usually a seaside resort such as Weymouth or Weston-super-Mare, London no longer being regarded as a cultural treat, and Boulogne, during the insular post-Second World War period, seeming more difficult of access than it had in Edwardian times. A special train (on occasion shared with the workers at Morris Cowley) would leave Oxford at 6.30 on a Saturday morning, sometimes arriving at the seaside in time for the whole party to be treated to breakfast at a hotel, and

A cartoon by Alan Course illustrating a cricket match between Morrell's Brewery and Hall's Brewery, 1948

returning at around midnight to be met by a small fleet of buses.[8]

Until 1938 such outings had included not only the brewery staff but all the Morrell domestic employees, some coming from Headington Hill Hall, others from Streatley House, joining the train at a scheduled Streatley stop on the southward journey from Oxford to Reading. This arrangement had naturally ended with the death of Emily Morrell. Streatley House, left to her younger son Mark, had been sold soon afterwards to pay double death-duties on Mark's unexpectedly early death in 1939. Headington Hill Hall, occupied by a Forces' nursing home until the late 1950s, had changed ownership when Jimmy, realizing that it would be impractical for him or his descendants ever to live there, sold the freehold to Oxford City Council in 1953 for £13,700.[9] Its subsequent history, as the home of the newspaper tycoon Robert Maxwell, is well known, and has culminated in the acquisition of a lease of the house and grounds by Oxford Brookes University in 1993.

Among the senior brewery staff, the retirement in 1962 of Morrells' first, long-serving company secretary, John Mundy, vacated his place for Charles Smith, one of the new generation of senior brewery employees who were eventually invited to sit on the Board. The son of the licensee of the Cape of Good Hope pub, at the junction of the Cowley and Iffley Roads with the Plain, he had first gone to work at the brewery as a clerk in 1936, and was not the only child of a Morrells' tenant to find employment in the brewery offices, where he remained until his retirement in 1981. After his return from the war he was considered too junior to be provided with a company car (only three members of the brewery establishment, the two Morrells, as managing director and assistant managing director, and their surveyor were awarded cars); but, having a car of his own, he was entrusted with the job of collecting the takings from Morrells' tied houses, which had until then been carried out more erratically by the returning draymen. From his earlier, pre-war years in the brewery office, he remembered how, before the Second World War, the draymen and labourers had been partly paid in beer tokens by the day – three lead tokens entitling them to three pints of ordinary fourpenny ale, or two brass ones to two pints of Morrell's best bitter.[10]

Louis Gunter, Charles's almost exact contemporary at Morrells (and, like him, a Board member from April 1976 until March 1987), was, like Charles, an immediate precursor of the generation that learnt to adapt itself to computerization in manufacturing and office work. Both, however, had organizational skills that were much in demand as the brewery's output increased and its paperwork became more complicated. Louis' judiciousness and adaptability as a brewer, especially in his acceptance of the new, high-powered technology of the 1960s and 1970s, combined well with the new spirit of competitiveness and determined survival at Morrells, as, all round the country, small local breweries supplying a few dozen pubs and off-licences with their own recognizably individual beer

J.H. Morrell with his wife and granddaughter, The Rise, 1963

were swallowed up and shut down by the larger, national companies.

On Jimmy's retirement as managing director, Colonel Morrell had succeeded him. The private, limited share-ownership of the Company still made forced take-over bids impossible, or at least unlikely; but various overtures were made from other, predatory brewing firms unsure of the younger generation of Morrells' determination to carry on as a family firm. To help him in the day-to-day business of running the company, Colonel Morrell appointed a new employee from outside the brewery, Miles Eastwood, a member of the family with a controlling interest in the Matthew Brown Brewery in Blackburn, as assistant to the managing director. Eastwood did not become a Board member; his successor, Tony Worth, who joined the firm in 1968 and was promoted to assistant managing director in 1970, broke ground for Morrells' senior employees in being the first of them to be invited to sit on the Board.

Jimmy died on 17 July 1965, a few weeks before his eighty-third birthday. The *Oxford Times* tribute to him, headed 'Served County in Many Spheres', emphasized the many public offices that he had held, while playing down the earlier University connections, which, it seemed, many people in Oxford had by then forgotten.[11] Within a few years a developer had purchased and demolished The Rise, replacing it with a block of luxury flats overlooking South Park, and breaking the last of the 150-year-old links that bound the Morrell family to Headington Hill.

CHAPTER ELEVEN

MORRELLS BREWERY LIMITED, 1965–93

After his father's death Colonel Bill Morrell, already managing director, inherited the position of chairman of Morrells Brewery Ltd, which he held until 1991 when ill-health forced his retirement and he became non-executive president of the brewery company. Like the first James Morrell, his great-grandfather, Jimmy had lived to the age of eighty-two, handing over the business to his son to manage a few years before his death. Like the second James, his own great-grandfather, Colonel Bill was devoted to hunting, and for many years combined his duties at the brewery with membership of the committee of the Heythrop Hunt, taking Mondays off work for hunting until well into his seventies. Here, however, the parallels between the mid-nineteenth and the late twentieth century cease. The younger James Morrell, the builder of Headington Hill Hall, had appointed a brewery manager in 1857 for the obvious purpose of releasing himself from all immediate responsibility for the brewing business or his farms. Colonel Bill actively directed the work of the brewery for twenty-six years before retiring as managing director in 1986, from the vantage point of his large, first-floor office with its bay window overlooking the tun room and the yard gates, and continued working there until he ceased to be chairman five years later. Although absent on Mondays in the hunting season, he could be found in his office on most Saturdays, reading through the week's entries in the current letter-book, one of a succession of several hundred dating from the 1870s, in which is to be found a copy of every letter sent out from the brewery. This, together with the Friday cheque-signing routine when he inspected every invoice, gave the Colonel a clear view of the day-to-day activities of the business.

During the mid- to late 1960s, expansion and modernization were in the ascendant in brewing as in most other branches of industry and of public and institutional life. This was the period during which the building trade seemed to be engaged in turning most of urban Britain into a mass of pre-stressed concrete, plastic, ceramic tile and glass. Happily most breweries (unless declared redundant after take-over) escaped being torn down for rebuilding or other reasons. More often it was their pubs

The Jolly Bargeman, Speedwell Street, St Ebbe's, Oxford, showing late 1960s demolition

that suffered, either through rebuilding in garish colours and undignified shapes or through being isolated, sometimes as the only surviving building at the corner of a demolished terrace or street.

In the centre of Oxford the number of freehold and leasehold pubs belonging to Morrells continued to diminish, while many of the surviving ones were refurbished and made more attractive, in particular as places in which to find good lunchtime food. The Old Tom in St Aldate's, the Grapes in George Street and the Queen's Arms in Park End Street are all examples of older Morrells' pubs in or near the city centre which have gained new reputations in the past twenty years. Before the Second World War urban redevelopment and the activities of the licensing justices had caused the disappearance of a number of older city centre pubs, among them the Air Balloon in Queen Street (demolished in 1937), the Blue Pig at Gloucester Green, and the (Jolly) Post Boy(s) in High Street, whose name was transferred to a new pub in outer-suburban Florence Park. Later, in the major upheaval of the late 1960s and early 1970s which accompanied the building of the Westgate Centre and the demolition of much of St Ebbe's, Morrells lost the Paradise House on the corner of Paradise Street and Castle Street, a property formerly leased from the City, and a number of small neighbourhood pubs and beerhouses in St Ebbe's. The Anchor, New Road, one of Sir Richard Tawney's original

The Paradise House, Castle Street, Oxford, 1968

The opening ceremony at the Pennyfarthing, Westgate Centre, Oxford, 1974

freehold acquisitions of 1779, was rebuilt as the Westgate in 1982, the year of the brewery's 'Bodleian Bicentenary' (see Appendix 1). Eight years earlier the Pennyfarthing, a completely new Morrells' pub held on a lease from the City, had been opened as a finishing touch to the Westgate Centre, almost on the site of the Victorian St Ebbe's Brewery in the former Church Street (now a traffic-free area between St Ebbe's church and the back entrance to Lewis's department store in Bonn Square).

In the country the brewery lost a handful of pubs to the increasingly prosperous free trade. These included two of Sir Richard Tawney's freehold acquisitions, the Red Lion at Tetsworth and the White Hart at Benson. (Tawney's other two country pubs, the Red Lion at Eynsham and the King and Queen at Wheatley, have remained tied to the brewery after more than 200 years.) Many of the country pubs lost were at some distance from Oxford, among them the Red Lion at Tetsworth, the Swan at Streatley, the Beetle and Wedge at Moulsford, and others at Stokenchurch and Watlington. Morrells' sphere of influence, however, remains as far-flung as in the days of the late Victorian Trustees, for the brewery still possesses three tied houses at or near Swindon, three at Banbury, one at Goring-on-Thames, and three in Buckinghamshire (the Plough at

The Grapes, George Street, Oxford, with tenants, 20 June 1969

The Fountain, Cardigan Street, Jericho, Oxford, with tenants, 1975. The tower in the background is that of St Barnabas's church, which features in Thomas Hardy's *Jude the Obscure*

Marsh Gibbon, the Royal Oak at Kingshill and the Carpenters Arms at Marlow). Most rural houses occupy traditional, older buildings – some unassuming; but some, like the Plough at Marsh Gibbon with its deep tiled roofs, or the stone-built, E-shaped, sixteenth- or seventeenth-century Bear and Ragged Staff at Cumnor, of historic interest and beauty. Modern pubs, dating from the 1960s or 1970s, include the Rowing Machine at Witney and the White Horse at Bicester.

By the early 1970s many of Morrells' city centre pubs were in need of repair and improvements. The growing general demand for good lunchtime food as an adjunct to, or substitute for, beer in pubs opened up the possibility that city centre pubs in prime sites might be completely refurbished and provided with full and varied lunchtime menus. Morrells' contract with Buccaneer Inns, an independent company (acquired in 1990 by Whitbread and renamed Cherwell Inns), granted Buccaneer the option to take out leases on twenty of its pubs to develop their potential as eating places and to modernize them generally. Sixteen Morrells' pubs, mainly in Oxford city, joined the Buccaneer franchise, but all remained the property of the brewery and continued to be tied to it for the sale of beer, wines and spirits.

* * *

While pressed for space in its St Thomas's Street premises, Morrells has been spared the compulsion to move which (for example) prompted Hall's Brewery to give up its Swan's Nest site off Paradise Street and transfer the brewing operation to Hanley's City Brewery after taking this over in 1898. Instead Louis Gunter, as head brewer from 1959, devoted much of his energies to carrying out brewhouse improvements in order to use the limited space to its best advantage. Between 1966 and 1976 the brewery received a thorough, if piecemeal, renewal and modernization of its brewing and fermenting equipment. Ten years later, in 1986–7, after the Company had acquired a licence to brew Harp Extra, it underwent the installation of a new, dual-purpose, computer-controlled brewing system capable of producing both ale and lager. Although outwardly late Victorian in its most prominent buildings, the brewery now houses the latest technology in a vertically and horizontally expanded brewhouse encompassing the former bottling hall, which was closed down in 1985.

From the balcony of the sample room, built out over the Back Stream between the rear of the tun room and the side of the Marlborough Arms in 1983, the view of a large bricked-up opening in the back wall of the brewhouse commemorates one of the more dramatic moving operations in the brewery's history. After years of coal firing had burnt a hole in the older copper, Louis Gunter found a second-hand, 6,660-gallon boiling copper for sale by a firm of whisky distillers in Scotland. At the same time one of the steam boilers had to be scrapped, enabling the brewery to acquire the most modern type of coal-fired boiler (GWB Vekos) with a pneumatic stoking system and a much greater steam-raising capacity than the earlier boiler. More steam meant that the replacement copper could be heated indirectly by steam from a remote boiler, fed into heating coils through steam mains. A firm of engineers was engaged to transport the new copper down to Oxford and to provide the necessary steam heating coils. Like other items installed at the brewery since then, this copper was too big to bring in through the main gates or lift into the brewhouse through any existing opening, even in the three separate sections in which it arrived ready for assembly inside the building. Part of the back wall was therefore demolished so that the sections of copper could be lifted in through the breach by crane from a punt on the Back Stream. The punt itself, a venerable piece of brewery property, was brought from Donnington Bridge, just south of Oxford, to St Thomas's by motor lorry, and launched on the Back Stream near the Swan's Nest, where the sections of copper were loaded on to it one by one. Purpose-built for the Isis public house at Iffley Lock, which has no immediate road access, the punt had been used by two generations of the Rose family, the father and the grandfather of the present licensee, to collect the deliveries of beer deposited by brewery lorries on the far side of the river below Iffley

The Prince of Wales, Walton Street, Oxford, with tenant, 1974

The Plough, Wolvercote Green, 1969, before Dutch Elm disease and the removal of the pub's picket fence

The Isis Tavern, Iffley Lock. This pub is reached only by river or towpath from Oxford

The Isis Tavern: bringing back the beer

village, close to the weir. Not long afterwards the punt was superannuated and replaced by a handcart, which in turn gave way in the late 1980s to an electric handcart, previously used as a milk-float, for the carriage of supplies along the towpath between the bridge and the pub.

The new Vekos boiler went into operation in October 1966, shortly before the first brew in the newly installed copper on 2 November. This was such a success that in 1967 the smaller copper was also converted to steam using second-hand coils and a calorifier acquired from the recently closed Starkey, Knight and Ford Brewery in Bridgwater. Energy-efficient brewing became a major theme in the modernization of the brewery, and long before any serious debate about the Greenhouse Effect (but spurred on by occasional complaints to the local authorities about emissions from the brewery chimney), Louis was examining ways of reducing the amount of coal burnt. The boiling time for wort in the copper was reduced to an hour (a third of its pre-war length); steam condensate from the brewhouse and bottle store was recovered and returned to the boiler feed-tank. A heat exchanger was introduced for wort-cooling, using the energy saved to heat the mashing liquor for the following brew. Some heat from the effluent was also recovered to help with economy in cask-washing. This work was summarized by Louis Gunter in a paper entitled 'Energy Saving in the Brewhouse', which he presented to the Brewing Energy Conference in 1979.

It was in the interests of conserving space, rather than improving energy efficiency, that the early nineteenth-century steam engines which had powered much of the lifting equipment in the brewhouse were banished to make way for electric motors. Louis' month-by-month brewhouse record states that on 5 March 1964 the steam engines were used for the last time, and that four years later, in March 1968, the beam engine was removed to the Leicester City Museum (at Coalville), where it functions as a working exhibit.[1] The table engine was donated to a Birmingham museum. Ironically, since that time several breweries have begun to make a feature of old-fashioned equipment. The Hook Norton Brewery, for example, proudly retains its Victorian steam engines in daily use, while the Tolly Cobbold Brewery at Ipswich exhibits one of two even older brewing vessels. The idea of a 'living museum' was less attractive to many 1960s industrialists than it subsequently became, otherwise the engines might still remain in place and be a focus of interest to visitors to the brewery.

A constant problem existed in connection with maintaining the cleanliness of the old copper fermenting vessels and the yeast skimming plant, which dated from the building of the tun room in 1896. Louis Gunter explains:

After each brew the vessels and internal cooling pipes were cleaned by men with scrubbing brushes and pumice powder. So vigorous were they over the years that the metal became paper thin, particularly at the yeast line. Replacement of the vessels was essential, and thinking and planning for the future was urgent. Meanwhile in-place cleaning methods were devised whereby caustic detergent was forcefully sprayed over the vessel surfaces and then rinsed thoroughly with clean water.

At about this time in the mid-'60s our big brothers at Whitbreads and Watneys discovered mutants or variants of British ale yeast which after fermentation would settle out at the bottom of the fermenter like lager yeast rather than come to the top for skimming – the traditional British way. The brewery achieved a break-through in 1969 when it acquired two eighty-barrel conical-bottomed Nathan fermenters – rather like large laboratory test-tubes with cooling panels welded on the outside, which Whitbread had used before building their new Luton brewery. Here was a most hygienic vessel, in stainless steel, ideal for in-place cleaning – about 6 ft in diameter and approximately 18 ft deep. One spray-ball fitted at the top ensured that all the internal surface was covered with detergent and then rinsed. Moreover the conical bottom ensured good drainage – a very important factor. Morrells had always used the 'dropping' system, which is a way of cleansing the fermenting wort of sedimentary matter which forms in the early phase of fermentation. Cooled wort pitched with yeast was collected in an open square and sixteen hours later dropped into a fermenter leaving the sediment behind. The 'dropping' system was continued with the Nathans and by good fortune a yeast was acquired which would settle at the bottom of a Nathan but would come to the top of a relatively shallow open skimming vessel. The new system of collecting yeast from the bottom of a conical vessel was greatly favoured. It was simple, most hygienic and labour saving. Yeast could be collected for immediate pitching into a subsequent brew or collected and stored in the refrigerator.

So successful was this method that, in January 1971, the four fermenting vessels that had been in use since 1896 were scrapped and the fermenting room gutted, before a new top storey was added to this early nineteenth-century part of the building at right angles to the tun room. Meanwhile, in March 1971, three further conical fermenters, each weighing 3 tons and capable of holding 140 barrels of wort, were acquired for the brewery and lowered one weekend by mobile crane through the fermenting room roof. Three further conical vessels have since joined them, and remain in constant use as part of Louis' legacy to the brewery.

The third, if less dramatic, innovation introduced during Louis' twenty-four years as head brewer was the use of powdered, and later pelletized, hops in brewing. Quite by chance the discharge pipe from the copper boiling vessels fed into the hopback at a tangent, causing a natural swirling of the wort. In 1971 Kurt Rosenfeld of Hop Developments Ltd noticed this while visiting the brewery and urged Louis to make use of it as the ideal system for trying out powdered hops, a new development that reduced storage problems associated with hops in their natural state. Not only were powdered hops less bulky than the 'pockets' (sacks) of untreated hops, but they could also be stored unchilled, since they were vacuum packed and did not need atmospheric protection. The main problem associated with the powder was that, in normal conditions, it inhibited the separation of the 'trub' (malt protein and hop residue) from the wort. Kurt Rosenfeld believed that the whirlpool effect caused by the tangential feed to the hopback would cause the trub to form a cone in the centre of the vessel, allowing clear wort to be run off from the outer edges. This idea proved successful when tried out at Morrells, and, unlike the system of dropping from open squares to conical fermenters, has now been adopted by many other breweries.

The range of beers brewed by Morrells had continued to expand during the 1950s and 1960s. Light and Brown (or Dark Mild) Ale, with original gravities of 1032° and 1033°, were now stronger than they had been during the years of austerity in the 1940s, and were available both as cask-conditioned (draught) beers and in bottle. The standard 'best bitter', which between the wars had been brewed to an original gravity of 1045°, was now back as a draught beer with an original gravity of 1036°. XXXX, the original of the popular Castle Ale, had reappeared in draught form as Varsity Bitter, with an original gravity of 1041°. In addition to Castle, winner of medals at the Brewing Exhibitions at Earls Court in 1968 and Birmingham in 1980, Morrells' bottled beers included malt stout, light and brown ale, and College Ale (also available as a winter-brewed draught beer) with the highest original gravity of all Morrells' beers at 1073°. Celebration, a strong pale ale with an original gravity of 1066°, was first produced as a bottled beer in 1973 to celebrate the wedding of Princess Anne (the Princess Royal) with Captain Mark Phillips, and continued, through popular demand, to be produced in cask and in bottle. For a time, in the 1970s and early 1980s, Morrells made a speciality of celebratory brews, such as the Royal Wedding Ale of 1981, costing the (then) unprecedented price of 60–65p. a half-pint, and the Ashmolean Tercentenary Ale of 1983. Like Celebration Ale, these brews shared a quality of alcoholic strength allied with a bright, rounded, nutty-tasting clarity.

While Morrells' superior cask-conditioned beers appealed to the growing band of those who looked for old-fashioned qualities in beer, there was also a new demand for kegged beers, carbonated in the barrel and therefore slightly gassier than ordinary cask-conditioned beer. Varsity Keg, the kegged version of Castle Ale, was first brewed on 23 August 1963, in time for the Beatle-dominated era of the 'swinging sixties'.[2] Pale Ale keg, a lighter alternative, was a gassier version of the ordinary Light Ale, with an original gravity of 1032°. By 1974 Morrells' sales of bought-in, kegged Harp Lager had grown to such an extent that it seemed viable to keg it at the brewery, together with Morrells' own two kegged beers. New kegging machines were installed in 1974 and 1976, and in late February 1977 the brewery commissioned a new layout for its kegging plant, followed by the installation of kegging conveyors six months later.[3] Production volumes increased by 40 per cent between 1970 and 1979, with the bottling hall busy packaging Morrells' beers and continuing its contract bottling for a number of national brewers, and the kegging plant working flat out to keep up with the demand for lagers. Harp now came in two strengths, Blue or Extra, with an original gravity of 1041° (the strength at which the lager had originally come on to the market), and Yellow or Standard, a new, milder version with an original gravity of 1032°.

Louis Gunter retired in 1983. His successor Michael Sullivan, who had brewed at the Phoenix Brewery and with Grand Metropolitan Brewers at Mortlake, was, significantly, experienced in lager brewing, while the second brewer David Polden, who had joined Morrells in 1976 from Gibbs Mew of Salisbury, was a qualified engineer with much kegging experience. These two worked together in the mid-1980s, in consultation with the Harp Lager Company, for the creation of the new, dual-purpose, high-technology brewing arrangements at Morrells for the alternate production of ale and lager.

In April 1982 Charles Eld, Colonel Bill Morrell's thirty-year-old nephew, had joined the brewery staff as assistant to the managing director. Like his uncle and grandfather, Charles combined military with scientific interests, and had gained an engineering degree in the course of twelve years' service with the Royal Artillery. At the end of 1983, when Tony Worth was taken ill, Charles became assistant managing director in his place; and when Tony Worth resumed his work, which included the computerization of the administrative side of the business, he did so as joint managing director with Colonel Morrell. Between 1986, when Colonel Morrell relinquished the management of the business, and his own retirement in 1988, Tony Worth was sole managing director, with a seat on the Board that he kept (as a non-executive director) until 1992. From his home near Oxford he still maintains a lively interest in the brewery and the improvements to its various tied houses.

In 1988 Charles Eld became managing director; and in 1991, when Colonel Morrell retired as chairman, he was succeeded by a colleague on the Board of the Aylesbury Brewery, Bill Leyland. The presidency and managing directorship of the company are therefore in the hands of family members, and the chairmanship in the hands of a non-family member, while the composition of the Board is divided fairly equally between members of the family and others. In 1985, to prevent any alienation of shares leading to a possible take-over bid, a new rule was written into the Company articles stating that if shares came on to the open market they could be purchased only by an existing owner of at least 1 per cent of the Company's assets. This effectively limited purchases of such shares to family members, or, failing them, to an employee benefit fund that was set up specifically for that purpose.

Despite the flourishing state of Morrells' bottling activities in the 1970s, the bottling equipment was rapidly becoming worn out or obsolete. Louis Gunter's notes record a succession of major overhauls to various items in November 1981 and February 1982: to the labelling machine, the filling and crowning machine, the pasteurizer, and a large compressor in the bottle store. To renew all these items together seemed too costly in view of the narrow profit margin attached both to contract bottling and to sales of Morrells' own bottled beers. Instead the board decided to close down the entire bottling operation, and in 1985 placed a contract with Morlands of Abingdon to bottle Morrells' beers.

With forecasts that lager would occupy over 50 per cent of the market for all beers by the end of the 1980s, Morrells' necessary strategy for survival now seemed clear. In the space left by the former bottling operation there would be room to expand the brewhouse to produce lager, despite the difficulties of doing so while ale was still being brewed on the site. After protracted negotiations, the Harp Company agreed to grant Morrells a licence to brew Harp Extra and to benefit from the profits of distributing it. Conversion of the brewhouse to dual-purpose use began soon after the bottling hall shut down in June 1985, and was carried out with advice and technical assistance from Harp and Guinness. (The Harp Lager Company had developed from a consortium of Guinness, Courage, and the Scottish and Newcastle Brewery.) David Polden, as engineering project manager, was responsible for installing the new brewing plant, while Michael Sullivan agreed specifications with Harp and, as head brewer, also looked after the continuing production of Morrells' beer.

Only three days' production of ale were lost before the first brews of ale and Harp Extra took place in the reconstructed brewhouse in June 1987. The large, second-hand copper installed in 1966 remained in place, but the mash tun installed when the tun room was built in 1901 was replaced by a new mash conversion vessel and lauter tun. The project, costing £4½m in all, included a new liquor treatment plant, new dual-purpose fermentation and maturation vessels, a new filtration room, and a two-lane automated kegging line. An investment of this magnitude clearly indicated the intention of the board and the family to continue brewing against all foreseeable odds.

Morrells' range of cask-conditioned, keg and bottled beers altered somewhat as a result of the changes in brewing and bottling procedure. Cask-conditioned beers no longer included Light Ale or Celebration Ale, since these could not be sold in adequate quantities as draught beers all the year round. Instead a new, super-premium bitter, Graduate Bitter, was introduced; while Dark Mild, which had previously had a low original gravity of 1033°, increased its strength to 1037°. The extra-strong College Ale was limited to production between November and January and made available only through selected outlets. Pale Ale Keg and Varsity Keg were discontinued in favour of a single Morrells' keg beer, Friars Bitter, named in allusion to Oxford's monastic past. Bottled beers of the special commemorative type also ended, as did bottled Malt Stout and Brown Ale. Morrells' present portfolio of beers is therefore as follows:

	OG	ABV
Draught		
Bitter	1036°	3.7%
Mild	1037°	3.7%
Varsity Bitter	1041°	4.3%
Graduate Bitter	1048°	5.2%
College Ale	1073°	7.5%
Keg		
Friars Bitter	1032°	3.3%
Bottled Beers		
Light Ale	1032°	3.3%
Castle Ale	1041°	4.5%
College Ale	1073°	7.5%

In 1989 Michael Sullivan left the brewery, and David Polden, after fourteen years as second brewer, took his place. During his period as head brewer the brewery's record has been exceptional, winning the Class 2 gold medal and being championship runner-up for draught lager, in competition with seventy-six other British and foreign brews, at the 1990 Brewing Industry Annual Awards at Stoke-on-Trent. Two years later Graduate Bitter won a class silver medal and Mild was adjudged Champion Mild at the same event.

The financial crisis which affected the whole of British industry from

1989 onwards did not leave the brewery completely untouched. Its difficulties, however, were the long-term ones suffered by other small breweries rather than the immediate consequences of inflation followed by slump. Despite the well-expressed appreciation of traditional, cask-conditioned beers by a small, discriminating section of the drinking population, beer sales as a whole have dropped or remained static as wine sales have risen. At a meeting attended by most of the 118 licensees of Morrells' pubs in early February 1990, Charles Eld pointed out that sales of Morrells' own beers through the tied estate had halved during the previous decade, and that, because of greater overheads resulting partly from pub improvements (on which the brewery had spent £870,000 the previous year), profits from that sector of the business had dropped by four-fifths during the period. Morrells had no intention of closing down or selling out, but its survival would depend on the sale of several pubs and an increase in rents to tenants, which would probably be passed on in the form of higher beer prices to customers. At the brewery the Company planned to begin producing Harp Lager in addition to the Harp Extra already brewed there. A new distribution warehouse was shortly to open at Osney Mead, under the direction of Bill Senior, the distribution director, to help increase the sales of beer and other drinks.[4]

Since that time the number of Morrell-owned public houses has begun once again to increase, rising from 127 in 1991 to 139 in late 1993. This has partly been due to the recommendation of the Monopolies and Mergers Commission that the large conglomerate brewing companies should be restrained from controlling the great majority of British pubs. Morrells have also ceased their involvement with managed houses (i.e. pubs that are tied to the brewery for the sale of beer and other drinks, but are leased out so that their management, and profits, are outside the brewery's control). The Board's intention in future is to keep its houses tenanted, on the pattern laid down by Sir Richard Tawney with his first handful of pubs over 200 years ago.

In 1993 Morrells Brewery has preserved the solidity of a family business and has helped to keep intact the character of an important part of historic, industrial Oxford. In a city with a shifting academic population and with relatively few long-standing commercial dynasties, the continuity between the eighteenth-century Tawneys and the present members of the Morrell family is remarkable in itself. The present managing director Charles Eld is one of the eighth generation in line of descent from the early eighteenth-century boatmaster and brewer Richard Tawney, whose great-granddaughter in the female line, Jane Wharton, married his younger son Edward's successor at the brewery, James Morrell. He is also one of the seventh generation in line of descent from Jeremiah Morrell, who practised brewing in his later years in Wallingford and left his brewing equipment to his son, the miller Mark. Down this line has perhaps descended that streak of obstinate self-determination which revealed itself in the character of James Morrell, the younger of the two brothers who took over Edward Tawney's brewery business. Without this spirit, especially as shown in the careers of Jimmy Morrell and his son, Colonel Bill Morrell, the business would almost certainly have disappeared at some time during the past fifty-five years. Instead it has half a century as a limited company to its credit, and the expertise and potential for many more years to come.

APPENDIX 1

'1782'

In October 1982 the Bodleian Library, Oxford, mounted an exhibition entitled 'Town and Gown', which included photographs of Morrells Brewery and one of its pubs. The exhibition catalogue states (p. 48) that the brewery was 'probably established in 1782'. On the basis of this statement, apparently confirmed in person by a member of the Library staff citing documentary evidence that seemed to bear out the suggestion, Morrells Brewery adopted 1782 as the year of its foundation.

As this study has shown, the brewery as a continuous business is in fact 250 rather than 210 years old, and may indeed date back to the early eighteenth century when Thomas and later William Kenton were brewing on the site. Richard Tawney, first named as a brewer in 1743 nearby in Fisher Row, took over the future Morrells Brewery site in 1745 from William Kenton's widow Hannah. No documentary evidence has survived to indicate that Richard took over Kenton's business in addition to his brewhouse, although he may well have inherited the goodwill of the Kenton brewery, which had been in existence for twenty to twenty-five years since about 1718. We do know, however, that Richard passed on his own business to his elder son, and that his younger son Edward transmitted it to the Morrell brothers in 1797–8, the transaction being completed with the legal transfer of the Tawney-owned freeholds to the Morrells after Edward Tawney's death in March 1800.

APPENDIX 2

PUBS LOST OR RENAMED

	Renamed	New Ownership?
CITY CENTRE		
Air Balloon, Queen Street		
Albion, Littlegate Street		
Anchor, Cornmarket Street		
Anchor, New Road	Westgate	No
(Old) Anchor, St Aldates		
Beerhouse, High Street		
Bell, Cornmarket Street		
Black Lion, Kybald Place (Grove Street)		
Black Swan, George Lane		
Blue Pig, Gloucester Street		
Boar's Head, Queen's Lane (Exchanged for Red Lion, High Street, *c.* 1800)		
Britannia, Church Street, St Ebbe's		
Carpenter's Arms, Thames Street		
City Arms, Radcliffe Square		
Coach and Horses, High Street		
Coach and Horses, King Street		
Crown, Cornmarket Street		
Currier's Arms, Queen Street		
Druid's Head, George Street		
Duke of York, Broad Street		
Friars, Friars' Entry		
George, Cornmarket Street		
Globe, Queen Street		
Great Western Hotel, Hythe Bridge Street		
Green Dragon, St Aldate's		
Horse and Groom, St Ebbe's		
King's Head, Holywell		
King's Head, St Martin's		
Lamb and Flag, St Thomas's Street		
Leden Porch Hall, Pembroke Street		
Nag's Head, Hythe Bridge Street	Antiquity Hall	Yes
Oddfellows' Arms, George Street		
Paradise House, Paradise Street	Oxford Alehouse	Yes
Parrot, St Ebbe's		
Paviour's Arms, Castle Street		
Peacock, St Thomas's Street		
(Jolly) Post Boy(s), High Street		
Punch Bowl, George Street		
Red Lion, High Street		

PUBS LOST OR RENAMED

	Renamed	New Ownership?
CITY CENTRE		
Robin Hood, Rewley Road/Hollybush Row	Part of Royal Oxford Hotel	Yes
Royal Blenheim, Little Clarendon Street		
Running Horses, Hythe Bridge Street		
Shoulder of Mutton, St Thomas's Street	Marlborough Arms	No
Three Crowns, St Thomas's Street		
Three Cups, Queen Street		
Three Horse Shoes, Castle Street		
Turk's Head, St Thomas's Street		
Vulcan, Friar's Entry		
Welsh Pony (Corn Exchange Hotel), Gloucester Green		Yes
(Old) Wheatsheaf, St Aldate's		
White Hart, Friar's Entry		
Windmill, Park End Street		
Windsor Castle, St Thomas's Street		
SUBURBS		
Abingdon Road		
Old White House	Folly Bridge Inn	Yes
Jericho		
Baker's Arms, Jericho		
Beerhouse, Albert Street		
Beerhouse, Cranham Street		
Bird in Hand, King Street		
Brown Jug, Great Clarendon Street		
Clarendon Arms, Walton Street		
Cottage of Content, Cardigan Street		
Duke of Wellington, Wellington Street		
Fountain, Cardigan Street		
Guardsman's Arms, Great Clarendon Street		
Jericho House, Walton Street	Jericho Tavern	Yes
Littlemore		
King of Prussia/Allied Arms, Rose Hill	Ox	No
Swan, Kennington Island		
Marston		
Victoria Arms		Yes
North Oxford		
Moulder's Arms, St Bernard's Road		
Navigation House, Heyfield's Hut [Hayfield Road]		
Waggon and Horses, Woodstock Road		
Osney		
Beerhouse, 44 Bridge Street		
SUBURBS		
Beerhouse, West Street		
Holly Bush, Osney		Yes

	Renamed	New Ownership?

SUBURBS
White Horse, 26 Bridge Street

South Hinksey
Cross Keys

St Clements/Cowley Road
Beerhouse, Bath Street
Beerhouse (off-licence), Penson's Gardens
Beerhouse (off-licence), Princes Street
Bird in Hand, Cross Street/Princes Street
Black Horse, St Clements Street — Yes
Bullingdon Arms, Cowley Road — Yes
Burton Junction, James Street
Carpenters Arms, New Street
Fir Tree, St Clements Street
New Inn, Cowley Road — Yes
Prince of Wales, St Clements Street
Sovereign, George (now Cave) Street

St Ebbes
Ancient Briton, Blackfriars Road
Beerhouse, 6–7 Charles Street
Duke of York, New Street
Game Cock, Blackfriars Road
Hop Pole, Friars Street
Jolly Bargeman, Speedwell Street
Malt Shovel, Friars Street
Mason's Arms, Blackfriars Road
Nags Head, Bridport Street
Norfolk Arms, Norfolk Street
Prince of Wales, Paradise Square
Queen's Arms, Gas Street
Saddlers Arms, Speedwell Street

Summertown
Beerhouse
Wheatsheaf

Temple Cowley
Swan

COUNTRY
Abingdon
Britannia

Appleton
Horse Shoes

Ardington
Boar's Head

Astall Leigh
Crown — — Yes

PUBS LOST OR RENAMED

	Renamed	New Ownership?
COUNTRY		
Bampton Eagle		
Banbury King's Arms		
Basildon Crown		
Beckley Abingdon Arms		
Benson White Hart		Yes
Besselsleigh Greyhound		Yes
Bicester Crown		
Bloxham Railway Tavern		
Chalgrove White Hart		
Charlbury Royal Oak		
Cuddesdon Bat and Ball		Yes
Culham Jolly Porter Nag's Head Railway Hotel Sow and Pigs	Lion	No
Cumnor Weirs		
Curbridge Herd of Swine		
Denchworth Star		
Eynsham Britannia, Barnard Gate Queen's Head		Yes
Faringdon Duke of York White Hart		

153

	Renamed	New Ownership?
COUNTRY		
Fyfield		
White Hart		Yes
Great Milton		
Beerhouse		
Red Lion		
Harwell		
Crown	(Nursing Home)	Yes
Hempton, Nr Chinnor		
Eagle		
Hethe		
Beerhouse		
Horspath		
Chequers		Yes
Kidlington		
Six Bells		Yes
Kirtlington		
Dashwood Arms		Yes
Little Milton		
Three Horseshoes		
Longworth		
Royal Oak		
Moulsford		
Beetle and Wedge		Yes
Murcot		
Red Lion		
Shillingford		
Blue Bell		
Stadhampton		
Bear and Ragged Staff, Brookhampton		Yes
Stanton Harcourt		
Harcourt Arms		Yes
Stokenchurch		
Black Horse		
Streatley		
Sun		
Swindon		
Beerhouse		
Volunteer Hotel		
Sydenham		
Sun		

PUBS LOST OR RENAMED

	Renamed	New Ownership?
COUNTRY		
Tackley		
Sturdy's Castle		Yes
Tetsworth		
Red Lion		Yes
Thame		
Plough		
Wallingford		
Cross Keys		Yes
Oxford House		
Watlington		
Black Lion		
Hare and Hounds		
Wheatley		
Chequers		
Woodstock		
Bear Tap		Yes
Crown		Yes
Dog and Duck		
King's Head		Yes
Prince of Wales		

APPENDIX 3

PUBS LOST, c. 1880–90

(Undated List, Archives of Morrells Ltd, P.D6)

Name of House	Where Situate	
Bell	Cornmarket Street, Oxford	Purchased by Hanley Bros, Oxford
Bookbinder's Arms	Jericho	"
Baker's Arms	Jericho	"
Guardsman's Arms	Great Clarendon Street	"
Beerhouse (Clapton)	St Ebbe's	" (now City Brewery Tap)
Chequers	Horspath, Oxon.	"
Abingdon Arms	Beckley	"
Bullingdon Arms	Cowley	"
Beerhouse (Tyler)	Great Milton	"
Bat & Ball	Cuddesdon	"
King's Head	Woodstock	Leased by the Duke of Marlborough to Hanley Bros, Oxford
Navigation House	Heyfield's Hut	Free House supplied by Hanley Bros
Crown	Woodstock	Purchased by Simmonds & Sons, Reading
Duke of Wellington	Wellington Street, Oxford	"
Beerhouse (Jessop)	Cranham Street,	"
Masons Arms	Blackfriars Rd	Leased to Simmonds & Sons
Off licensed Beerhouse	Princes Street	"
Curriers Arms	Queen Street	"
Beerhouse (Smith)	West Street, Osney	"
" (Pigott)	Summertown, Oxford	"
Oddfellows Arms	George Street,	Leased to Phillips & Sons, Oxford
George Hotel	Cornmarket Street	" by Tender
Three Horse Shoes	Castle Street	" by Auction
Holly Bush	Osney	Purchased by Clinch & Co., Witney
Horse Shoes	Appleton, Berks.	"
Peacock	St Thomas's, Oxford	Purchased by Hall & Co., Oxford
Albion	Littlegate	"
White Hart	Friars Entry	Leased to "
Bear Tap	Woodstock, Oxon.	"
Swan	Kennington Island	Leased to Morland, Abingdon
Six Bells	Kidlington	Purchased by Mrs Shepherd, Kidlington
Britannia	Church Street,	Purchased by Weaving & Co.,
St Ebbes, Oxford	Oxford	

PUBS LOST, C. 1880-90

Name of House	Where Situate	
Norfolk Arms	Norfolk Street	Purchased by Saxby & Co., Abingdon
Royal Oak	Wantage, Berks.	Purchased by North Wilts Brewery Co., Swindon
Star	Denchworth,	Sold
Royal Oak	Charlbury, Oxon.	Sold. Converted into coffee tavern Licence dropped.
Beerhouse (Corp)	High Street, Oxford	Licence dropped by owner (premises converted into shops)
" (Perry)	Albert Street,	"
Royal Oak	Stow Wood, Oxon.	"
Beerhouse Off Licence	Pensons Gardens, Oxford	"
Boars Head	Ardington, Oxon.	Free House. Ceased dealing
Dashwood Arms	Kirtlington	Free House. Supplied by Brackley Brewery
George and Dragon	"	"
Burton Junction	James Street, Oxford	"
New Inn	Cowley Rd, Oxford	Free House. Ceased dealing on account of not being allowed 15 per cent
Cross Keys	Wallingford, Berks.	Short lease offered but declined on account of Lessees having to rebuild
Red Lion	Murcot, Oxon.	Short lease offered but declined, property being in very bad state of repair. Lessor requiring it to be put and kept in substantial repair
Coach & Horses	King Street, Oxford	Lease surrendered to University of Oxford Property pulled down
Black Swan	George Street	Property pulled down for City Improvements. Licence transferred to Crown Street
City Arms	Radcliffe Square	Lease Expired. Pulled down
Weirs	Cumnor, Berks.	Property of Earl of Abingdon. Pulled down being unsafe. Licence not removed

NOTES

Abbreviations.
OC2: Rev. H.E. Salter MA, *Cartulary of Oseney Abbey*, Volume II (Oxford Historical Society, XC, 1929)
AMB: Archives, Morrells Brewery, Oxford
OA: Oxfordshire Archives, County Hall, Oxford
PCC: Prerogative Court of Canterbury
PRO: Public Record Office, London

Introduction
1. OC2 523–4.
2. OC2 503.
3. Notably by T.E. Lawrence, who grew up in Oxford before the First World War and attended the Oxford Boys' High School and Jesus College; also, in the 1950s, by the author's husband.
4. OC2 378–80.
5. OA, Misc. Som. I/1.
6. *Victoria History of the County of Oxford*, IV (1979), 308.
7. Vivian H.H. Green, *The Commonwealth of Lincoln College, 1427–1977* (1979), 231n. James Bond and John Rhodes, *The Oxfordshire Brewer* (Oxfordshire Museum Services, 1985), 36.
8. *Aubrey's Brief Lives*, edited by Oliver Lawson Dick (Penguin edition, 1978), 343–4.
9.
10. See *Register of . . . Exeter College, Oxford, with a History of the College and Illustrative Documents* by the Rev. Charles William Boase MA (Oxford Historical Society, XXVII, 1894), clviii.
11. Peter Mathias, *The Brewing Industry in England, 1700–1830* (Cambridge, 1959), 343. AMB, P.A3/51.
12. Rev. H.E. Salter MA, *Oxford City Properties*, (1926), 258–9.
13. OC2, 402–4.
14. OC2, 523–4. For Cope, admitted a City freeman in 1647, see *Oxford Council Acts, 1626–1665*, edited by M.G. Hobson MA and the Rev. H.E. Salter MA (1933), 143.
15. Christ Church Archives, MS.1.C.2 (J. Willis, 'Book of Evidences'), 32.
16. OC2, 381.
17. OC2, 538.
18. OC2, 503.
19. Rev. H.E. Salter MA, *Oxford City Properties* (1926), 196–7.
20. *Oxford Council Acts, 1626–1665*, edited by M.G. Hobson MA and the Rev. H.E. Salter MA (1933), 73.
21. AMB, D.B1 (Deed of Sale of Chattels of Elizabeth Tawney, 24 October 1691).
22. OC2 499, 507.
23. Bodleian Library, Oxford, MS. Top. Oxon. d.247, fo.621. For a list of Sir Richard's expenses paid to the Royal Household on receiving his knighthood, see AMB D.A2.
24. AMB, F.1 and P.A.4, 51.
25. Oxford University Archives, LA 39/2 (Tidmarsh Lane). Christ Church Archives, 'Calendar of Estate Papers Oxon. 8', 90–101.
26. Rev. H.E. Salter MA, *Oxford City Properties* (1926), 200.

NOTES

27. OC2 381, 499–501.
28. See note 26.
29. Copy of will of Edward Tawney, 21 January 1800, AMB, D.A2.
30. Deed of transfer of property, Tawney's executors to Mark and James Morrell, 23 August 1800, AMB P.A.4, 51, and copy in OA, *Blake* XV/i/5.
31. See note 30 and *Jackson's Oxford Journal*, 22 December 1798.
32. AMB, D.D3.

Chapter One
1. Will, PCC, PRO, Prob/11 922.
2. Will, PCC, PRO, Prob/11 1162. AMB, A.3. (personal papers of Mark Morrell).
3. Bodleian Library, Oxford, MS.Top.Berks.b.10, p. 47, 'The Case of Mr Morrell ye now Ten[an]t of Wallingford Milles'.
4. Surrey Record Office, Guildford Muniment Room, 100/5 (31 October 1726), 100/8 (18/19 October 1728), and Records of St Nicholas's parish, Guildford (Burials).
5. J.K. Hedges, *The History of Wallingford*, II (1881), 246.
6. PRO, PCC, Administrations, 1733.
7. Copy, AMB, D.A1.
8. Berkshire Record Office, AC 1/1/3 (Wallingford Corporation Minutes, 1765–), 1 ff. J.K. Hedges, *The History of Wallingford*, II (1881), 246.
9. OA, Morrell V/s/4a (James Morrell to Mr Plumer, 21 August 1757). *Oxford Council Acts, 1752–1801*, edited by M.G. Hobson (Oxford Historical Society, New Series, XV, 1962), 40. *Jackson's Oxford Journal*, 5 December 1767.
10. Morrell, Peel and Gamlen, Oxford, Cash Book of James Morrell and Thomas Walker, 1763–6. Balliol College, Oxford, Deeds of 1 St Giles: Assignment of lease of the White Hart, Thomas Stevens to James Morrell, 10 October 1766. See also Lincoln College Archives, L/OMM/44, 45, 49 (Lincoln College to James Morrell, 14 December 1774, 19 December 1788 and 16 December 1802).
11. See Bodleian Library, MS. Autograph d. 9, Blackstone to James Morrell, 20 January 1769, and William Craven to James Morrell, 26 February 1768. AMB, A.1 (Diary of Robert Morrell).
12. Wills of William Willmott, 1691/92, PCC, PRO, Prob/11 408; George Deacon, 1775, PCC, PRO, Prob/11 1026; and Robert Baker, 1810, PCC, PRO, Prob/11 1539.
13. *Universal British Directory, 1790–1798* (Berkshire, Wallingford).
14. AMB A.1.
15. AMB A.3.
16. AMB A.1. Will of Mark Morrell, PCC, PRO, Prob/11 1162.
17. AMB A.1.

Chapter Two
1. Barclays Bank Archives, Ledgers of Parsons, Thomson & Co. (earlier Fletcher, Parsons), Old Bank, Oxford, 1792–.
2. Lincoln College Archives, Z/OMM/1, valuation of 1829.
3. Rev. H.E. Salter MA, *Oxford City Properties* (1926), 258–9. Balliol College Archive, Deeds of 1 St Giles: Memorandum of Agreement between James Morrell and Rev. John Price, 2 May 1803; Assignment of leasehold by Mrs and the Misses Morrell to Baker Morrell, 27 September 1813.
4. *Jackson's Oxford Journal*, 22 September 1798.
5. Christ Church Archives, St Thomas's Box VIII (Church House), *passim*; St Thomas's Box VII, lease to Edward Tawney of the 5th and 6th tenements in Fisher Row, with plan, 12 February 1772.
6. OA, St Thomas's parish, Oxford, Rate Book, 1812–35. Christ Church Archives, MS. Estates 78, 20.
7. OC2, 604 (plan).
8. OC2, 524.
9. Barclays Bank Archives, Fletcher, Parsons, Ledger B, 382–3, 346. AMB, B.A2 (bank

pass-book of Mark and James Morrell, 1797–1811).
10. See note 9 (also Ledger C, 174–5, 267, 445; Ledger D, 100).
11. See note 9: also AMB, B.A3 (bank pass-book, 1811–18).
12. The Wintles are a difficult family to disentangle. Robert (1773–1848), appears to have been the son of the Rev. Robert Wintle of Brightwell (i.e. either Brightwell Baldwin or Brightwell-cum-Sotwell, both near Wallingford). Thomas, according to the *St John's College Register*, was the son of the Rev. Thomas Wintle, vicar of the Morrells' home parish of St Peter's, Wallingford. Robert Baker, in his will of 1810 (PRO, PCC Prob 11/1539), left £5,000 each to his nephews Deacon Morrell and the Rev. Thomas Wintle, fellow of St John's College, with interest payable to the Rev. Robert Wintle, Rector of Compton Beauchamp, Berks. In addition he left £100 to Mrs Wintle, wife of the Rev. Robert Wintle senior, Rector of Brightwell. His uncle, George Deacon, in his will of 1775 (PRO, PCC Prob 11/1026), had left £50 to the same Mary Wintle, wife of the Rev. Robert Wintle of Brightwell. The younger Robert's diary for 1806 (in the possession of Mr and Mrs McLaren, Baker's Dozen, North End, Steeple Claydon, Bucks) records his life as a curate at Acton, since the living at Culham, to which he had been presented in 1797, had been temporarily bestowed on the Rev. Henry Wintle, who remained there with his wife and family until the mid-1820s. (In the diary, Robert also refers to the installation of a substitute vicar at Compton.) Evidently a widower, he refers to visits to the Oxford Morrells and to his only child Mary Ann, who must have been brought up by her maternal grandmother and aunts before marrying, at Culham, the Rev. Ashurst Turner Gilbert (who later changed his surname to Wintle to enable him to inherit her family estates). Robert's late wife's father appears as 'Mr Morrell', not 'Uncle James', but he writes familiarly of 'Tom' and 'Deacon' (often together) as if of cousins and close friends.
13. St John's College Archives, Ledger 5, 40, 16 December 1799. Magdalen College Archives, Libri Computi 1802, no. 2.
14. AMB, P.A4, 51 (release of property, Tawney's executors to Mark and James Morrell, 23 August 1800); F.1, 24 *verso*, no. 68 (notebook listing deeds). OC2, 88, 504; Rev. H.E. Salter MA, *Oxford City Properties* (1926), 77, 184, 237; *Oxford Council Acts, 1752–1801*, edited by M.G. Hobson (Oxford Historical Society, New Series, XV, 1962), 266.
15. AMB, P.A14.
16. AMB. F.1.
17. Christ Church Archives, MS. Estates 78, 18, 22; AMB, B.A2; OA, St Thomas's parish, Oxford, Rate Book, 1812–35.
18. *Oxford Council Acts, 1752–1801*, edited by M.G. Hobson (Oxford Historical Society, New Series, XV, 1962), 271, 278–9.
19. Barclays Bank Archives, Fletcher, Parsons (Parsons, Thomson & Co.) Ledger A, 187–9, 198, 219. Bodleian Library, G.A.Oxon.a.101, 2 and G.A. Oxon. 8° 900, no. 25 (rules of the Unanimous and Useful Societies, 1770, 1814). For a scathing view of the general usefulness of such societies, see Brian Harrison, *Drink and the Victorians* (1971).
20. AMB, A.2 (copy of Robert Morrell to Peter Green, 1808).
21. Barclays Bank Archives, Fletcher, Parsons (Parsons, Thomson & Co.), Ledger C, 9 verso–10 recto. AMB, D.A3 (copy, will of Ann Wharton, 1802); D.B3 (marriage settlement, James Morrell and Jane Wharton, 16 December 1807).
22. See Note 20 and AMB A.3 (dissolution of partnership, Baker and Robert Morrell), A.2 (Robert Morrell, fire insurance and other papers).
23. OA, Morrell VII/a/28.
24. AMB F.1, p. 28, no. 77 (note of deed of sale).

Chapter Three
1. For Malchair's Headington Hill drawings, most of which are precisely dated, see Bodleian Library, MS.Top.Oxon.c.475 and Corpus Christi College, Oxford,

NOTES

   Malchair Vol. I, 14; Vol. V, 9; Vol. VII, 11–12.
2. AMB, D.E1 ('Abstract of the Title to a Freehold Estate situate on Headington Hill in the County of Oxford', 1875).
3. OA, MS.Diocesan Papers d.562, Clergy Answers, St Clement's parish, Oxford.
4. See note 2.
5. AMB, 'A Survey and Plan of Bowl Shipton Farm belonging to Wm Smith Esq. in the Parish of St Clement's in the County of Oxford Survey'd by Jno Baker 1788' (traced copy). See also Malchair's drawing, dated 11 July 1774, of 'Dr Kay's Plantation Near Cabage Hall Heddington Hill' (Corpus Christi College, Malchair VII, 12), and *Oxford . . . Survey'd by I. Taylor in 1750 and Engrav'd by G. Anderton, Publish'd by W. Jackson Printed in High Street Oxford, October 19 1751.*
6. *Remarks and Collections of Thomas Hearne*, Oxford Historical Society, VI (1902), 174. Bodleian Library, MS.Top.Oxon.d.284 (Harry Paintin, History of St Clement's Parish). OA, MS.dd.Par.Ox.St Clement's, d.24 (tithe dispute, 1839). AMB, F.1, p. 28, no. 77 (note of sale).
7. AMB F.1, unpaginated section headed 'Sundry Deeds'. For the Garbetts, see Howard Colvin, *A Biographical Dictionary of British Architects, 1600–1840* (1978), 330. A map of St Clement's in OA, MS.dd.Par.Ox.St Clement's, d.24, dated 1839, states that James Morrell's house had been built 'within twenty years' of that date.
8. OA, MS.dd.Par.Ox.St Thomas, c.22 (Rate Book, 1812–37).
9. See AMB, C.1 (diary of Charles Morrell) and B.A3, B.A4 (bank books).
10. AMB, A5, Examination of Elizabeth Price and James Watts, 24 August 1819, and paper endorsed and headed 'Case'.
11. AMB, C.1, B.A3–B.A5.
12. AMB, F.7a, E.B1. E.A3 (Brewery and Farm Accounts, 1857–1858) shows that at that date the brewery was still paying rent for Charles Morrell's malthouse at Wallingford.
13. AMB, B.A4.
14. AMB, A.4 (draft will of James Morrell, 1830) and F.5 (notes on Sandford Farm, with plans). OA, Misc. Mul. 2a and 2b.
15. *Victoria History of the County of Oxford*, edited by Mary Lobel, V (1957), 270.
16. AMB, F.5 (plans).
17. See note 15, 274.
18. Christ Church Archives, MS.Estates 78, 27 and Calendar of Estate Papers, Oxon, 90, 98, 101.
19. AMB, F.1, p. 9, no. 20. Alderman William Fletcher had been Mayor of Oxford in 1782, 1796 and 1809, and had been the senior partner, with John Parsons, in the mercers' business which developed into Fletcher, Parsons' Bank. By 1821 the St Thomas's parish rate books show the Morrells paying rates on land 'late Fletcher', which they continue to lease from his trustees until able to buy it.
20. AMB, F.1.
21. OA, MS.dd.Par.Ox.St Clement's, d.1/17–18.
22. AMB, F.1.
23. OA, MS. Diocesan Papers d. 581 (Clergy Answers, St Clement's parish, Oxford).
24. AMB, A3. *Victoria History of the County of Oxford*, edited by Alan Crossley, XII (1990), 343, 356 (properties in Woodstock).
25. AMB, A.4 (draft will of Richard Cox), D.C1–D.C8 (Cox deeds).

Chapter Four
1. OA, MS. Diocesan Papers d.567, 569, 571 (Clergy Answers, St Thomas's parish).
2. OC2, 521.
3. W.E. Sherwood, *Oxford Yesterday. Memoirs of Oxford Seventy Years Ago* (1927), 32–3.
4. OC2, 610–14.
5. *Oxford Times*, 12 July 1913.

6. Census returns, St Thomas's parish, Oxford, 1861.
7. AMB, A4 (will of Mark Morrell). Bodleian Library, MS.Top.Oxon.c.211, fo. 131.
8. Census returns, St Thomas's parish, Oxford, 1841, 1851.
9. See note 8 (1851, 1861). AMB, A4 (will of Mark Morrell), D.A10 (will of James Morrell Jr).
10. Census returns, St Thomas's parish, Oxford, 1851, 1861. OA, burial register, St Thomas's parish; marriage register, St Mary Magdalen parish. AMB, D.A10.
11. Census returns, St Thomas's parish, Oxford, 1841–61.
12. AMB, A4.
13. AMB, C8 (brief in [?Spencer v. Morrell], an action or threatened action for breach of promise, Exchequer Court.)
14. AMB, D.A13 (will of Mark Theophilus Morrell).
15. OA, Morrell X/h/9, X/h/11, wills of Frederick Morrell, 1879, 1883, the latter revoking a £20 bequest to Frederick George Hall.
16. AMB, E.A3 (brewery general accounts, 1857–8).
17. AMB, F.1.
18. AMB, D.B4, 23 August 1851.
19. AMB, C.1 (diary of Charles Morrell), 20 October 1820; 4 April 1821.
20. *Ottoline, The Early Memoirs of Lady Ottoline Morrell*, edited by Robert Gathorne-Hardy (1963), 125.
21. AMB, F.5, notes on Sandford estate.

Chapter Five
1. Reproduced in Brent Elliott, *Victorian Gardens* (1986), 116.
2. W.H. Baxter, *Descriptive Catalogue of the Trees and Shrubs at Headington Hill Hall, Oxford* (1857).
3. AMB, F.5.
4. AMB, F.3.
5. AMB, B.A5.
6. AMB, E.A4.
7. AMB, E.A3, E.A4.
8. AMB, E.A4.
9. AMB, D.A10 (will of James Morrell), D.D3.
10. Census returns, St Thomas's parish, Oxford, 1861.
11. AMB, D.A10 (will of James Morrell), E.A3, E.A4.
12. AMB, E.A4.
13. *Oxford University Herald, City & County Advertiser*, 8 November 1856.
14. *Jackson's Oxford Journal*, 22 September 1860.
15. See note 14 and *Oxford University Herald*, 12 June 1858. In his will (AMB, D.A10), James expressed a wish that the school should remain free of parochial interference.
16. AMB, D.A10.
17. See OA, Morrell X/1/2a, 'Account of Expenses of Housekeeping, Horses, Carriages, Rates & Taxes Gardens &c &c connected with the Headington Hill Estate' [1863–4], and *Cottage Gardener and Country Gentleman*, 16 November 1858, 100.
18. *The Late James Morrell Esq.* (privately printed pamphlet, 1863). AMB, D.A10.
19. *Oxford University Herald*, 26 September 1863.
20. W.E. Sherwood, *Oxford Yesterday. Memories of Oxford Seventy Years Ago* (1927), 51.
21. AMB, D.A10. See also note 17.
22. AMB, D.A11, D.B9, E.A10. Census returns, St Clement's parish, Oxford, 1871.

Chapter Six
1. Mary Prior, *Fisher Row: Fishermen, Bargemen & Canal Boatmen In Oxford 1500–1900* (1982), 331.

NOTES

2. See note 1, 19.
3. *Oxford Yesterday* (1927), 47.
4. See Chapter Two, note 17, above.
5. Census returns, St Thomas's parish, Oxford, 1871, 1881, 1891.
6. See note 3, 12–13.
7. AMB, E.A7 (letters of Ward to Trustees, with garden accounts, 1865–6).
8. OA, Morrell X/1/3 (correspondence concerning Emily Morrell, 1869–74).
9. See AMB, W.1 (album of newspaper-cuttings, 1870-9), 1-17.
10. See note 8.
11. See note 9.
12. See notes 8 and 9.
13. AMB, D.B9.
14. AMB, N.A1, 23 April 1875.
15. AMB, V.1.
16. See note 9, p. 58.
17. AMB, K.1, 28 December 1886; N.A7, 31 October 1884.
18. AMB, N.A3, 9 November 1877.
19. AMB, K.1, 26 December 1886.
20. AMB, N.A1, 19 November 1875; N.A4, 9 May 1879.
21. AMB, N.A3, 15 March 1878; N.A7, 25 July 1884; N.A4, 14 March 1879.
22. Census returns, St Thomas's parish, Oxford, 1871.
23. AMB, N.A7, 20 June 1884.
24. AMB, N.A.6–7, 15 June, 19 October 1883.
25. See note 9 and AMB, D.E1.
26. See Chapter Three, note 1, above. The bailiff's house appears on A. Bryant's *Map of the County of Oxford* (London, 1824) but not on Sheet 13, Ordnance Survey map of England and Wales (1830) or the 1832 Parliamentary boundaries map (*Reports from Commissioners on the Proper Division of Counties and Boundaries of Boroughs*, IV).
27. See AMB, D.E1.
28. Census returns, St Clements' parish, Oxford, 1881.
29. OA, Morrell X/1/3, G.H. Morrell to F.P. Morrell, 25 June 1877. (Although writing from Streatley House, Herbert felt unable to ask Emily Stone about this directly.)
30. AMB, N.A3, 19 January 1877.
31. AMB, F.12.
32. AMB, N.A2, 12 May, 26 May 1876, and F.7a, p. 40.
33. Christ Church Archives, MS.Estates 78.
34. See note 33.
35. OA, Morrell X/1/5a, H.M. Dowson to G.H. Morrell, 26 May 1896, and G.H. Morrell to F.P. Morrell [1896].
36. AMB, N.A3, 12 October 1877.
37. Census records, St Thomas's parish, Oxford, 1881; AMB, N.A3, 20 July 1877.
38. AMB, J.C1, Ramsden & Son to Jorden, 7 October 1875 (three letters).
39. AMB, N.A3, 20 July 1877.
40. AMB, M.A2, M.A3, 20 July 1883, 6 September 1889.
41. AMB, F.7a, p. 40.
42. AMB, N.A4, 21 June 1878.
43. AMB, M.A2, 16 March, 22 June, 28 September 1883.
44. AMB, N.A4, 20 June 1879; K.1–5, *passim*.
45. AMB, Y (unnumbered plans), 'Fox Lane Maltkilns', two drawings, September 1883.
46. AMB, M.A2, M.A3, 31 October 1884, 27 February 1885, 9 October 1885.
47. AMB, W6, Emily Stone to G.H. Morrell, 9 July [1882].

Chapter Seven
1. AMB, K.1–5 *passim*.
2. AMB, loose documents with printed settlement of Culham Estate, Managing Director's safe.

3. AMB, M.A3, 16 September 1887.
4. AMB, K.2, 6 August 1887.
5. AMB, K.2, 11 October 1887.
6. AMB, M.A4, 15 May 1896.
7. AMB, M.A2, 11 May 1883.
8. AMB, M.A3, 9 July 1886; K.2, 8 July 1887; N.A3, 26 January, 2 February 1877; N.A4, 14 February 1879.
9. AMB, K.1.
10. AMB, K.2, *passim*.
11. AMB, K.3, *passim*.
12. AMB, K.2, 4 August, 10 October 1887; M.A3, 7 October 1887, 25 January 1889.
13. AMB, M.A3, 25 September 1885; 25 May, 1 June 1888.
14. AMB, K.3, 7 June 1888; M.A4, 9 June 1893.
15. AMB, K.3, 14 February, 12, 18 April 1888; M.A3, 12 July 1889, K.3, 28 March 1888.
16. AMB, M.A3, 6 November 1885, 13 January 1888, 26 August 1887.
17. AMB, K.5, 5 April 1890; J.C1.
18. AMB, K.6, 18 February 1891.
19. AMB, M.A3, 18 March 1887, 12 April 1889.
20. AMB, J.C1; M.A4, 26 July 1895, 8 May 1896.
21. AMB, M.A2, 21 March 1884.
22. AMB, N.A3, 15 June 1878.
23. AMB, P.B1.
24. AMB, N.A7, 16 November 1883.
25. Advertisements, *Jackson's Oxford Journal*, 1892 *passim*.
26. See note 25 and Bodleian Library, John Johnson Collection, Oxford Trades 2 (Brewing).
27. 'HS', *Brewery Companies. A reprint from 'The Statist' of a series of articles Appearing from August 25th to December 15th, 1894, furnishing for the First Time Full Particulars and Authentic Data concerning all Brewery Companies Registered up to November 30th 1894* (London, The Statist, 1895).
28. *Encyclopaedia Britannica*, 14th edition (1929), Vol. 14, 191 ('Liquor Laws').
29. AMB, M.A4, 3 November 1899.
30. AMB, M.A4, 29 July 1898.
31. AMB, M.A4, pp. 39–45 and 7 September 1894, 14 December 1900.
32. AMB, M.A4, 2 December 1894; M.A5, 20 September 1907.
33. John Burnett, *Plenty & Want, a social history of food in England from 1815 to the present day* (3rd edition, 1989), 257.
34. AMB, M.A4, 27 October 1899.
35. Bodleian Library, John Johnson Collection, Oxford Trades 2 (Brewing). AMB, S.E1.
36. AMB, M.A4, 25 January 1895.
37. For example, the textile-manufacturing firm owned by John Heathcoat at Tiverton, Devon, whose staff outings to the sea at Teignmouth are recorded from 1836 onwards. (W. Gore Allen, *John Heathcoat and his Heritage* [London, 1958], 89, 96).
38. AMB, U2.
39. AMB, M.A4, 28 July, 5 August 1892, 15 November 1895, 15 May 1896.
40. AMB, 3 February 1899.
41. Magdalen College Archives, R.T. Günther Papers, MS 583 (iii).
42. *Jackson's Oxford Journal*, 10 October 1906.

Chapter Eight
1. AMB, M.A5, 21 May 1909.
2. AMB, M.A6, 9 February, 15 March, 6 November, 6 December 1912; 28 March, 4 April 1913.
3. AMB, M.A4, 25 January 1901, and dated plaque on brewery chimney.

NOTES

4. AMB, M.A6, 24 January, 14 February, 7 March 1913; Y (unnumbered plans), drawing of proposed Labour Exchange on Old Wheatsheaf site.
5. *Oxford Times*, 12 July 1913.
6. AMB, M.A6, 18 July, 25 July 1914.
7. AMB, M.A6, 15 May 1914.
8. Information from Archivist, Oxford University Archives. Jimmy Morrell was reappointed a University demonstrator in 1931 and continued as such until 1933–4.
9. AMB, M.A6, 4 August 1914.
10. Oxford University OTC records, Yeomanry House, St Cross Road, Oxford, 1915–16.
11. AMB, M.A6, 6 August 1914.
12. Berry Ritchie, *An Uncommon Brewer, The Story of Whitbread 1742–1992* (1992), 83
13. AMB, M.A6, 27 September 1912, 7 February 1913.
14. AMB, M.A6, 14 August, 2 October, 27 November 1914; 3 September 1915.
15. AMB, M.A6, 5 November 1915; 11 February, 12 May 1916.
16. AMB, M.A6, 9 July 1915, 4 August 1916.
17. AMB, M.A6, 4 December 1914.
18. AMB, M.A6, 7 December 1917.
19. AMB, M.A6, 2 March, 30 March 1917.
20. AMB, M.A6, 3 August 1917.
21. AMB, U.10.
22. Olive Gibbs, *Our Olive* (1989), 75.
23. AMB, U.10 (Mrs Hounslow to Colonel Morrell, 28 September [1983]).

Chapter Nine
1. AMB, J.3–4 (Brewing Books, 1903–19, 1919–29).
2. See note 14 and J.5 (Brewing Book, 1946–57).
3. AMB, M.A6, 2 January, 2 May 1919; 2 January 1920.
4. *Oxford Journal Illustrated*, 23 October 1921; *Oxford Chronicle*, 20 January 1922.
5. AMB, M.A6, 30 April 1920.
6. Oxford City Council, Deeds of Headington Hill Hall. Alfred Davenport and James Rose to Trustees, 17 February 1920.
7. AMB, M.A7, 27 April 1923.
8. AMB, M.A7, 29 May, 30 October 1931; 23 December 1932.
9. AMB, M.A7, 31 October, 26 November 1926.
10. AMB, M.A8, 24 August, 5 October 1934.
11. Oxford City Council, Headington Hill Hall deeds. Emily Morrell to James Herbert Morrell, 8 April 1933 (copy).
12. Queen's College, Oxford, Archives, FB 1509 (Brewhouse file). Additional information from Louis Gunter.
13. AMB, M.A8, 14 January 1938; W.5 (price list, 29 April 1940).
14. AMB, W.5 (comparative table on verso of Morrell's beer-label).
15. Oxfordshire Local Studies Library, printed Headington Hill Hall sale catalogue, October 1939.
16. AMB, M.A8, 1 September 1939; 3 July 1941.
17. AMB, M.A8, 1 September 1939, 20 January 1933.
18. AMB, M.A8, 5 May 1933, 26 April, 25 July 1940; 23 April 1942. See also AMB, G.3, price list, 29 April 1940, amended 29 July 1940.
19. AMB, G.3, J.H. Morrell to Leonard Mortimer, 15 September 1942 (copy).
20. AMB, G.3, Frank Jefferis to J.H. Morrell, 22 October 1945, and conversation between the author, Mrs Mary Luard and Mrs Margaret Eld, 11 March 1993.

Chapter Ten
1. AMB, M.A8, 12 September 1943. Conversation between the author, Mrs Mary Luard and Mrs Margaret Eld, 11 March 1993.

2. AMB, G3, Frank Jefferis to J.H. Morrell, 22 October 1945.
3. AMB, J.A5, Brewing Book, 1946–57.
4. *Oxford Times*, 23 March 1956.
5. Oxford University Archives, LA 39/2, H.W.J. Morrell and others to the University of Oxford, 18 June 1957.
6. *Oxford Times*, 7 December 1956.
7. *Morrells Brewery: A Drinker's Guide to Morrells' Houses* (1975).
8. AMB, U2, *passim*.
9. Oxford City Council, Deeds of Headington Hill Hall. Release by James H. Morrell to the Mayor, Aldermen and Citizens of Oxford, 24 June 1953.
10. Information from Charles Smith, March 1993.
11. *Oxford Times*, 23 July 1965.

Chapter Eleven
1. AMB, 'Summary of Brewings', 1942–82 (uncatalogued).
2. See note 1.
3. See note 1.
4. *Oxford Mail*, 8 February 1990.

INDEX

Abingdon, Earls of, 10–11, 38, 46, 61, 96
Ale, beer, xi, 47–8, 87, 109, 116, 124, 143; duties on, 97–8, 105, 120; sales, prices of, 20, 87, 97–8, 105, 120, 147; strength of, 58–9, 105–6, 109–10, 116, 120–1, 124–5, 143; *see also* Brewing, Bottling
Allied Breweries, viii
Allsopp & Co., brewers, viii, 87, 111, 116, 123
Aubrey, John, xi

Back Stream, St Thomas's, viii, xiii, 33, 86, 138
Baker family, Moulsford, 5, 12, 38
Baxter, William, Curator of the Oxford Botanic Garden, 53–4
Beer, *see* Ale
Beer Act, 1830, 47
Benefit Societies, Oxford, 26
Blackbird Leys, farm at, 54–6, 74–5, 80–2, 91
Blackstone, Sir William, jurist, 10–12
Bottling, 84, 108, 126, 144–5
Bradley Farm, Cumnor, 21, 34, 43–5, 56–7
Breweries, Oxford: City Brewery (Hanley's), 47, 66, 87–8, 111, 138; Eagle Brewery (Weaving's), 66, 110; St Clement's Brewery, 111; St Giles Brewery, 47, 88; St Ebbe's Brewery, 66, 136; Simonds, H.G., 66, 78, 87; Tower Brewery (Phillips'), 66, 87, 111; *see also* Morrell's Brewery, Hall's Brewery, Swan's Nest Brewery
Brewers, Oxford: Allen, Edward, x; Bishop, John, xvi; Bosworth, Henry, xvi; Chillingworth, William, xvi; Hall, Daniel George, 47; Kenton, Thomas, vii, xv, 18; Kenton, William, vii, 18; Loader, Francis, xvi–xvii; Loader, Thomas, xvii; Newman family, ix–xi; Smyth family, viii; Treacher, John, xvii; Treacher, Sir John, viii, xvii, 23, 47; *see also* Hall, Morrell, Tawney
Brewing, 20, 58–9, 86, 109, 120, 124–5, 138, 141–4
Buccaneer Inns (later Cherwell Inns) franchise, 137
Burton-on-Trent, beer from, 48

Canal, Oxford, viii, 64; shares in, 27
Castle Ale, 87, 125–6, 143, 146
Castle Mill, Oxford, viii–ix, xviii–xix
Castle Mill Stream, viii–ix, xiv, 17
Chamberlain, Rev. Thomas, Vicar of St Thomas's, 51
Colleges, Oxford: Balliol, 11; Christ Church, ix, xiii, xv–xvi, 17–18, 23, 34–5, 38, 75–6; Corpus Christi, xii, 115; Jesus, 48; Lincoln, xi; Magdalen, 23, 28, 93, 102, 115; Magdalen Hall, 32; Merton, 21, 34; New College, xix, 115; Oriel, 115; Queen's, 108, 115; St John's, 11, 22–3, 61; Trinity, xi, 22
Collins, Bernard, Morrell's trustee, 102, 114; Collins, Henry, Morrell's trustee, 70, 101–2
Cox, Richard, banker, 16, 27, 38–9; estates of, 38, 49, 57, 76; Cox, Richard Ferdinand, banker, 27, 38–9
Cox, Morrell & Co., Bank, later J. & R. Morrell, 27, 38–9, 52, 57
Cricket Club, Morrells' Trustees, 90
Culham, farms at, 55, 94

Deacon family, Streatley, 12
Drinkwater, H.G.W., architect, 78, 80–1, 86–7

Eld, Charles, Managing Director, 4, 144–5, 147–8
Excise duties, 22; *see also* Ale, beer, duties on

Fisher Row (Lower), Tawney property in, vii, xix–xxi, 18; Morrell's Brewery house in, xxi, 27–8, 32, 37, 41, 46, 50, 57, 63, 70
Fletcher, William, alderman, 35; Fletcher, Parsons, bank, 16, 21, 27, 32, 39

Gamlen, John Charles, Morrell's trustee, 102, 114, 123; Gamlen, W.B., Morrell's trustee, 70, 85, 96, 101
Garsington, 2, 23, 54, 81, 112
Garbett, E.W., architect, 32, 42
Gibbs, Olive, Oxford City councillor, 106–7
Gilkes, John, Blackbird Leys farm bailiff, 74–5
Ginger beer, *see* Mineral water
Ginger wine, 89
Godfrey, Thomas, carrier, 31–2

Hall, Colonel A.W., MP, brewer, 70, 95, 100; Hall, William, brewer, xvii, 23, 34–5
Hall's Brewery (Hall & Tawney's Brewery), viii, 34, 41–3, 46–7, 66, 71, 78, 87, 100–1, 110–11, 138; *see also* Swan's Nest Brewery
Harcourt, Simon, 1st Earl, xii, 10
Harp Extra, Harp Lager, 126, 138, 144–5, 147
Headington Hill, James Morrell senior's house on, 1, 28, 37, 53; Headington Hill Hall, 1, 53–4, 56, 59, 62, 66–70, 72–4, 81, 90, 94, 111–12, 131
Hucks, William, and Wallingford Mill, 8

James II, accession celebrations, xii
Jaques family, Wallingford, 12, 28

Kettell, Dr Ralph, President of Trinity College, xi
Knapp family, Headington Hill, 73–4

Leyland, Bill, Chairman, Morrells Brewery Ltd, 145
Licensing Acts, 95, 97–8
Liddell, Alice, 69
Linke, Robert, senior, xiii–xv; Linke, Robert, junior, xv

Malchair, John Baptist, 30
Malt, barley, supplies of, 20, 25, 34, 55–6, 82–3, 111, 120–1, 127–9

167

Malthouses: Fox's, 25, 78–9, 82–3, 111, 127–9; Goundrey's, 78; Symms's, 25, 40, 64; Ward's, 78; other (Dorchester, Shillingford, Wallingford, etc.), 33, 78–9

Marlborough: George Spencer, 4th Duke of (d. 1817), 10–11; George Spencer, 5th Duke of (d. 1840), 45–6; George Spencer, 6th Duke of (d. 1857), 46, 52; John Winston Spencer-Churchill, 7th Duke of (d. 1883), 46, 61; Duchess of (wife of 7th Duke), 68; 8th Duke of, 96

Matthias, Peter, xiii

Mileways Act, 1771, xix

Mineral water, production of, 89, 105

Morrell Avenue, Oxford, 1, 112

Morrell: Mr, Wallingford miller, 7–8; Alicia (née Everett), 4, 50–1, 60, 62; Ann (née Baker), 5, 12, 15; Ann (née Jaques), 3; Baker, attorney (solicitor), 5, 12, 17, 27–8, 51–2, 67; Charles, son of Jeremiah, 8; Charles, son of Mark, of Wallingford, 2–3, 8, 22, 79; Charles, son of Charles, of Wallingford, 3, 32, 50; Rev. Deacon, 5, 12–13, 38, 52; Elizabeth (née Fludger), 3, 8; Elizabeth (née Parker), 51; Emily, 4, 6, 28, 38, see also Stone, Emily; Emily Alicia, 4, 12, 38, 51–3, 62–3, 67–70, 72, 79, 92, 96, 112, 114, 118; Frederick Joseph, solicitor, 2, 5, 51, 55, 61–2, 67–8, 70, 113; Frederick Parker, solicitor, 2, 5, 51, 68, 70, 74, 112; George Herbert, 4, 67–70, 72–5, 88–96, 104; George James, 122; Rev. George Kidd, 67; George Mark, 89, 94, 131; Harriette (née Wynter), 51–2, 68; James, attorney, xxi, 1–3, 7–8, 15–17, 27; James senior, brewer, vii, xxi, 1–3, 13–18 et seq.; James junior, 28, 38, 45, 49–62; James Herbert ('Jimmy'), 79, 85, 89–90, 93–6, 98–9, 102–8, 113 et seq.; Jane (née Wharton), 3–4, 6, 27–8, 147; Jeremiah, Wallingford miller, 2–3, 7–10, 22, 147; Jeremiah, London corn-factor and brewer, 8–9, 22; Julia (née Denton), 4, 98–9, 132; Margaret (Eld), 4, 122; Maria (Wintle), 5, 13, 15, 22; Mark, son of Jeremiah, of Wallingford, 2–3, 8–10, 148; Mark, brewer, vii, xxi, 1–3, 13–18, et seq.; Mark Theophilus, 28, 38, 46; Mary (née Smith), 3, 8–10; Mary (Luard), 107, 122; Mary (Stone), 3, 13–18; Ottoline, Lady, wife of Philip, 2, 5, 112–13; Philip, MP, 2, 5, 112–13; Robert, senior, 3, 9, 27; Robert, junior, solicitor and banker, 3, 9, 12–15, 26–8, 34, 38–9, 52; William ('Bill'), Colonel H.W.J., chairman and president, 4, 107, 122–4, 133, 145, 148

Morrell's Brewery, employees: Achurch, Brian, second brewer, 117–18; Burrows, counting-house clerk, 71; Campbell, cooper, 84, 96; Clemson, Jonathan, drayman, 43; Cousins, Violet (Mrs Hounslow), 106–8; Cunliffe, Gordon, brewer, 118, 127–8; Dowson, Henry, manager, 85, 88–90, 97, 103–8, 110, 113; Dry, William, engine-driver, 77; Eastwood, Miles, assistant to managing director, 132; Fillmore family, 106; Fletcher, James, senior, brewer, 42; Fletcher, James, junior, brewer, 42, 63; Fletcher, Robert, brewer's man, 42; Fletcher, William, brewer's man, 42; French family, 106; Green, Ralph, brewer, 108, 117–18, 123, 126; Gunter, Louis, brewer, 115, 118–19, 123, 131, 138, 141–5; Haines family, 96, 106; Harvey, maltster, 79; Haslett, brewer, 83, 85, 96, 108, 110, 117; Hearne, Henry, brewer, 42–3; Hearne, William, maltster, 42–3; Heritage, brewer, 83; Hill, George, clerk, 58; Hutt, Charles, brewer, 44, 58, 63, 72; Hutt, Joe, drayman, 43–4, 63; Hutt, Thomas, drayman, 44; Jaggar, Henry, cooper, 45; Jorden, Arthur, manager, 69–72, 77–8, 80–5, 95; Lord, George, clerk, 58; Mundy, John, company secretary, 108, 123, 131; Paine, night-watchman, 71; Polden, David, brewer, 145–6; Price, lorry-driver, 119; Senior, Bill, distribution director, 147; Sherwood, Thomas, manager, 57–8, 63, 65–6; Smith, Charles, company secretary, 123–4, 131; Stone, Richard, maltster, 45; Sullivan, Michael, brewer, 145–6; Tremlett, John, second brewer, 117; Webb, John, clerk, 18–19, 41, 44, 50, 58; Weller, maltster, 90, 96; Whittle, maltster, 78–9, 85; Worth, Tony, managing director, 123, 132, 144

Morrell's Brewery, equipment, 33, 77–8, 83–4, 86, 127, 138, 141; site and buildings, vii, xiii–xv, 18–19, 75–6, 78, 86, 99–100; staff outings, 90–1, 130–1

Morrell's Trustees (1863–74), 62, 66–9; Morrell's Trustees (1875–1943), 70–1, 73–122; see also names of individual trustees

Mortimer, Charles, Morrell's trustee, 101; Mortimer, Leonard, Morrell's trustee, 102, 114, 121–3

Motor transport, 88, 105, 109

Norton, Cornelius, attorney, 10

Old Berkshire Hunt, 39, 46, 50, 54, 60–1

Oseney Abbey, vii–ix, 47; brewhouse built by, ix–x, xvi

Oxford University: and assizes of bread and ale, xi; Boat Club, 116; buys Fox's Malthouse, 127; Laudian statutes of, xi; Officers' Training Corps, 93, 102, 104; Volunteer Rifle Corps, 67, 93, 104

Oxford (City) Volunteer Rifle Corps, 59–60, 67, 104

Parsons, Herbert, banker, 62; Parsons, John, banker, 26, 32

Public houses owned or leased by Morrell's Brewery (see also Appendix 2): Air Balloon, Queen Street, 35, 134; Albion, Hollybush Row, 41, 101; Anchor, Cornmarket Street, 72; Anchor, later Westgate, New Road, xviii, 23, 26, 134–6; Ancient Briton, St Ebbe's, 106; Bear and Ragged Staff, Brookhampton, 48; Bear and Ragged Staff, Cumnor, 137; Beetle and Wedge, Moulsford, 136; Black Horse, St Clement's, 35–6, 49; Black Swan, George Lane, 49; Blue Bell, Shillingford, 48; Blue Boar, Longworth, 36; Blue Pig, Gloucester Green, 49, 87, 134; Boar's Head, Queen's Lane, xviii; Bookbinder's Arms, Jericho, 49; Cape of Good Hope, The Plain, 23, 131; Carpenters Arms, Marlow, 137; Chequers, Cassington, 48; Chequers, Wheatley, 23; Coach and Horses, King Street, 49; Coach and Horses, St Clement's, 59, 106; Coach and Horses, St Giles, 49; Cross Keys, South Hinksey, 49; Crown, Bicester, 36; Crown, Charlton on Otmoor, 23; Dog and Duck, Woodstock, 23; Druid's Head, George Street, 49;

INDEX

Duke of York, Broad Street, 35; Duke of York, Faringdon, 48; Duke of York, St Ebbe's, 48; Folly, Faringdon, 48; Friars, Friars' Entry, 35; Gamecock, St Ebbe's, 106; Gardener's Arms, North Parade, 106; General Elliot, S. Hinksey, 49; George, Botley, 49; George, Cornmarket Street, 49; Globe, Queen Street, 49, 86; Golden Ball, Littlemore, 36, 48; Grapes, George Street, 134, 136; Great Western Hotel, Hythe Bridge Street, 86; Green Dragon, St Aldates, 35; Holly Bush, St Thomas's, 49; Horse and Groom, St Ebbe's, 49; Horse and Jockey, Woodstock Road, 49; Isis Tavern, Iffley Lock, 109, 137, 140–1; Jericho House, Walton Street, 49; Jolly Bargeman, St Ebbe's, 48; Jolly Porter, Culham, 86; (Jolly) Post Boy(s), High Street, *later* Florence Park, xviii, 23, 134; King and Queen, Wheatley, xviii, 136; King of Prussia, *later* Allied Arms, *later* Ox, Rose Hill, 36, 88; King's Arms, Banbury, 86; King's Arms, Nethercott, 48; King's Head, Holywell, 49; King's Head, St Martin's parish, 35; Lamb and Flag, St Thomas's Street, 49; Lamb, Bladon, 23; Marlborough Arms, St Thomas's, *see* Shoulder of Mutton; Nag's Head, Fisher Row/Hythe Bridge Street, 23, 49; Oddfellows Arms, George Street, 49; Old Tom, St Aldate's, 134; Old White House, Abingdon Road, 49, 86; Paradise House, St Ebbe's, 23, 134–5; Parrot, St Ebbe's, 48; Paviour's Arms, St Ebbe's, 23, 49; Pennyfarthing, Westgate Centre, 135–6; Plasterer's Arms, St Clement's, 35; Plough, Dorchester, 48; Plough, Marsh Gibbon, 136–7; Plough, Wheatley, 36; Port Mahon, St Clements, 35; Punch Bowl, George Street, 49; Queen's Arms, Park End Street, 23, 103, 134; Railway Hotel, Culham, 86; Red Lion, High Street, xviii; Red Lion, Eynsham, xviii, 136; Red Lion, Tetsworth, xviii, 136; Rose and Crown, Blackthorn, 49; Rowing Machine, Witney, 137; Royal Blenheim, Little Clarendon Street, 72; Royal Oak, Kingshill, 137; Seven Stars, Piddington, 49; Shoulder of Mutton, *later* Marlborough Arms, St Thomas's Street, 41, 64, 85, 99, 101; Swan, Islip, 48; Swan, Streatley, 136; Swan, Sutton Courtenay, 36; Swan, Temple Cowley, 36, 48; Three Crowns, St Thomas's Street, 35; Three Cups, Queen Street, xviii, 17, 23; Three Goats' Heads, St Mary Magdalen parish, 23, 49; Three Horse Shoes, Garsington, 23; Tree, Iffley, 49; Turk's Head, St Thomas's Street, 23, 41, 44, 101; Two Hands, 49; Union, Thrupp, 48; Vulcan, Friars' Entry, 35; Wagon and Horses, St Giles, 49; Welsh Pony, Gloucester Green, 86; Westgate, *see* Anchor, New Road; Wheatsheaf, High Street, 86; Wheatsheaf, St Aldates, xiii, xviii, 23, 100; White Hart, Benson, xviii, 153; White Horse, Bicester, 137; Windsor Castle, St Thomas's Street, 41, 49, 100–1

Rewley Abbey, vii–viii, xviii, 47

Sandford on Thames, farms at, 34, 49, 54–7, 91
School, Mrs Morrell's, 60–1, 68–9, 99
Sherwood, Rev. William, 61, 63–5, 82
Smith family, Headington Hill, 30, 73
Spencer, Georgiana, 45
Stone: Emily, 52, 62, 67, *see also* Morrell, Emily; William, and Susannah, of Basildon, Berks., 13; their son, of Englefield, Berks., 14; their grandson, husband of Mary Morrell, 13–14; William Henry, their great-grandson, husband of Emily Morrell, 38, 52
Streatley House, Berks., 12, 38, 62, 69, 94, 131
Sugar in brewing, 89, 106, 109–10, 120, 127
Swan's Nest Brewery, viii, xix; *see also* Hall's Brewery
Swindon, Morrells' public houses at, 86, 121, 136

Tawney: Ann, *see* Wharton, Ann; Bradnam, xix, 6; Charles, brewer, xix, 6, 41, 46; Edward, miller, brewer and alderman, vii, xvi, xvii–xxi, 6–7, 17–18, 21, 23, 46, 148; Elizabeth (later Clarke), xvii; Elizabeth (née Rowles), xvii, 6; Henry, carpenter, xix, 6; Jane, wife of Richard (d. 1717), xviii, 6; Jane, daughter of Richard and Jane, xviii, 6; Nicholas, xvii; Richard, boatmaster and brewer, vii, xiii, xvi–xvii, 6, 147; Sir Richard, brewer and alderman, vii, xvii–xix, 6, 17–18, 147; Richard, canal engineer, xix, 6; Robert, boatmaster, xvii, 6; Robert, carpenter, xvii, 6; William, xix
Telephone, at brewery, 88
Tew: Sarah, 8; Thomas, 8
Thomas, John, architect of Headington Hill Hall, 53

Ushers' Brewery, Trowbridge, 121–2

Walker, Thomas, attorney, 10, 16
Wallingford, Morrells at, 2–4, 7–10, 32
Watneys Brewery, 118, 142
Wells family, Wallingford brewers, 7, 10, 23, 33, 79, 121
Wharton: Ann (née Tawney), xix–xx, 6, 27; Brian, 6, 27, 74; Jane, *see* Morrell, Jane; Theophilus senior, xx, 6, 27; Theophilus junior, 6, 27, 74

Whitbread, Samuel, 41
Whitbreads Brewery, 47, 87, 104, 124, 137, 142
Wick Farm, Headington, 28, 74, 94
Wilmott family, Cholsey, 12
Wintle, Rev. Robert, 13, 22–3
Wood, Anthony, xii
Wynter, Rev. Philip, 51, 61

169